The Gift of
Peaceful Genes

ALSO BY WARREN JOHNSON

Muddling Toward Frugality

The Future Is Not What It Used To Be

Economic Growth vs the Environment (with John Hardesty)

Public Parks on Private Land in England and Wales

The Gift of Peaceful Genes

Cultural Evolution on a Finite Earth

Warren Johnson

The Other Way Press

THE OTHER WAY PRESS
An imprint of BookSurge.com, Inc.
Charleston, South Carolina
www.booksurge.com

Permissions

Material condensed from Richard Critchfield's *Villages,*
printed with the permission of Doubleday, a division
of Random House, Inc.

Material from Arnold Toynbee's *Civilization on Trial*
printed with the permission of Oxford University Press.

Material from Richard Pipe's *Russia Under the Old Regime*
printed with the permission of the author.

Graph of the Genuine Progress Indicator used with the permission of Redefining
Progress, San Francisco, California (info@progress.org.)

ISBN:1-58898-261-0

Printed in the United States of America

To the people ahead,
May they be blessed with wisdom and good fortune

CONTENTS

ACKNOWLEDGEMENTS

In this age of the specialist, it is a solitary activity to be a generalist, especially when arguing a case few want to think about. Thus I am happy to express my gratitude for two good friends, Gary Suttle and Burr Keen, for their continued willingness to help with my stumbling, searching efforts over the years.

I would also like to thank Melissa Harrison, the other people at BookSurge.com, and electronic publishing in general for the opportunity to present thoughts and ideas that at one time could be published conventionally. I would also like to express my appreciation for the encouragement of my editor, Rita Samols, my son Aaron for the cover art that so beautifully symbolizes the book, and my son Blake for his knowledge of the economy.

It is also my pleasure to thank George Helmholtz, Diana Richardson, Charles Moutenot, John O'Brien, Sara Lewis, Danny Moses, Sandra and David Ballard, and Richard White. At the same time I accept responsibility for the errors that accompany most books but especially one by a generalists.

And finally, I would like to express my appreciation for two of the truest forms of abundance we enjoy—libraries, for the treasures they hold, and travel, for the opportunity to see if the world agrees with what they say. They made this book possible.

.

INTRODUCTION
The Inevitable Future

Our passion for growth, progress, and the new makes us different from traditional peoples around the world with their equally strong passion for known ways, continuity, and stability. Yet in one way we are like them—when we fear where change is taking us. This undoubtedly contributed to the movement toward conservatism in recent years, but the irony in this is that conservatives support the most powerful force for change the world has ever known, the free-market economy. Still, what alternative is there, given our dependence on a strong, growing economy? It seems to be the only way of keeping this huge, complex society functioning—and increasingly the world, too.

A dispassionate view of our circumstances requires that we face the implications of Figure 1.

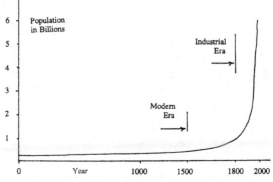

Figure 1. World Population Growth

The numbers are for population, but the lines are similar —if steeper—for economic growth, technological advance, environmental impact, resource use, and other of the revolutionary changes of the modern era. In the evolutionary time frame, they are growing at a rate that is close to vertical. That such growth cannot be sustained may be hard for us to accept, but mathematicians have long told us that any positive rate of growth leads toward infinity, and we are beginning to feel the uncomfortable reality behind this simple mathematical statement. The only real questions are when growth will slow, stop, and begin to decline, under what circumstances, and what will take its place? This assumes, of course, that humans do not destroy the environment or revert to the "nature red in tooth and claw" of Darwinian survival.

Thinking in the Evolutionary Way

The future cannot be known, but the process by which it will be reached is known: it is cultural evolution. The history of cultural evolution throws light on how humans emerged from the animal world to create the great array of cultures on Earth— including today's modern industrial society. Much of value has been created with the spectacular technological advances of our times, but they were not done with an eye toward achieving stability or balance with the environment. Cultural evolution always involves change, but never has change been so explosive, so worldwide in scope, or placed such heavy demands on the environment that supports all life. The problems being encountered now are the initial stages of the long evolutionary movement toward the sustainable ways that cannot be avoided if humans are to occupy the Earth for a long time yet.

This will be a new kind of challenge for us, but our ancestors faced similar challenges, including the most difficult one of all—the gradual movement away from the ways of our primate ancestors to create the first human societies. This occurred in the small bands of hunters and gatherers that existed during most of the millions of years of human evolution. The pace of cultural evolution quickened with the invention of agriculture and herding a mere 10,000 years ago, and quickened again with the invention of urban-based civilizations 5,000 years ago. Still, the pace was slow until the Renaissance, when it can be said that the modern era began. The rate of change then accelerated with the Enlightenment, the Industrial Revolution, and literally exploded in the fully evolved urban industrial way of life of the present.

Each of these major leaps in the evolutionary process brought problems for people who had evolved in small bands of hunters and gatherers, often quite serious ones that included violence and exploitation. The challenge facing cultural evolution was to find ways of utilizing the benefits of the new technologies while overcoming the problems they brought with them. This is what cultural evolution has proven itself capable of doing, and it will do so again with the technological advances of the modern era. But the changes this will entail are so threatening to our present way of life that we block them out of our minds. The dynamism of the modern economy is so powerful that there is no longer any debate about whether it is desirable or not, only that we have built our lives on it and have no other choice. This means we must work to preserve a strong and growing economy—just what cannot be sustained. At some point barriers to this way of life will appear, probably in a number of forms— social, economic, political, and environmental—to slow it down; some already have, as reflected in many of the problems we face, of congestion, rising prices, unemployment, global warming, anger, even terrorism. The process is not apt to be a pleasant one, especially after the heady growth of recent centuries. But as time passes, there will be less choice but to adapt to the circumstances our experiences have not prepared us for.

All living things face such evolutionary challenges if they are to survive, but those we face are of a different order of magnitude because of the high levels of population and economic activity that have already been reached. These may be unparalleled circumstances for cultural evolution to deal with, but this will not fundamentally change the process. It will still be those who adapt most effectively to the circumstances they find themselves in who will do well and set the tone for the future. Cultural evolution will remain what it always has been, a process of ordinary people taking steps to make their lives better, but there will be more traps and dead ends than our ancestors faced when the Earth was less crowded and cultures could evolve more freely in their own directions. Ahead there will be less tolerance for errors and false starts, and more reason to be aware of what can be learned from the vast panorama of the human exper- ience—not only what has worked but what has not, and why. Of all the over-arching questions that can only be speculated about today—whether world population will peak at 10 billion, 50 billion, or crash; whether economic growth can double a few more times or is already unsustainable; and whether issues such as global warming and declining bio-diversity will mark the end of an era or simply provide new challenges for technological society to conquer—none will alter the inevitability of cultural adaptation, only the timing and conditions under which it takes place.

One thing, though, is certain: no society was ever strengthened by denying the reality of its circumstances. Our society makes a number of fine claims for itself, but one of the most persistent is that we have moved to a higher plane of consciousness that makes the ways of other times and places of little value to us. This may be flattering, but just because our experiences have been different doesn't make us superior. Such a view, if justified, would have to be limited to our technological achievements, since in other ways we have lost ground, especially in the capacity to work together and in balance with nature. And the machines that give us such great powers carry risks of equal magnitude. We are heavily dependent on them now, even as we consume the fossil fuels that drive them, while modern weapons have escalated the capacity to kill just as reasons to kill increase—to gain control of oil fields, markets, or water supplies.

The challenges we face may be unprecedented, but we have equally unprecedented advantages in dealing with them. A list would be long, but the history of cultural evolution tells us quite clearly that one asset has been critical to the evolutionary success of our species. It is a gift, pure and simple, from our earliest ancestors: the capacity to work together peacefully.

The Gift of Peaceful Genes

Human nature has the potential for good as well as for ill—for peacefulness, generosity, and cooperation as well as for violence, greed, and divisiveness. The role of culture from the beginning has been to encourage the good and discourage the bad. In a process that seems so improbable as to be almost miraculous, our hunting and gathering ancestors managed to overcome instincts as basic as those for sex and dominance, and in ways that encouraged the cooperation that left humans more fit in the evolutionary struggle. Those who could work together easily and comfortably found things going well for them and were able to pass their genes forward in children who grew up well-adjusted, productive, and happy with their lives. Those with strong drives for dominance and aggressiveness were thwarted in this; the killer genes, in effect, killed themselves off, if not in fighting then in failing to reproduce effectively in the more cooperative circumstances that were shaping human development. Over the millions of years of human evolution the balance slowly shifted in favor of peacefulness, and as this occurred a way of life evolved that gave humans their critical advantage in the evolutionary struggle. If evolution is the survival of the fittest, then the fittest turned out to be those who could work together effectively, not the strongest and most aggressive that wasted energy—and lives—in conflict.

The ways in which cooperation overcame aggressiveness were deemed so valuable that they were enshrined in cultures that were held to tenaciously over vast periods of time.

They survived until disrupted by the invention of agriculture, which led to the violence and exploitation of the early civilizactions, but this too was overcome by the ways of traditional agricultural societies that survived for thousands of years. This is the way of life that is now being displaced by the spreading power of the urban industrial way of life that is now taking over the world at such an explosive rate. The problems it is creating will be overcome in the same way, by the reestablishment of stable ways of life in balance with the environment; either that or we will die out as a species. This much can be known, but not the manner in which it will be accomplished, or what the final results will be. Only the process of cultural evolution can determine that.

There have been setbacks in this process as well, many of them; cultural evolution is a halting process, one full of false starts and dead ends. The modern era is unique in the extent to which the advantage has shifted back toward aggressiveness, even if in the more ordered form of free-market economics that has replaced the warfare of recent centuries—hopefully not just temporarily. As individual worth came to be based on economic achievement it was inevitable that the tone of society would change to reflect the importance of drive and competitiveness, but also that the institutions that depend on peaceful cooperation would weaken, the family and the community especially. People find such changes uncomfortable, and everything imaginable is blamed for them—everything except the economy, which, with the fall of communism and the decline of socialism, is accepted as immutable as the air we breathe. Governments and corporations are the most common targets for the discontent, but behind them is usually culture, the "system," that is seen as constraining our freedom. The left and right may see the specifics differently, liberals tending to see wrongs as stemming from corporations and the power of money while conservatives see government as the culprit. But neither seek ways of rebuilding cooperation when individual achievement and the self is the basis of what is good and valuable.

Freud played a role in this when he argued that the restraints culture placed on instincts, especially sex, were the source of emotional problems. It was an appealing argument at a time when Victorian restraints were vainly trying to hold back changes caused by the Industrial Revolution, with religion the main device used. The issue became moot as freedom and individualism became essential for living in the cities and working in the large-scale enterprises that made the free-market economy so efficient; indeed, individual freedom was essential to make the market work in the first place. There is logic in this, as reflected in the achievements of modern society, but in the evolutionary context it is all wrong. The restraints culture placed on individual instincts and behavior are what made us human. Controlling the instincts for aggression and dominance enabled our ancestors to separate themselves from the other primates in the first place. Marx, that other great error maker of our times, at least saw the importance of human solidarity, but he erred on the side of a totalitarian solidarity rather than a totalitarian individualism.

The challenge, as it always has been, will be to build peaceful, satisfying ways of life within the limits established by the environment that supports all life. Which of the technological advances of our era will be a part of the new stability cannot be known, but the individuals and groups who can use them peacefully and constructively will be the ones able to enjoy secure and satisfying lives in balance with the environment. One thing is certain: It will never be possible to meet the needs of a society driven by the quest for more—regardless of how wealthy, free, or powerful it becomes. The proven alternative is to find satisfactions more as our ancestors did, in the emotional, social, and spiritual realms rather than the competitive and the material. We have inherited the genes for both, and even if competitiveness has been so heavily encouraged in recent times that it is hard to imagine how cooperation will ever come to the fore again, it will. There is no other choice, not if the Earth is to be a secure home for humankind for a long time to come.

Reaching this goal may entail a long and difficult process, with new dark ages always a possibility. But it could go smoothly, too. The violence of our times could cause a recoiling from the threat of more, and after the long loneliness of a market-driven way of life there could well be a yearning for more cooperative ways. The process of moving toward a new stability may be smooth or halting, but the human experience confirms that in the end the peaceful will inherit the Earth. There is probably no other choice if there is to be a future for humans on this small but beautiful planet.

Let Us Think Together

The name *Homo sapiens* flatters us by describing humans as "thinkers" and "wise," the meaning of the Latin word *sapiens*, but let us try to live up to this name. I offer no solutions for the future, only what can be learned from the evolutionary experiences of the past and a clear-eyed understanding of our present circumstances. It begins with a brief chapter about the cultural evolutionary process, leading to Chapter 2 that makes the case for the peaceful genes being the critical factor in human evolution. It deals with the ways peacefulness was encouraged during the long era when hunting and gathering was evolving as a way of life, and then was tested in painful ways by the invention of agriculture, nomadic herding, and urban civilization based on irrigated agriculture. Stable, peaceful ways were finally recovered in the varied forms of traditional agricultural society, ways that, although not fitting human nature as well as hunting and gathering, still permitted the growth of richer cultures and larger populations. The peacefulness of hunters and gatherers was regained mainly through the great world faiths, which all ask for selflessness in one form or another.

Chapters 3 through 6 apply this evolutionary perspective to our society and the changes it is bringing on so rapidly. Chapter 3 deals with the disappointments that have eroded the optimism of the post-World War II era, when progress seemed to promise solutions to age-old problems, not their replacement by new ones. Chapter 4 looks at how human relationships have changed in a market-based society, especially the way the competitiveness required by the market has worked against the core cooperative institutions, the family and community. Chapter 5 deals with the forms of environmental resistance that have the greatest potential for ending the era of growth, while Chapter 6 looks at the role of world trade, especially its implications for sustaining population growth and the rapid depletion of world resources. Much of the material in these four chapters is covered in the media, and most of it is disheartening since it reflects the barriers our way of life is coming up against. If they offer something unique it is because the evolutionary lens encourages a longer-term view, but readers who wish to can skip them without significant loss to the main discussion—of how we can move toward sustainable ways as smoothly as possible.

Chapter 7 takes on the difficult task of identifying policies that could at least begin this process. This means politics, with the argument made that our society is democratic, and that it will move toward sustainability once the majority of the voting public sees this as the right thing to do. But it also depends on finding good ways of doing this, and without jeopardizing the ongoing stability of the way of life we are all dependent on, including the mainstream economy. The ways proposed for this do not depend on changing the economy so much as encouraging the evolution of a sustainable economy that functions in parallel with it. The key turns out to be finding ways of enabling those who would like to live in more sustainable ways while still contributing to the stability of the mainstream economy. The ideal would be for the new sustainable economy to grow as the mainstream economy declines, with the challenge being to find policies that benefit both economies while also holding off inflation and depression.

At some stage, however, more fundamental cultural changes will be needed—ones that move more clearly toward peaceful cooperation. "Putting Economics in Its Place" is the title of Chapter 8, and it describes how other societies have met their material needs without letting economics shape everything. Religions have been important in this, mainly by placing economics in the context of the higher truths each faith strives for. This worked best in the fortunate circumstances enjoyed by India and China, but even under the less fortunate circumstances of Africa and Russia, economic impulses were organized in ways that may have been as satisfactory as possible given the circumstances. The strains in Islamic societies today are seen as relevant to the West, since the two civilizations have much in common, including the propensity for violence that has plagued the West throughout so much of its history.

Chapter 9 looks at this Western heritage, and why industrial society evolved here rather than elsewhere. The role of Christianity is important in this because, even though it restrained economic impulses during the long medieval Age of Faith, with the Reformation it gave momentum to the changes that would lead to the Industrial Revolution and the challenges we face now.

The concluding chapter looks at the advantages and disadvantages we have in dealing with the task ahead. Technology is an important part of this since it could improve the quality of sustainable ways of life in the future, but it involves risks, too, especially of violence. A hopeful sign is the remarkable convergence in the ethics of the world's great faiths, since it was a common ethical pattern that permitted hunters and gatherers to live peacefully without fear of being preyed on by the aggressive. Such an ethic in the future would be the most direct route toward secure and satisfying ways for our species, but there are many possible pitfalls, too. In the West, the disregard of the ways Christ asks for at least means the original faith is still there, and could replace our market-based ways as they become less useful. The ways of the past with proven evolutionary value could well be the greatest assets we have in coping with the times ahead.

Warren Johnson

CHAPTER ONE

Challenge and Response

The economy can be thought of as a powerful train with the unusual characteristic of having to keep speeding up all the time. It is going very fast already and taking us to new places, many of them quite exciting, but it is also generating a good deal of anxiety about whether the train will be able to stay on the track, get the fuel it needs, and what life will be like on a train that is going faster all the time. Yet the prospects of it failing are so terrifying that we feel we have no choice but to do everything we can to keep it going. The driver's compartment is crammed with highly trained technicians and complex instruments, and together they have been able to get past obstacles with names such as Chrysler, the savings and loan industry, and Mexico written on them. But the bigger one named Asia required the whole world to keep it on track. What if the props under it do not hold? Or Japan fails, or Europe, or even the United States? The dark visions are terrifying, of unemployment trapping millions of people in cities, businesses going bankrupt, banks failing, falling tax revenues tearing holes in the social safety net, and money being printed to deal with such problems but only adding runaway inflation to the list of ills.

It is unfortunate to speak of such fears when so many of us have good jobs and are living in nice homes in well-tended neighborhoods. But even if unstated, such fears are in the backs of people's minds. If someone knew a way of slowing the train down without adversely affecting the economy, it would probably be a politically popular proposal. But it is hard to say

11

this with any assurance, since Americans are so proud of the achievements of their economy and the dynamism and creativity that drive it. We are the winners in this game, and success has reinforced the regard with which it is held—especially now that so much of the world is following our lead. Public opinion polls report greater feelings of confidence and well-being at times of strong economic growth, and there are even measurable drops in suicide rates when unemployment declines.

But it may be that success is all that is propelling us forward now, since the polls that for decades have asked people how happy they were peaked in the late 1960s, and since then the percentage of people reporting themselves as very happy has declined 40 percent. What economic growth has brought with it is of evidently less value than what has been lost in the process. The postwar decades were full of optimism about what the new machines being invented would do for us, but now technology is mainly a defense against problems such as unemployment, pollution, congestion, resource depletion, and terrorism. The hope is that we can hold onto what we have, especially as emerging economies become more competitive and add their demands to the world's resources. Rather than the optimistic vision of more leisure, less poverty, and richer lives, the focus now is on preserving the nation's competitive position. Talk of moving toward sustainable ways seems more like wishful thinking than realism.

But growth lines do not rise forever. This is reflected in the familiar S-shaped growth curve, shown in Figure 2, that has been found to describe most growth processes, from a new species introduced into an environment to a new office technology in the workplace. The first half of the process reflects the easy growth in wide-open circumstances, as when a species expands freely into a niche suitable for it or everyone is interested in the new office product. Growth rates are strong and steady, resulting in the upward curving line of exponential growth. At some point, however, growth begins to slow; this is the inflection point shown in Figure 2, the point at which the first resistance to growth is encountered. The market for the office product experiences the first indication of saturation, while the ecological niche for the new species begins to fill up, with food supplies becoming harder to find and more predators arriving on the scene. The biological example is the most useful for our purposes, since our way of life ultimately depends on the productivity of the environment that supports it. As population and economic activity continue to increase, environmental resistance increases, too, slowly at first but then more rapidly, until it brings growth to a halt.

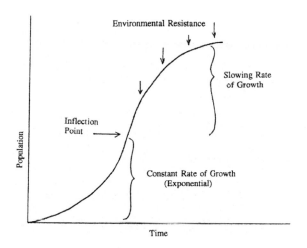

Figure 2. The S-Shaped Growth Curve

Where our society is on the S-shaped growth curve cannot be known since there is no experience to base prediction on, but it is clear that environmental resistance is growing. It takes many forms, including higher costs of housing, energy, and pollution control, longer commutes, more congested airports, fewer urban pleasures, and many pressures and frustrations compared to the easy growth of the post-war decades. The optimism then can be understood as reflecting the wide-open niche for industrial society of the times and the rapid gains being made against the age-old plagues of poverty, ignorance, and disease. There were also gains in individual freedoms, economic opportunities, and civil rights, all while the world's peoples were being drawn closer together. With everything appearing to be opening out into a brighter future, there was no consideration of halting the growth process at the stage that turned out to be its most benevolent. Who among all the young people who enjoyed the opportunities of the sixties would have predicted that today's youths would feel so pressed to find a job that can support a family. No longer is it possible to enjoy the luxury of taking a few years off to explore different ways and still be confident of finding a decent job later. Now, with barriers to growth appearing in all directions, we simply organize to drive over them, regardless of the costs—personal, social, environmental, and military. Growth has brought with it a whole new series of plagues, ones associated with the fast-paced, highly competitive, and self-oriented way of life that has brought with it high rates of divorce, violence, alienation, drug use, and depression. Survey research adds other, more private torments of insecurity, aloneness, and fear of failure.

Which plagues are worse, the old or the new, is of course a personal matter, but as time passes the question will become academic; there will be little choice in the matter. At some point increasing environmental resistance will force the economy down. The growth that at one time was desirable will have been carried to the point where its costs so outweigh its benefits that it will be folly to push on with "business as usual." Growth will be brought to a halt by the economy's own vigor and dynamism. Already there is a tendency to look back on the times when incomes were lower but life was simpler, cities were smaller, the air cleaner, jobs more secure, streets and schools safer, marriage and raising children easier, and taxes and regulations fewer even as government worked better.

There is no way of knowing when the urban industrial economy will peak, but thoughts of this are so unattractive that we try to avoid them. It is easier to proceed as we always have on the assumption that things will work out—as they always have. All societies tend to stay with ways that work for them, and this could be the case with us, too. The economy could continue to expand for some time yet, perhaps quite a while if everything is done right, but it cannot be a long-term solution. It may be called the information economy now, but that is only because information is the current growth sector. Underneath it is still the industrial economy, with its steel mills, power plants, 18-wheeled trucks, huge cities, and the rest of the paraphernalia necessary to produce and distribute the incredible output of urban industrial civilization. We are letting the market economy shape our lives, and it is taking us where it will—as opposed to where we might go if we had more choices in the matter. Those who would like to be small farmers, for instance, or shopkeepers, or craftsmen working with their hands in the context of a community have ever fewer opportunities to do this. All of those who do not thrive in the ways of a competitive high-tech economy may just as well hunker down and endure, enjoying the abundance it offers while hoping for changes that will permit more choices in the future.

Beyond the Peak

What is beyond the high point of the S-shaped curve is even less knowable than how and when it will be reached. But the patterns in nature provide a number of useful insights, not pleasant ones, perhaps, but still helpful in deciding on the best course of action ahead.

In nature, what follows the topping out of the S-shaped growth curve has been extensively studied, and the resulting pattern is known as overshoot and collapse, and shown in Figure 3. As a population grows beyond the capacity of the environment to sustain it, it over-exploits the environment, damaging it in ways that reduce its productivity, leading first to malnutrition, then diseases and more effective predation, and finally starvation. Population falls, often precipitously, but this gives the environment a chance to recover, and then population, too. The process repeats itself until the population finally stabilizes at a level that can be sustained—the definition of the term *carrying capacity*.

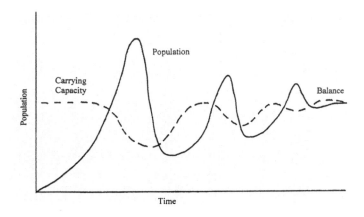

Figure 3. Overshoot and Collapse

Humans differ from animals in that we can modify the environment to raise its carrying capacity, and success in this is the essence of the modern achievement. (Kates) In following this path, however, the carrying capacity of the environment is not only being exploited but also being consumed in ways that animals never could. This is most clearly reflected in the consumption of the fossil fuels that power industrial society— oil, natural gas, and coal—and enable large populations to be supported at high material standards of living. With no energy alternatives on the scene with anywhere near the capacity of the fossil fuels, even after decades of research and development, the threat of overshoot and collapse is no longer remote. There are low-grade fossil fuels available—oil shales, tar sands, and heavy oils—but in addition to being costly to convert into usable forms of energy, they also generate more greenhouses gases—the wild card in the game of overshoot. The fusion reactors that were to be the utopian way of sustaining industrial society indefinitely into the future turned out to be quickly damaged by the high-energy particles that come off them at close to the speed of light. Renewable resources have the capacity to support simpler ways of life but not urban industrial society as we know it. Chapter 5 will provide a fuller examination of the energy alternatives, but for our purpose here, of learning from natural processes, the human response to overgrowth cannot be to press harder for growth. That would only leave our descendants in more difficult circumstances, with critical parts of the environment damaged or depleted.

Still, human resiliency and adaptability are great, much greater than other species, as demonstrated by all the changes people have adapted themselves to. This makes the concept of carrying capacity of less value for us than for wildlife, since our needs are not as fixed as those of other species. Even in the distant future when the fossil fuels are gone, the human population that can be sustained will depend on many things, but especially how much is demanded from the environment to meet everyday needs. And the end of the era of growth does not mean an end to the era of challenges, excitement, and new opportunities. Just the opposite: the most important stage of cultural evolution is just beginning—the movement toward the sustainable ways that will support a long human presence on this planet. And it is not just survival that is at stake; the quality of life will also be determined by the evolutionary process ahead.

The Immediate Need

The difficulties inherent in dealing with overshoot and decline suggest that reaching sustainability will be easier—and the final result better—if it can be reached in a long, smooth evolutionary process rather than a series of booms and busts as shown in Figure 4, each of which could end in a reversion to "nature red in tooth and claw."

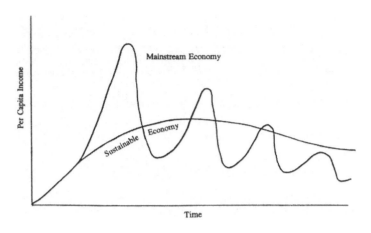

Figure 4. Two Paths To Sustainability

These two ways of moving toward sustainability provide the frame of reference for this book, and its purpose, too—of discouraging the all-too-human tendency to stay with what is working, no matter how difficult it gets. Change may be hard, but avoiding change will be harder yet since it leads to change in its most brutal form—the crushing declines that make the dark-age scenarios so fascinating for science fiction writers. These are the worst-case scenarios, the ones that leave people hungry and cold, or worse, struggling with violence and predation, since killers thrive on such circumstances. This is the kind of future that could leave people brutalized, both in body and spirit. The best possible path would be the long, slow—evolutionary—one that permits a wide range of experiments under diverse circumstances. This has been the path of evolutionary success in the past, and there is no reason to believe that it will not be so in the future.

Nor does this mean that radical change is necessary. Just the opposite; evolutionary progress comes out of tentatively moving in one direction and then another, but avoiding the risky plunges that could jeopardize a way of life, even decimate a population. *Nothing I say should be taken as arguing for radical change* It is simply too risky, especially given our present dependence on the smooth functioning of the modern economy. That economy can certainly be made more efficient, which would help significantly by increasing the time available for the transition. But it is hard to imagine how the economy could be transformed in ways that would make it sustainable; even to attempt to do so would be so expensive and require such fundamental changes that it would risk bringing the whole thing down. The process must be a gradual one that explores different ways of living and working, the more the better. But, the luxury of exploring the sustainable economy under such fortunate circumstances is only possible with the continued productivity of the mainstream economy, especially when it is considered that the physical plant of our society may have to be largely rebuilt. With enough time to fully explore the alternatives, none would have to be given up prematurely, before missteps could be corrected or critical elements altered. Think of how long it took to learn how the market economy worked and then to manage it for steady growth.

The slow but steady movement toward a sustainable way of life shown in Figure 4 is the most that can be hoped for. Ideally, the sustainable economy would emerge in parallel with the mainstream economy, meaning there are two parts to the task—creating opportunities in the sustainable economy while preserving the soundness of the mainstream economy. The productivity of the mainstream economy would provide most of people's needs but also the materials to build the physical plant of the sustainable economy—whatever forms it takes, including a good deal of experimentation. There is little question that many Americans would like to participate in building a sustainable way of life while living in simpler, less stressful ways more of their own choosing, but for the present there are few chances to do this. Creating these opportunities could well be the most challenging task, especially since it would have to be done in ways that contribute to the stability of the mainstream economy.

Thoughts on the economic aspects of this matter are offered in Chapter 7, but it may not be until some of the high-powered talents presently going into keeping the economy strong are diverted into allowing it to slow down gracefully that the real nature of the process will begin to emerge.

With skill—and luck—the sustainable economy will grow as the mainstream economy encounters greater resistance. As it peaks and begins a long and hopefully slow decline, the sustainable economy will be there to take up the slack, the two economies being interdependent but driven by different motivations. The movement toward sustainability would be under way when the sustainable economy advances in balance with the slowing of the mainstream economy, a process that could continue for a long time. The vertically rising lines that make the modern era so dangerous would gradually be turned downward, and in the process ways of living would be created that, while simpler in material terms would be richer in emotional, social, and spiritual terms, as well as more in balance with the environment. Such is the ideal to strive for.

Are We Flexible Enough?

Free markets have been good to the United States, but this does not mean this will always be the case. Even now, in the heyday of the free-market era, when natural gas or electricity shortages appear there is a tendency to blame producers for the price rises that follow, rather than accepting that something is getting scarce. The only effective way of bringing prices down is to bring demand into balance with supply.

At any point in time markets favor the ways that best fit the times, and for a long time this has been the ways of the advanced industrial nations, the U.S. especially. The free-market economy turned out to be the most effective way of bringing forth the new technologies that could put the abundant natural resources of this nation to work, but as this way of life spreads rapidly the world's resources are being consumed at an ever faster pace. When it becomes clearer that this cannot be sustained, the adaptability of more and more nations will be tested. Markets have already turned against many Third World countries as the price of their exports declined compared to the cost of their imports, but the greatest tests could well be in the nations that have been most thoroughly shaped by market ways. Still, these countries have proven themselves quite adaptable in dealing with change, and even when not wanted, as with the closing down of older industries and small farms.

The energy crisis of the late 1970s provided the most useful insights as to how market forces will drive change, especially as energy grows scarce—and thus expensive. The response to higher oil prices then was vigorous and effective; individuals, governments, and corporations all changed in constructive ways once higher prices made clear the necessity of doing so. The world would be in a better position today if the higher oil prices then had held, and continued to encourage energy conservation, the use of renewable resources, and the movements in toward cities and out toward rural areas to reduce transportation. But the high oil prices of that time stemmed from the actions of a cartel; there was more oil in the ground, and as it was discovered and prices dropped, the economic lines resumed their upward trend. The return of cheap energy meant the market economy could return to what it did best, and the growth that followed was rapid. But that episode told us something important, that change will occur when the need for it is clear—when it hits our pocketbooks and threatens our jobs.

Until this happens, however, there will be a tendency to block out information we do not want to know about. This is the only way to explain the absence of media attention to reports in the nation's premier scientific journals, *Scientific American* and *Science* (the Journal of the American Association for the Advancement of Science) which suggest that world oil production will peak sometime between 2003 and 2018. (Campbell, 1998; *Science,* 1998) The actual date will be an important one, since the only way to bring consumption in line with falling production is through higher prices—either that or a global recession that reduces demand enough to keep prices down, the alternative that could well be more likely as the global economy weakens. If the economy remained strong, however, the peaking of world oil production would mark the start of a long climb in oil prices.

Even the reason why the dates for the peaking of world oil production vary so much is interesting. The discrepancy is not due to differences over how much oil remains to be found. No giant fields have been discovered since Prudhoe Bay in Alaska in 1969, and the smaller fields being found now will not significantly extend the oil era. The large additions to proved reserves in recent decades have come primarily from the increased sizes claimed for existing fields. This is possible, since original field sizes were calculated with data from test wells, and new technology is finding oil left in depleted fields. But there is skepticism about these uniformly higher claims, especially since they justify higher production quotas under OPEC rules, higher stock values for oil corporations, and more loans for Third World countries—all powerful incentives. With today's focus on the short run, the bottom line, and political advantage, such ways are almost expected of corporations and governments, especially if competitors are claiming them—and benefiting from doing so.

As significant as the two articles about oil resources are, however, they have received no coverage in the main-stream media (at least by the time this book was published three years later). There is no government censorship in the U.S., but there is a market-based censorship, since consumers gravitate toward the media sources that say what they want to hear, which is not that oil production will begin to decline relatively soon. More important yet is avoiding anything that clouds the future of the economy, since that could undermine the stock market and the confidence that keeps everything going. Even if the claims for increased field sizes are valid, the years of abundant—and cheap —oil are numbered. At present, only Saudi Arabia has the capacity to increase output to meet rising world demand, and when their production peaks the price increases that follow will be market driven, not cartel driven. There is much potential for using energy more efficiently, and it could be encouraged with higher taxes on fossil fuels, but this is the kind of thing our society is not interested in. It is easier to see OPEC or the oil companies as gouging us, or that higher taxes on oil is only the government getting into our pockets again, rather than a efficient way of diverting oil consumption from the present to future generations—to those who will be forced to get by on less while rebuilding the economy in sustainable ways. It is through our answers to such questions that the new century will be shaped—for good or for ill.

The Real Challenge

If anything separates humans from the other animals, it is the capacity to look ahead and see where our actions are taking us. There are alternatives to pressing on with overgrowth, good ones, too, but our collective national mind has been so shaped by the needs of the economy that virtually no thought has been given to how the economy could be allowed to slow down gracefully. Perhaps more important is that our own personal growth is tied to the opportunities the economy provides us with. Growth is the one national goal that is supported by liberals and conservatives, labor and management, the old and the young—in short, by everyone. It could even be said that growth has become an obsession with us, perhaps even an addiction, or enough so that we feel we have no choice but to work ever harder to develop new technologies, move into new markets, and create the high-paying jobs that will keep us ahead of the competition—all the things that make the modern way of life so stressful.

To suggest that growth is an addiction is not to say that dealing with it will be easy. It will not; that is the nature of addiction. There is a physical basis for it now, too, since we have built our lives around the needs of the economy—around big cities, for example, vast transportation and industrial facilities, and the heavy use of fossil fuels to keep it all functioning. The main problem, though, is in our minds, since our well-being is so heavily associated with growth, individual as well as economic. Everyone has been shaped by what it takes to do well in today's economy and to stand out from an increasingly formless crowd. To even think about moving away from growth—in any form—creates deep resistance, especially as memories of more cooperative ways fade with the passage of time. There is a powerful logic in what we are doing, but a substantial part of it is based on the logic of the free-market economy that is shaping this society ever more pervasively, including now sports, entertainment, education, the arts, religion, and politics. Yet this is the world we live in, and there is a sense that it cannot be changed. And besides, it is what made the U.S. a strong, unified nation, its economic supremacy the basis of its military supremacy. We are the winners in this game, and it makes any talk of moving toward more sustainable ways seem almost irrational, as detached from reality.

The discomforts of modern economic society are telling us things we should hear, but we are so absorbed in its ways that we fail to hear them. We blame everything except the economy for what troubles us while accepting its platitudes without question—that greed is good when it creates jobs, ostentatious consumption, too, since it keeps workers on their jobs, and advertising since it sells more of the things that keep the economy going. Even the religious right doesn't balk when mothers are deemed more productive when working than when raising their children. Such is the nature of our addiction. Its logic is deeply embedded in the world we live in, and we seem bent on following it wherever it takes us.

Overcoming these ingrained beliefs is the essence of the challenge we face, since we have the skills, the tools, and the resources to move in directions that will leave our descendents with better evolutionary prospects. The next few decades could set the tone of life for a long time to come—for better or for worse. If we fight ever harder to preserve something that cannot be preserved, we risk leaving our children with little beyond depleted oil fields, damaged environments, assets of little value, and who knows what social and national security problems. It would be a far cry from what we were left by our ancestors from softer, more generous times.

CHAPTER TWO

The Changing Fortunes of Dominance and Cooperation

That humans are still close to other primates is demonstrated by the 98.5 percent of our genes that are the same as the chimpanzee's, our closest relative. That percentage and a half of difference is of course important, but still, the 98.5 percent that are the same should remind us of how close we are to the primates—and how easy it would be to revert to their ways.

In this age when humans are such a dominant force on Earth, there is a tendency to idealize nature, which is healthy in many ways. But it should not be taken to the point of forgetting that there is still much truth in seeing nature in harsh Darwinian terms, as "red in tooth and claw." Culture managed to find a better way than this, one that enabled humans to occupy all the varied environments on Earth, and even if this process may have been taken too far, the achievements of our ancestors should not be denigrated. Nor is this to deny that there are many biological influences in human behavior, as the sociobiologists tell us, only that their arguments, too, should not be taken too far. This is much in fashion today, especially in seeing all behavior as driven by selfish genes. (Dawkins, 1990; Ridley, 1996) This is flattering, since it justifies seeing our market-based society as the culmination of human evolution, as the "end of history." (Fukuyama, 1989, 1993) But it also provides an excuse for everything from infidelity to alcoholism: "my genes made me do it." There certainly are selfish genes, but it is probably more correct to see them as the source of the will to live in all living things—one of the many miraculous things about life on Earth. But to follow them alone is to respond only to the instincts for dominance—as reflected in some of the most unsavory societies. The early supporters of Darwin's *Origin of Species* gravitated easily toward the Social Darwinism that justified Europe's exploitation of much of the world, just as the selfish genes justify today's market-based behavior. But in the book written later in his life, *The Descent of Man,* Darwin pointed to the evolution of the moral sense as the measure of the human achievement, and to factors such as conscience and sympathy controlled by reason and habitual behavior. (Loye, 2000) Petr Kropotkin, too, in *Mutual Aid*, pointed to the many forms of cooperation that occurred in nature as well as in primitive human societies. Things are obviously much more complicated than the socio-biologists suggest, not only in the incredible diversity of life but in the varying degrees of benevolence and malice in human societies.

The genius of the human species has been its capacity to institutionalize the peaceful, cooperative ways that permitted the steady evolution of richer, more satisfying, and more secure cultures—those that suppressed the selfish genes or directed them in constructive directions. Still, Gandhi was undoubtedly correct when he warned that we should never hope for a social system so perfect that people will not have to strive to be good. As humans, we are still members of the primate family, for good and for Ill. The ongoing task of restraining the instincts for aggression and dominance should reinforce the respect we have for our distant ancestors who controlled the selfish genes in the first place.

The Hunters and Gatherers

The case for the evolutionary achievement of our hunting and gathering ancestors was made most clearly by the anthropologist Marshall Sahlins in an article in *Scientific American*, "The Origin of Society." (1960) Rather than studying inanimate bones and stone tools to learn about human evolution, he compared the societies of hunters and gatherers that survived to our own times to the societies of chimps, with the differences taken as the measure of the human achievement. There were of course a good number of similarities, as would be expected with so many genes being the same. But Sahlins' study pointed to the critical difference: hunters and gatherers controlled sex.

In chimpanzee societies sex is the cause of much fighting among males as they struggle to gain the dominant position that permits them to mate with the females. This makes sense from the Darwinian perspective since the genes of the dominant male are passed on to all the females so their offspring will be most apt to survive. But the costs of this are significant, in fighting, injuries, and deaths, plus a good deal of wasted effort. In suppressing this drive our proto-human ancestors were able to direct their energies into more productive activities. One does not have to be a trained naturalist to notice how much energy goes into the mating process of animal species all across the spectrum, from dogs and cats fighting to dragonflies attacking each other, song birds defending their territory, and chickens with their pecking orders. Even lions, with no predators, turn to killing other lions as one male tries to eliminate competing males in order to expand his pride and the territory it controls. A huge surplus of young are born to most species, with all but the strongest dying or being killed. Those that survive are those apt to be most successful in carrying on the evolutionary process.

Humans are certainly not immune to such behavior; the genes for sex and dominance are still there, and still strong. But hunters and gatherers managed to control them, and Sahlins argues that the most important step in this was making the family into the peaceful, productive center of life that it has been ever since. He saw the incest taboo as critical in this, since in restricting sex to parents the family was freed from the disruptive effects of the almost indiscriminate sex of primate societies. But the incest taboo did more than create peace in the family; it spread that peace to other families, since it required that children marry outside the family. Kinship became the cement that held the band together but also contributed to peaceful relationships with neighboring bands, since the small size of bands necessitated mating outside them to avoid the consequences of inbreeding in a small gene pool. Kinship ties encouraged inter-band visiting and hospitality, in contrast to the enmity that characterizes relationships between groups of other primates, which often ends in fighting and death.

Many other restrictions were placed on sex by hunters and gatherers, on where it occurred, when, and under what circumstances; privacy, for example, is only required in human societies. Sex was simply too disruptive to the harmony of a band to be allowed free play. And controlling it worked; cooperation led to other advances, such as language, which was necessary if cooperation was to be effective and also stimulated brain development. Cooperation enabled hunters and gatherers to live in environments as hostile as deserts and the Arctic, while other primates have been left in the restricted habitats they still occupy. Cultural evolution was paying off in impressive ways.

If our earliest ancestors had one critical advantage in their movement toward cooperation it was the incentives for cooperation that hunting provided. When a large animal was killed, a good part of the meat would be lost to spoilage if the hunter and his family kept it for themselves. If they shared it with others, however, they not only earned their appreciation but could count on reciprocity later when others were successful in the hunt. Sharing avoided the waste of food while also tying the members of a band together into a group that could be counted on for assistance when needed. Sharing became a universal requirement of hunting and gathering societies, and it was done with special generosity at times when food was scarce. To refuse to share was cause for ostracism, which was akin to capital punishment when survival outside the band was so doubtful. But refusing to share was rare; the more frequent problem was competition over trying to give away more than others could return. This may have been a benign way of gaining dominance, but it was still dominance and could lead to discord, and thus had to be restricted. When an animal was brought down by a band of hunters, all would drive their spears into it to signify that all had been a party to the kill. The Eskimos, who often hunted as independent family units, placed all of the animals killed on a common meat rack from which anyone could take what they needed.

The leadership of a band gravitated to the most respected individual. Often this was the best hunter, but general understanding was important as well, especially of how to preserve harmony in the band. Those who became leaders were the ones who, when they spoke, were most apt to be listened to, the ones others naturally turned to for their thoughts and suggestions. This is reflected in the names for leaders, "the talker" among the Shoshoni and "he who thinks" of the Eskimos. Leaders were never formally chosen, nor could they give orders to anyone; a leader of a band of Congo Pygmies told an anthropologist that there was no point in giving orders, "as nobody would heed them." Wisdom and good judgment were what led to leadership which, in the relatively unchanging circumstances hunters and gatherers lived in, often meant older and more experienced individuals. A leader received no benefits from the position; if anything, it required the greater generosity that reflected greater capacities. The role is reminiscent of the biblical one: "Whoever wants to be great among you must be your servant."

The other leader was the shaman, the member of the band who could be thought of as having the best psychological insights; often it was a woman—the "witch doctor" in Tarzan terminology. The shamans' skills reflect the animistic religions characteristic of hunters and gatherers in which the world was seen as full of spirits, in animals, birds, trees, water, even stones. If a problem arose, it was felt to be due to something the band had done to offend the spirits, and if the shaman was in close touch with the spirits, the band changed its ways so as to live harmoniously with them again. Elaborate rituals were developed to get in touch with the spirits, discern their wishes, and placate them. The effort to preserve harmony with the spirits was an ongoing part of life; the Pygmies in the Congo basin still sing to the forest as they walk along its trails, referring to it as their mother who cares for them and provides for their needs.

In hunting and gathering societies, men did the hunting and women the gathering. The role separation seems to have been complete, and supported by powerful taboos. The Eskimos believed, for example, that the seals they depended on during the winter would leave if a woman hunted them. Does this mean sexism right from the start, of men oppressing women and keeping the higher status activities for themselves? Or does it reflect the differences between men and women, especially the role of childbearing and the strength required for hunting? Arguments can be made both ways, but anything that is so universal must have some positive value; evolutionary success does not come from preserving arbitrary distinctions, especially ones that could cause dissension. The most common explanation for roles is, again, that they facilitated cooperation. Clear role separations made men and women dependent on each other, and this helped to weld the family into a strong unit. The gathering of plant foods by women usually provided more food than the men's hunting; only in environments such as the Arctic, where there was no food to gather most of the year, did hunting produce more food than gathering. But as Peter Freuchen makes clear in *The Book of the Eskimos* (1967), in the Eskimo society he married into, a man was virtually destitute if he lost his wife and had little choice but to try to attach himself to another family to survive. Roles assured that necessary tasks were done, and in ways that pulled the band together in mutual interdependency. Roles not only strengthened marriage but helped assure that children were cared for in secure and stable circumstances. They were an important part of the confidence members of the band could have in each other and the continuity of the way of life they all depended on. And one of the great advantages of hunting and gathering societies is that their roles reflected the innate differences between males and females, the greater aggressiveness and physical strength of males and the more intimate, nurturing qualities of females.

The great majority of hunting and gathering societies for which there are records were quite peaceful. Sahlins writes that "many are reported to find the idea of war incomprehensible" and that "Thomas Hobbes's famous fantasy of a war of 'all against all' could not be further from the truth." It seemed not to be in the nature of hunters and gatherers to fight, and this was true even without any formal government or laws. (This changed with agriculture, and radically so with herding, distinctions that are important to keep in mind and will be returned to.) Much of the peacefulness of hunters and gatherers was due to the importance of kinship, but customs also evolved that led to clear knowledge of proper behavior. Breaches in etiquette led to punishment in the form of avoidance, gossip, and ridicule, ways that were highly effective in a small band. Gifts were important too, and entire books have been written about the role of gifts in primitive societies. (Hyde, 1970) Visitors were often showered with gifts, often to the point of embarrassment. One of the most striking accounts of both peacefulness and generosity is in the first letter Columbus wrote to his royal patrons in Spain describing the people he encountered in the New World.

> Initially they were so timid that they fled, but when they perceive that they are safe, putting aside all fear, they are of simple manners and trustworthy, and very liberal with everything they have, refusing no one who asks for anything they may possess, and even themselves inviting us to ask for things. They show greater love for all others than for themselves; they give valuable things for trifles, being satisfied even with a very small return, or with nothing.

Ominous words, these, since the people Columbus wrote about would all be dead several decades later, those not succumbing to the diseases introduced by the Spanish being worked to death by their obsession with gold. One of the tragedies of the peacefulness of hunters and gatherers is that it left them terribly vulnerable to outsiders with more aggressive ways. Those who survived into the era when anthropologists could study them did so primarily by living in unproductive areas that more numerous agricultural peoples could not use. The persistence of their peacefulness while being squeezed into less productive areas is remarkable.

The conclusion about the peacefulness of hunters and gatherers is not complete. The people Columbus encountered spoke of the dangerous people known as Caribes who, moving from island to island in their long canoes, periodically attacked them. The Indians of California benefited from the abundance of acorns from the state's oak trees to become more numerous than any other part of the U.S., but they were at times disturbed by tribes, often smaller ones, from the mountains above the Central Valley. (The settlers looked down on the California Indians for their peacefulness, while the Plains Indians were admired for their fighting skills.) In *The Book of the Eskimos*, Freuchen notes that violence occurs at times in Eskimo society, especially in dealing with individuals who have been ostracized from family groups, but also in dealing with the long, dark winters. Yet these exceptions to the general rule about the peacefulness of hunters and gatherers did not turn them from their peaceful ways; they did not have to develop martial skills in order to survive. It is unfortunate that the good information is restricted to the hunters and gatherers that survived into the modern era, since that means little is known about the vast lengths of time before that, and how it was that peaceful ways were favored in the evolutionary process.

This conclusion about the peacefulness of hunters and gatherers has been challenged, as seems inevitable whenever any view gains wide acceptance—especially one that goes against the expectations about what "primitive" peoples were like. Most of the criticism of the peacefulness of hunters and gatherers has come from anthropologists influenced by the sociobiologists, with the strongest challenge being by Napoleon Chagnon in his influential book *Yanomamo: The Fierce People.* (1968) Selling more copies than any other anthropological book, it described a people in an almost continuous state of warfare in a remote part of the Amazon Basin. But this account of the Yanomamo has been challenged by Patrick Tierney in *Darkness in El Dorado: How Scientists and Journalists Devastated the Amazon* (2000), which was nominated for the National Book Award for non-fiction. Tierney argues that the intertribal conflict the Yanomamo were involved in was induced by Chagnon and other outsiders, mainly by the large number of metal tools brought in, including many machetes. Also, the people were farmers as well as hunters and gatherers, and while many farmers are peaceful, others have been quite violent; the people of the highlands of New Guinea provide the most striking example. (Rappaport, 1984)

Yet even before the invention of agriculture, the peacefulness of hunters and gatherers would seem to have left them vulnerable to the more aggressive peoples who coveted the environments they occupied. It would seem to be an unstable situation, one that would lead to the "war of all against all" that Enlightenment philosophers reasonably assumed was the way of primitive societies. Why this was not the case cannot be known without more information than can be gleaned from stone tools and bones. Speculation is hard to avoid, but there may be one piece of evidence that is relevant—the role of territoriality, which is common in nature, too. After occupying one territory for great lengths of time, a band of hunters and gatherers would feel uncomfortable when they moved outside of it. They knew the spirits of their own territory well and how to preserve good relations with them, but the spirits of neighboring areas would be alien—and possibly hostile. This could have undermined the courage of people with aggressive ideas, causing them to return to the safe haven of their own territory. And if defending their territory was necessary, people could take heart from their own benign spirits who had sustained the band for such a long time.

Still, this is primarily speculation; all that can really be known is the final outcome, that in the evolutionary process the aggressive genes turned out to be less functional than the peaceful genes—for whatever reasons. Hunters and gatherers could organize their lives around peaceful cooperation without having to fear being taken advantage of by more warlike groups; they did not have to honor fighting skills and martial attitudes in order to survive. It is unfortunate that there is no evidence as to how such an unlikely conclusion came about, since it could be important in encouraging peacefulness in the future. All we know is the conclusion, that in the end, at least, the peaceful genes triumphed.

Nomadism also tended to discourage competitiveness among hunters and gatherers. Rarely could they obtain enough food in one place to stay there, so they moved in a regular pattern through their territory to meet their needs. They enjoyed this, and resisted later efforts to settle them in one place, even when it meant the comforts of houses, heavy items such as beds and ceramics, and clothes rather than skins to wear. Nomads had to get by with the few possessions they could carry from camp to camp, but this discouraged competition over the accumulation of things. And with few things to take care of, they enjoyed a surprising amount of leisure, most of which was spent playing games, telling stories, playing musical instruments, and taking long naps. After killing an animal and gorging themselves, they would often lay around for as long as it took to consume the rest of the meat before going out again. Such characteristics led Sahlins to describe hunters and gatherers as the original affluent society in his book, *Stone Age Economics.* (1972)

Even the exception to this pattern confirms it—in the environments where an abundance of food made nomadism unnecessary. The best documented case here is the Native American tribes of the Pacific Northwest, where heavy runs of salmon provided the assured sustenance that permitted settled ways of life. With material needs easily met, more energy could go into economic competition, and in the Northwest it evolved in the form of the potlatch, in which powerful individuals sought to demonstrate their superiority by giving away more than others could. When first encountered, this was seen as extraordinarily generous, but it soon became apparent that it represented the degradation of sharing to a form of economic competition much like in our society. Achievement may have been demonstrated differently, by conspicuous giving rather than conspicuous consumption, but the motivation was the same—to demonstrate superiority and humiliate competitors. Both were driven by the genes for dominance rather than peacefulness.

Hunters and gatherers were excellent conservationists. This was partly due to their limited capacity to exploit the environment. Hunters tried to put themselves into the bodies of the animals they hunted and to think as they did, with the best hunters having an almost instinctive feeling for where animals might be at different times and how best to approach them. But such skills could also lead to the overkill that threatened the group's survival. There is evidence that excessive hunting caused the extinction of some large animals in North America, but this would lead to the demise of the hunters, too. It was the groups that put their activities on a sound ecological basis that survived, and this required that they be acute observers of the environment. When unwanted changes occurred, such as those resulting from the over-harvesting of a favorite plant or animal or the disruption of reproductive cycles, they took steps to change their ways. This was usually understood in religious terms; their animistic beliefs led them to see unwanted changes as stemming from ways that offended the spirits of the environment. But they changed their ways much as if they were following scientific methods of resource management, if for different reasons—to be reconciled with the spirits of the environment. And to wantonly kill or waste anything would be certain to offend the spirits. It was in such ways that hunters and gatherers gained a deep understanding of the environments they lived in. Most of the rain forest plants which have medicinal value were brought to the attention of ethno-botanists by

Warren Johnson

indigenous peoples who had found uses for them.

A striking thing about hunters and gatherers is that their ways were the same in all the different environments they occupied. This is surprising, since it would seem that temperate, tropical, desert, and Arctic environments would bring out different ways. That this was not the case suggests that there was something fundamentally "right" about the way of life that came out of the long evolution of the hunting and gathering societies, a rightness that overwhelmed the effects of environmental differences. This brings us to an important question.

Is Human Nature the Creation of Hunters and Gatherers?

Why does it feel so good to help a person stranded by the side of the road or a blind person to cross a busy street? Why are people glued to their television sets when efforts are under way to reach a child who has fallen into a well or the survivors of a disaster, and why do volunteers seem almost thankful for the opportunity to help raise dikes against floodwaters or stop the spread of a fire? Unlike success in business, sports, or politics, where there are many losers for each winner, in collective efforts all are winners. All are drawn together by the common bonds created when a community accomplishes something that benefit all. Is this why there is so much discontent in this the most materially affluent society the world has ever known? Could the opportunity for selfless service in a community be something our genes remember, even if our culturally shaped behavior has moved in other directions? Is this why helping others has that rightness about it —because it is "gene deep"?

Keep in mind that the hunters and gatherers we know of are the product of a long evolutionary experience. Our ancestors drew away from the primates at an almost imperceptible rate in a process that went on for millions of years. If the bones of *Homo erectus* are used as a marker—those who walked upright, used stone tools, had fire, and buried their dead—it would still be some 1.8 million years before the invention of agricultural a

37

mere 10,000 years ago. The modern era began only five centuries ago, and industrial society about two, but even the agricultural era is only a brief instant compared to the time spent as hunters and gatherers. It is hard to avoid the conclusion that human nature was formed during the long evolutionary experience as hunters and gatherers. The accelerating rate of social change since the invention of agriculture has certainly changed behavior, but not genes so much, since agriculture and industry both provided the assured sustenance that preserved most individuals—along with their genes. This is not to deny the importance of cultural change, but to recognize that we still have the peaceful genes we inherited from our hunting and gathering ancestors. It is also to accept that many of the seemingly petty complaints in this affluent era have a deeper source—the frustration of the instincts for cooperation and the dearth of peacefulness.

It is not necessary to claim that the peaceful genes are stronger than those for sex and dominance; almost certainly they are not. It is important, however, to see the peaceful genes we have inherited as a true treasure, the great gift of our supposedly primitive ancestors, those we ridicule as apelike and dragging a club behind them—if not a woman by the hair. What monstrous injustice! Then we claim a higher consciousness to justify liberating ourselves from limits in any form while finding someone else to blame when things go downhill, and selfishness and anger take over where comfort and security once were. Even incest is becoming common now, and with dreadful consequences. We are reverting back toward the ways of the other primates and calling it liberation.

Even though genes cannot be destroyed as easily as culture, culture is still necessary if peaceful ways are to be possible in everyday life. Only through culture can the peaceful genes be safely expressed and the aggressive genes effectively repressed. The body of literature that deals with how hunters and gatherers accomplished this is a true treasure. (See hunters and gatherers in References)

Birth Control, the Garden of Eden, and the Fall

The old accounts of explorers and missionaries report that hunters and gatherers seemed to be living almost in a Garden of Eden, and it was assumed that their numbers were kept low by high death rates, from war and starvation especially. But more careful work by anthropologists led to a different conclusion; population was kept below the carrying capacity of the environment by controlling the number of births.

With few effective predators, the numbers of hunters and gatherers must have grown beyond the carrying capacity of the environment, which was relatively low when limited to the edible foods naturally available in it. Migration to unoccupied areas was initially possible as a response to growing population, but this could be risky if it turned out that there was little food in the direction moved. And in time, all nearby land would be occupied, and trying to take it by force could lead to injury and death. But when a band's population went above the carrying capacity of the environment, troubling problems were caused. Stresses began to undermine the cooperation the band depended on, stresses that would be multiplied if malnutrition appeared and the specter of starvation led to painful questions about who would live and who would die. Too many people jeopardized the good life, especially the solidarity that was so important to their evolutionary success.

It can be imagined that, after going through several periods of population overshoot and die-off, people got the idea that the spirits of the environment were trying to tell them something—perhaps that they were dominating it with their excessive numbers. The unpleasant task of keeping their numbers down inevitably fell to women, and over time modestly effective methods of birth control were found. Prolonged breast-feeding was the most important one, with children nursed until they were five years of age, sometimes longer. Researchers were surprised to find this was effective as a form of birth control, since it does not work in our society, where it had come to be seen as an old wives' tale. But it works when mothers do not have the abundance of food and the ease we have. Prolonged breast-feeding also functioned to space children, since it was not possible for a mother to carry more than one infant when moving from one campsite to another. Abstinence was common as well, with all manner of taboos on when and where sexual intercourse was allowed. To early observers, these often seemed arbitrary, even bizarre, but they make sense as part of the general effort to keep the number of births down.

It was when such methods failed that things got tough. Primitive methods of abortion were used, ones which are terrible to even think about, such as jumping on a pregnant woman's stomach, pushing sharpened sticks up her vagina, or trying to cause infections that would lead to spontaneous abortions. As today, abortion represented the failure of birth control. Infanticide was also practiced, usually by exposing a newborn infant in the environment. Almost always taboos supported this. With twins it was required that one be exposed, sometimes both, since a mother could not carry two babies. This was also the fate of any child with a birth defect, since hunters and gatherers could not support unproductive individuals as we can. It is hard for us to imagine how a mother with all the same maternal instincts of mothers today could leave her newborn child to die in the forest or on a hilltop. The taboos made the difference; if not followed, the whole band would suffer, so the mother had no choice; the taboo served to reduce the guilt she would otherwise feel. Gericide was practiced as well, although in this case the old people themselves usually made the decision—generally during a time of difficult circumstances when they felt they were a burden to the rest of the band. They saw themselves as having outlived their best times, while death was seen as leading to the next place in the journey—a good place, too.

Population control was thus the painful part of life for hunters and gatherers, but it was one that was absolutely essential if the good things in their lives were to be preserved. Still, it can be assumed that women were always looking for new forms of food to reduce the burden of birth control, and there is little question that they used the seeds of the wild grasses that were so nutritious, even if they were hard to harvest and cook. Also used were root crops such as potatoes, yams, taro, and cassava. This leads to the fascinating question of why, when they knew plants so well, did women not start agriculture earlier? Remember, they had been gathering food for eons, and there can be little doubt that they had noticed that seeds sprouted in garbage heaps. Root crops are almost impossible not to grow; potatoes sprout in our cupboards. Why didn't agriculture begin earlier?

We can still only speculate on this, but here at least there is an ancient myth to help us. If agriculture was tried, it may have led to unfortunate results that were interpreted as offending the spirits of the environment. This could have caused a taboo to grow up against agriculture, one that, if violated, meant a penalty—such as expulsion from the Garden of Eden. The Garden can be thought of as the environment hunters and gatherers lived in, with its fruits free for the taking. There was only one exception, the fruit of the tree of knowledge—of agriculture. The woman took the first step, since there is little question that women invented agriculture. In Genesis 3, "She took the fruit thereof and did eat," and Adam, because he listened to his wife and also ate the forbidden fruit, is cursed with "painful toil. . . . You will eat the plants of the field by the sweat of your brow." And there was no going back once God—or the taboo—had been disobeyed; agriculture generated a population too large to be supported by hunting and gathering. The garden was no longer an alternative; the expulsion was final. "The Lord sent him forth from the Garden of Eden, to till the ground from which he was taken."

There were other penalties for eating the forbidden fruit. As soon as they had eaten it, "their eyes were opened, and they realized they were naked; so they sewed fig leaves together and made coverings for themselves." In the small, closely knit bands of hunters and gatherers, nakedness was not a threat to the family, but with the larger populations that agriculture made possible it was too dangerous to be allowed; it threatened the family. God also said to them, "I will put enmity between you and the woman." Why? Because agriculture reduced the straightforward role separation between men and women enjoyed by hunters and gatherers. Men could till the fields just as well as women, especially when only digging sticks were used, but working with plants was women's work, and this made men doubly reluctant to give up the excitement of the hunt for farming. And if they did, the loss of the role separation with women led to conflicts over who did what tasks. But if men stayed with hunting, even tougher problems were caused; more hunters meant each one could take fewer animals, so hunting provided less food to meet the group's needs. Traditional agricultural societies would create new roles for men and women, but they were of necessity more arbitrary than the roles for hunters and gatherers, with the result being more friction between the sexes. Such frictions are now growing severe as the last of these role differences are being eliminated under the impact of modern technology, which does not require large muscles. Now one of the main issues is who will do the less rewarding tasks around the home, including the one absolutely essential task of any society—the raising of children.

Agriculture was a significant fall from the relaxed co-operation of hunting and gathering. Not only was farming hard, unexciting work, it also discouraged sharing, since farmers could not be expected to share the fruits of their hard labor in the sun with those who preferred to sit in the shade of a tree. The end of nomadism also permitted competition over the accumulation of things. Life would forever be different with agriculture, and the losses would not be compensated for by the advantages of a settled, farming way of life because it did not fit so well with a human nature that was the product of hunting and gathering. It would be up to culture to make the best of the situation by creating something with a better fit. The limited record of the earliest agricultural societies suggests that, even though progress was made in this, problems soon appeared, major ones, too, many of them created by the men who managed to avoid taking up farming.

Men undoubtedly hoped there would be some way of preserving a way of life associated with animals, but as they continued hunting they found themselves marginalized by the declining returns to hunting as farming expanded. Hunting declined further when farming forced the end of nomadism, which was necessary to protect the crops from the wild animals attracted by the nutritious grains being grown. Agriculture has always been feminine, and not just because of women's association with plants; there was also the sexual symbolism of placing seeds in the dark, moist earth. The time of early agriculture seems to have been the time when matriarchal societies appeared, since women were carrying out the main economic task, and also the time of the goddess in religions. (McNeill, 1963, p.35) Everything pushed men toward giving up hunting, but since this meant giving up both their ancient role and a satisfying form of work, it was hard to accept.

The Plague of Unstable Equilibriums

The region in which agriculture first appeared presented men with another alternative—herding—that could preserve a life associated with animals and be nomadic as well. The oldest agricultural settlements that have been found date from between 7000 and 10,000 B.C. and are located in the hills around the valley of the Tigris and Euphrates. The rich biological resources of this region led to it being called the Fertile Crescent, and included the wild ancestors of wheat and barley, sheep, goats, asses, and cattle. The animals with natural herding instincts, sheep and goats, were the easiest to domesticate, especially with the help of dogs, which were almost certainly the first animals to be domesticated. They were probably volunteers initially, attracted by the bones thrown into waste heaps, and then making themselves useful by barking at intruders, helping with hunting, and then herding animals. With the help of dogs men could move their animals to places where feed was available and protect them from predators to form a living food supply that could be harvested as needed. But in the absence of effective fencing to protect the growing crops, herders increasingly came into conflict with farmers, as reflected in the Old Testament story of the hostility between Cain and Abel. If a way of life associated with animals was to be preserved, it would be necessary to leave the agricultural areas and live by herding alone.

It was long assumed that herding appeared before agriculture, that it was a step in the process of moving from hunting to agriculture, but newer evidence points quite clearly to agriculture coming first, followed by herding. (Khazanov, 1984) It was a fateful splitting of the ways when groups moved off to live as nomadic herders, especially since the men who did so must have been the most masculine, proud, and spirited ones—those least interested in settling down to do women's work. The obvious direction for them to move from the Fertile Crescent was north, to the grasslands of Central Asia, where the horse was domesticated around 3000 or 4000 B.C. Initially they were a source of meat, but later, when riding them was learned, horses became a formidable military weapon. Warfare on the steppes quickly resulted as groups fought to acquire the horses that would give them the power to control large areas of grazing land. Once supremacy was achieved, however, a successful leader found himself in a difficult position, since the violence that had been triggered could not be stopped. There was a tendency for it to be turned inward, and the best way of avoiding this was by directing the violence outward, with a logical outlet being to the south—to plunder the settled agricultural communities in the Fertile Crescent. There was little reluctance to do this since the farmers there were seen as debased men doing women's work; they had no worth anyway. The raiders initially took the grains they could not produce themselves, but over the millennia they came to be known as barbarians—those who spread death and destruction wherever grasslands took them, from China to the

Danube Plain of Hungary.

The domestication of the horse was a decisive event in human history, since it virtually forced the adoption of a violent way of life. The many herding peoples in the savannah environments of Africa who did not have horses did not become violent. (It is extraordinary that out of Africa's vast array of wildlife, none have yet been domesticated.) The instability triggered by horses is illustrated by the rapid transformation of the Plains Indians in North America once they obtained horses. Prior to 1600 they lived primarily as farmers raising corn on the bottomlands along rivers. Buffalo were common but difficult enough to kill that they could not be counted on as a food supply. The Apaches were the first to capture horses that had escaped from the Spanish and then learn to ride them, as they had seen the Spanish do. With horses, hunting the buffalo became an easier, more exciting way of obtaining food, and they soon become nomadic so they could follow the herds. As they did this, however, they began to turn on the settled tribes to get the stored corn that nomads could not produce themselves. The victims, facing starvation before another crop could be planted and harvested—assuming they had the seeds—had no choice but to adopt the same predatory ways if they were to survive. Raids to capture horses became the central feature of tribal warfare on the Great Plains, the way one group became powerful and another was subjugated. Within a century, the Plains Indians were transformed from peaceful farmers into the brave but cruel warriors so familiar in American history. (Secoy, 1953)

Whether in Central Asia or the Great Plains, the horse was the first technological advance to create the "take or be taken" dynamic that has characterized the worst periods of human history. Horses created a situation in which the only alternative people had to submitting to warriors known to be harsh and cruel was to adopt their ways, and do so more successfully than their enemies—to be harsher and crueler yet. There was no other choice in the circumstances they found themselves in; either they took their enemies or their enemies took them.

The development of the mounted herding way of life in Central Asia is a classic example of a technological advance creating an unstable equilibrium. In Figure 5, the two balls are both in equilibrium; they will stay where they are as long as nothing disturbs them. But when the balls are nudged, the results are quite different. In the stable equilibrium, the ball will roll back and forth a bit and then return to its original place; this is characteristic of traditional agricultural societies. In the unstable case, however, the ball, once nudged, picks up speed as it descends from the high point at an ever accelerating rate. Once triggered, change is unstoppable—the result of the domestication of the horse.

Figure 5. Equilibrium Stability

People caught up in such unstable circumstances may have had no taste for the violence they were enmeshed in, but they had no choice; it was "take or be taken." This is one way of explaining the pervasive violence of the indigenous peoples of northern Europe, since the mounted herders who moved so freely across the fertile grasslands of southern Russia and Hungary drove the peoples they encountered westward. Even if not initially violent, the people displaced had no choice but to fight to take land from those they encountered farther west if they were to survive. And if successful, the people they displaced had to do the same thing. Violence spread out from the eastern steppes like waves in a pond until it reached the Atlantic. No groups could avoid it. A similar process occurred among the more advanced societies in the Middle East, with a more sophisticated but still quite violent heritage reaching Europe by way of the Mediterranean. Together they virtually assured the heritage of violence that would be one of the most unfortunate characteristics of Western civilization. William McNeill, in his fine *The Rise of the West: A History of the Human Community*, states that "The barbarian inheritance . . . made European society more thoroughly warlike than any other civilized society on the globe." (1963, p. 592)

Dynamism and Its Afflictions

For thousands of years there was no force capable of halting the mounted warriors who spread out from Central Asia in wave after wave. With no cavalry to send against them, armed with rifles and supplied by railroads, they could not be subdued as the Plains Indians could, and the civilized world knew them only as the barbarians who plundered and killed until the time of the Renaissance, when advances in technology finally ended their military supremacy.

There is little knowledge of the internal characteristics of these warrior peoples except for the Mongols, who were among the last of the conquerors as well as the most destructive. Genghis Khan may have achieved a sort of hero status as the greatest military leader of all time, but for our purposes here it is more important to know what life was like among the Mongol people themselves. Fortunately, China had sent spies to collect information about these people living on their northern border and known to be dangerous, and they described the Mongols as intensely self-seeking and power-oriented, with loyalty and honor playing minor roles. Individual insecurity was high, and trust was so dangerous that it was rare; the most treacherous leaders were often the most successful. Those with power were vengeful and cruel, but this was approved if they were successful in battle or taking booty. Strength was everything, with leadership having to be demonstrated continuously, especially by having orders obeyed. Failure meant weakness, which encouraged challengers to move in for the kill; often it was a leader's own kin. When a leader died, his sons would fight among themselves until all were dead except one—the most effective killer. Mongol families had similar characteristics: they were highly patriarchal, with the father relying on force to assure obedience. Arrogant and condescending when in power, they groveled before those with more power. Hostility was pervasive, especially between brothers, and there was contempt for the weak, the old, and the sick. In Mongol folk tales, the hero's quest for attachment found its outlet in his horse, since it could be trusted, and was often cared for better than members of his own family. Mongol religions reflect this world view; the gods were tyrannical and corrupt, often hideous, and often in the form of women. Cultures are all of a piece; a violent culture will not have a peaceful religion. (Thomasic, 1953)

How familiar much of this sounds, since our era is crowded with the technical advances that generate the "take or be taken" dynamic of the mounted herders. The dynamism we are so proud of could be driving us in similar directions—to the importance of strength, control, power, and independence, however achieved. The decline of trust and kinship is clear, as is the increase of insecurity, isolation, and fear. Even if the ways of the modern economy are not as harsh as those of the mounted nomads, they still demand the same intense, self-centered drive. We are also protected by a benevolent heritage, but there are the same workings of a disequilibrium in which the harshest competitors get the greatest rewards, while the cooperative find fewer outlets for their urges and tend to be held in contempt, as weak and powerless. The most effective killers now are those who can take over competitors and build corporate empires, regardless of the human costs. Many of the films that bring in the largest audiences can be thought of as reflecting Mongol ways, with vicious men doing violent things to each other and to women. And if we were in the position of having to create a religion today, can anyone imagine that its central commandment would be to love others as ourselves, or that the way of dealing with aggressors would be to turn the other cheek?

The history of the West since the Renaissance can be understood as a long series of unstable equilibriums created by technological advances—in maritime skills, the arms to take the richer colonial prizes, exploit them, and overcome foes in Europe. Peasants had to be turned into soldiers, and then into workers in the Industrial Revolution once it was demonstrated that economic power was the basis of military power. Once the U.S. had the atomic bomb, Stalin had no choice but to do everything he could to produce a Soviet bomb, and then the means of delivering it. Few countries can stand away from the global economy now, even if they want to, and hard-hearted ways are necessary for dealing with a whole array of demands, from young people seeking work to corporations trying to avoid being taken over. Economics has been described as war on a peaceful basis, and it is more than a coincidence that the best fighters in World War II now have the strongest economies—the U.S., Germany, and Japan. There are good things associated with the modern economy, significant ones, but they should not cause us to close our minds to the costs involved or the directions that "progress" is taking us.

With the Mongols, however, we can follow their subsequent experiences, and two things stand out that are particularly striking. One is that the population of Mongolia is today 2.8 million, a tiny fraction of the more peaceful peoples they conquered. Then, in the early seventeenth-century the Mongols converted to Tibetan Buddhism, one of the most peaceful forms of Buddhism, and today travelers to Mongolia describe the people they meet as warm, generous, and trustworthy. History is not destiny; cultural evolution occurs.

Equilibrium Lost and Regained

Let us return to where we were in the evolution of agricultural societies before being drawn away by the destructive role of the mounted herders. In accepting their fall from the Garden of Eden, the more peaceful men took up the digging stick and then the hoe (draft animals would come later) and moved to reestablish the peaceful, collective ways of their hunting and gathering heritage. But they had to come to terms with their new circumstances as farmers, and this was not easy.

The greater productivity of agriculture meant women were freed from the need for birth control, so population grew, and as it did farming spread down from the hills of the Fertile Crescent toward the broad river valley of the Tigris and Euphrates. The deep, alluvial soils there were very productive if irrigated, and the first irrigation works were organized by a priestly class who also developed the first use of cattle, for sacrificial purposes. But the earliest records also speak of the warfare that disturbed the peacefulness of the early farming communities, initially the attacks of herding peoples. The process by which the farmers lost their freedom seems to have stemmed from the defensive units they organized to protect themselves from their mounted attackers, only to have their defenders turn on them and demand more and more food. Food was essential to feed soldiers and trade for copper and tin to make bronze for spear points and shields. After forcing all the food they could out of their own farmers, military leaders moved to take other areas to get the food being produced in them. If a chieftain was successful in this, he could make himself into a ruler of one of the early states for which there are records in Mesopotamia, the land between the rivers. But he could also suffer the fate he had in mind for his neighbors, the consequences of which were so unattractive that they justified dangerous actions. Another unstable equilibrium had been created; it was "take or be taken" again, this time triggered by the productivity of irrigated agriculture.

The word civilization is based on the Latin word for city, *civitas*, a definition that says nothing about the quality of life in the emerging cities. Kenneth Boulding called the early civilizations a protection racket, since rulers demanded food from farmers in return for protection. The time between one harvest and the next planting was turned from a time of rest for farmers into one of continuous labor, on irrigation systems, walled cities, and monuments to warlord kings. Any reluctance to work was sure to be dealt with harshly; troublemakers were quickly put to death, but by public torture as a lesson for other workers who had to be kept alive, since their labor was the basis of the warlord's power. He had every reason to force farmers to produce as much as they physically could, and slavery was inevitable as conquered peoples were put to work for a new master. But other things were necessary, too, if a warlord was to be successful in dealing with the challengers all around him. Architecture, mathematics, and engineering skills were needed to build fortifications, granaries, and irrigation works, and astronomy was necessary to make the calendars that assured crops were planted at the right times. New social organizations were needed to manage large operations, and writing was necessary to communicate over long distances. Art advanced, too, sponsored by kings intent on building up their prestige to strengthen their rule, which often included making themselves into god-kings.

Such advances are the reason we honor the early civilizations today. Of such things there are records, but there are no records of how the mass of people felt about life in their new, supposedly civilized circumstances. For them, it must have been an unmitigated disaster. From being peaceful, independent farmers, they were turned into pawns in the power struggles of great lords, forced to work as much as physically possible while having all the food surplus to their needs taken by the state, perhaps even to go to war if ordered to. On top of this, they often had to worship the king as a god. Caught up in the workings of an unstable equilibrium, they were forced into a way of life that was radically at odds with what they had lost.

The origin of civilization has long been seen as a voluntary process, of people coming together for the advantages offered by large-scale social organization. The historical evidence, however, suggests that it was more of a coercive process. Robert Carneiro of the American Museum of Natural History makes an environmental case for this in "A Theory of the Origin of the State" in *Science.* (1970) He points out that civilizations appeared only in places where the environment acted as a prison to keep people from fleeing. Mesopotamia is this way, with the Arabian Desert to the south the only direction to flee once the hills of the Fertile Crescent were fully occupied. The Nile Valley is perhaps the best example of an environmental prison, a narrow strip of green surrounded by empty deserts on both sides. Fleeing into it meant certain death, which undoubtedly contributed to the early rise of the pharaohs and their long reign. One result was the unimaginable labor that went into building pyramids and other grandiose monuments; imagine spending one's life doing such work. To the east, Indian civilization began not in the fertile Ganges Valley but on the lower part of the Indus that flowed through the Thar Desert. In China, it was not the warm, humid rivers of the south where civilization began, but the upper parts of the Yellow River in the north that depended on irrigation—which the rulers controlled. In the Andes, people were trapped between the snow-covered peaks and infertile soils of the Amazon Basin to the east and the deserts along the Pacific Ocean to the west. The negative evidence is strong, too, since civilizations did not appear in fertile Europe or North America, where there were no environmental prisons for people to be held in, or in Africa either. Rather than being forced to work for warlords, people could simply flee, maintaining their independent ways in smaller groups closer to those of their hunting and gathering ancestors but not benefiting from the advances of urban-based civilizations either. The question of which way was better hinged on whether the technological advances could be incorporated in more benign cultures than those of the early civilizations—the same challenge we face today.

The warlord civilizations in the West rose and fell one after another: Sumeria, Assyria, Babylon, Persia, and many smaller ones; Greece and Rome only employed greater sophistication in following the same pattern, and it resumed with the Renaissance. As in our own era, the new technologies had the potential to make life better, but only if the instabilities could be overcome. For this, the second great leap in cultural evolution was required, and it can best be understood as reestablishing ways as similar to those of hunters and gatherers as possible in the new agricultural circumstances.

The Second Great Achievement

The people trapped in the early slave civilizations must have felt an overwhelming sense of powerlessness. How could the warlords be displaced, especially when backed up by their armed henchmen and with everyone dependent on the continued smooth functioning of the irrigation systems that the warlords controlled. The lords might fight among themselves, but they would never give up control of the farmers who were the basis of their power. How could such oppressive ways be replaced with peaceful and cooperative ways? The manner in which this was accomplished is almost as miraculous as the first great evolutionary achievement of hunters and gatherers.

The turning point seems to have been the sixth-century B.C. when so many of the founders of the world's great religions lived: Buddha in India, Confucius and Lao-tzu in China, Zoroaster in Persia, and the Old Testament prophets in Israel. The world's great faiths differ in many ways, but all have one thing in common: all ask for selflessness in one form or another. The religions of Indian origin, Hinduism and Buddhism, ask for it in the form of ceasing to desire; Confucianism in China in the ways that bring honor to the family and the nation; with Islam, it is in surrendering to the will of Allah; while with Christianity it is in loving others as ourselves. The form of selflessness may be different, and the theologies even more so, but the cultural objective was the same, to create circumstances that favored peacefulness and discouraged aggressiveness.

The genius of the great faiths is that they had the capacity to mold conflicting individuals into a force that strove to make brothers and sisters of all people—to turn the often selfish and unruly human nature into a moral community. For little would be gained if there was a great gulf between high spiritual ideals and an everyday world full of conflict, exploitation, and ugliness. All religions, to be effective, had to get down to the nitty-gritty, down to the everyday problems of people living and working together. It was never easy, especially given the inevitable tensions between self and selflessness in every human being, but when they worked, good things came of it. They provided the sense of being a member of a community organized in a benevolent way that also provided transcendental meaning for ordinary lives. How else can the longevity of the great faiths be explained, or that people held to them tenaciously even as modern ways eroded the selflessness they were based on? So important have these faiths been in shaping cultures that the major cultural realms of the world are still defined by the religions that shaped them.

A key advantage of the order provided by religions is that their controls are internalized by faith, as opposed to the external controls of secular society, the laws and regulations that can be evaded. This means there must be a penalty of some kind for violating religious laws, one that is usually levied in the after-life. It is surprising that people obeyed such laws in the absence of any evidence that the penalties would be applied. This must say something about human nature, perhaps that people wanted their lives to be shaped by the selflessness of the great faiths, that they reflect the urges of the peaceful genes. Affluence may permit us to be more independent, but its costs are high in the aloneness and insecurity that are so different from the ways of traditional societies shaped by the great faiths. It brings to mind Dostoyevsky's words: "Without God anything is permitted."

The appearance of so many religious leaders in the sixth-century B.C. may just have been a coincidence, but it could also reflect the emergence of a strategy for dealing with the warlords.

The military strongmen of the time would not seem to be the types likely to tremble at the threat of burning in hell or being reincarnated as a dog, but they could not know for sure. And if such beliefs were gaining wide acceptance, suppressing them could be dangerous. Not only does suppression often strengthen a religion, it could encourage a challenger to adopt the faith in order to gain the people's support in overthrowing the ruler. A wiser course of action for a warlord king, one apt to assure a long reign, would be to accept the religion, including its restraints on his behavior, but receiving in return the respect and support of his subjects. This is familiar in Western history, the high regard a good Christian king received compared to one who was rude, violent, and apt to take his subjects into wars or other tribulations.

The process is less clear in the East, mainly because warfare did not shape it so pervasively as in the West. This could well be due to the different geographical circumstances of India and China, especially their greater isolation from the mounted nomads that permitted the evolution of civilizations shaped more by the peaceful ways of agriculturalists than the attacks of mounted warriors. The terrain between Central Asia and India and China includes mountain ranges that fan out in several directions from the Pamirs and are all over 20,000 feet —the Hindu Kush to the southwest that divides Afghanistan; the Karakoram and Himalayas between India and Tibet; and the Tien Shan to the northeast of Central Asia that separates Siberia from the high deserts of western China, an area known as the dead heart of Asia. The nomads found Siberia's endless forests claustrophobic, and its harsh weather spreads south into Mongolia, the one grassland area China was vulnerable to. Invaders came to both India and China, but not before stable agricultural civilizations had evolved to the point where they could resist the militarization that occurred so early and so pervasively in the Middle East. It was not until 1211 that a hundred thousand Mongols under Genghis Khan conquered a hundred million Chinese. The Mongols then set about slaughtering Chinese to turn the land to pastures for their horses, something that was only stopped when Chinese officials promised to feed their horses for them. The nomads were rarely able to effectively rule the areas they conquered, and the Mongol reliance on Chinese administrators soon led to the end of their rule there.

The route from Central Asia into India was shorter and more direct than into China, but it still meant crossing the Hindu Kush in Afghanistan and then dropping through the Khyber Pass into present-day Pakistan and the Indian sub-continent. Invaders came earlier to India than China, but they encountered little resistance. This was partly because India was rarely unified enough to resist them effectively, but even this is a reflection of its otherworldly character. India's highly evolved religions provided the unity that enabled it to hold together through some murderous invasions, but also to take what they found useful from their invaders while at the same time turning them toward Indian ways; Tamarlane brought Mongol ways to India from Afghanistan, but his heirs ended up the Moguls, and more Indian than Mongol. This passive response may have been the most effective way of preserving a cultural heritage, since China's ancient, proud, and unified empire collapsed under the impact of superior European weaponry in the nineteenth-century. India, in contrast, absorbed English influences while preserving its own heritage more effectively than any other major culture.

In contrast to the relative security of India and China, the Middle East was wide open to an early and steady stream of mounted invaders. It was almost a straight-shot to Mesopotamia from Central Asia, most of it across the high-plateaus of western Afghanistan and Iran, terrain that mounted nomads could cover quickly and easily. But most nomad attention was focused on control of the prime grasslands due west of Central Asia, the broad, fertile steppes of southern Russia. The names of the early groups of nomadic warriors are unfamiliar—Cimmerians, Scythians, Sarmations, Shakas, Juan-Juan—until later when they turned their attention on the settled West—Huns, Goths,

Mongols, and Turks. It was not just the fall of Rome that they caused; the Mongol invasion of the Middle East in 1221 ended the Great Age of Islam there, destroying the irrigated agriculture of Mesopotamia and leaving Baghdad devoid of life; Islamic civilization was dealt a blow from which it never fully recovered. Kievan Russia suffered the same fate in 1239, with the remnants of Russian culture driven north into the protective forests around Moscow that were so much less fertile than the steppes of present day Ukraine. It is interesting to speculate on what the results of the planned Mongol invasion of Europe would have been if the nomads had not been discouraged by the forests still covering so much of Europe at the time. They intimidated people who felt most at home on the open steppes.

Jared Diamond, in *Guns, Germs, and Steel* (1998) makes a number of interesting observations about the factors that influenced cultural evolution, but much of it reflects the selfish gene perspective that sees dominance as the measure of success. Diamond says little about the human costs of such ways, not only of warfare but the other horrors of history, including slavery, torture, and genocide. If evolutionary advances are to have ongoing value, they must be sustained by the voluntary allegiance of people who value them highly enough to hold to them firmly. That which is forced on people by occupying armies, colonial authorities, or repressive religions is unlikely to survive. Religions can be the worst offenders, especially when they try to convince the oppressed that any resistance will be punished in the after-life. It is because religion can be such a powerful organizing force that it can be an equally powerful force for evil, as was so often the case in the unstable conditions of the West, but increasingly so worldwide now.

In the West it was only the fall of Rome that gave Christianity its opportunity to rebuild Europe in the ways of a traditional agricultural society. This occurred much later than in India and China, but still, the medieval Age of Faith was the longest period of relative stability in Western history, a matter that will be returned to in Chapter 9.

Traditional Agricultural Society

The evolution of traditional agricultural society was thus an irregular process, but as with hunting and gathering societies, a common pattern emerged in the villages where the vast majority of people lived. (Urban peoples followed different and more varied ways, ones that often included preying on villagers.) The distinctive characteristics of village life was the lifelong focus of the journalist Richard Critchfield who, while writing for a magazine as worldly as *The Economist*, spent much of his life in villages all over the world. With interpreters initially, but only until he learned enough of the languages to get by on his own, he got to know villagers in a way that is only possible by living with them for extended periods of time. In doing so, he gained a deep respect for them, and late in his life he consolidated his experiences with those of anthropologists, historians, and travelers in a book titled simply *Villages*. (1993) It concludes with a sketch of the common elements of village life worldwide, ways Critchfield considered to be "universal village qualities." They are summarized below. In reading them, compare them with the ways of hunters and gatherers presented earlier, and consider whether they reflect the same characteristics—the same human nature—but modified to reflect the requirements of a settled agricultural way of life.

Villagers are present-time oriented, concrete-minded, and have a capacity for spontaneous enjoyment. They are fatalistic, plain, straight, and conservative. The father is usually the head of the family and responsible for providing food, shelter, and clothing, giving his authority an economic basis. Family life tends to be centered around the mother, and marked by crowding, gregariousness, and lack of privacy. Blood ties and kinship carry heavy weight, and marriages are usually arranged, more on a practical basis than romantic. Marriages are characterized as "dogged partnerships" of closely related work and family life, but deep affection can develop based upon compassion and mutual need. Single people are rare, adultery is harshly punished, and early marriage reduces the frustration of sexual prohibitions. There is no prostitution or homosexuality.

Hard physical labor is the central fact in every villager's life, but agricultural work is felt to be good work. There is great enjoyment when periods of labor end, but morale rises with labor, while periods of prolonged idleness can cause disorientation. Children perform useful tasks from toddlerhood, and are eager to perform work as proof that they are growing up. Industry and thrift are prime values, and there is an exaggerated fear of illness or disability—but not of death—because one falls in status if unable to work. Villagers have a love of their native land, an intense attachment to their ancestral soil, and a personal bond to the land. They live close to their animals, and communicate with them in special languages. The reverence for nature and ancestral ways can lead to an organic relationship between a man, a woman, their work, and the land.

There is a strict moral code, and even though there is skepticism toward priests and other religious officials, especially from outside the village, there is a deep faith in a personal god who is concerned with their lives. A significant percentage of family spending goes for religious rites, while low percentages go for medicine, education and clothing. There is an almost universal belief in the supernatural, including omens, magic, demons, and spirits [which Critchfield saw as creating the greatest psychological divide between villagers and ourselves].

The village is the fixed point by which people know the world and their position in it, and their interests extend only as far as the places they have traveled or are likely to travel. There are mutual relationships with neighboring villages, but most social life takes place within the village itself. The village community is the one that people are bound up with by common and familiar tasks, and values which are expected to go on forever. The fear of a neighbor's censure is a more potent force molding behavior than the fear of god or government laws. Life is governed in harmony with the weather and seasons, festivals, and births, marriages, and deaths, with traditional ceremonies carefully observed. There is little difference in dwellings or clothes, much visiting, including gossip, and a great deal of courtesy and traditional forms of greeting.

Cities are feared, as are the city people who come to the village. Commerce is suspect, and there is an almost universal belief that a preoccupation with wealth would destroy the fellowship of the village. Villagers want to be left alone, with all outside authority avoided if at all possible. There is little awareness of world problems unless they impinge directly on the village.

Condensed from *Villages*, pp. 341-346.

Critchfield points to exceptions in this pattern, such as the "ostentatious virility" of *machismo* in Latin America and the greater male-female role separation in the Middle East, as well as the differences in temperament and personality between all cultures. But the overall pattern holds, and it explains a good deal of the stability of traditional agricultural societies that enabled them to resist the modernization that seemed so logical to outsiders. The changes that ultimately came to villages were those that altered their internal circumstances, especially population growth and changing market conditions. Still, Crutchfield reached the end of his long career with confidence that village ways will survive, perhaps better than modern ways.

Where We Stand

The village ways summarized above can be thought of as a measure of the distance between traditional and modern societies. The physical differences between villages and modern cities are clear, too, with both reflecting different worldviews—ways of understanding the world and how to live in it. Villages provide little room for the expanding prospects that are so important to us, and there are virtually no opportunities for the novelist, scientist, inventor, military hero, business leader, or any of the other change agents in our society. The role of villagers in history is rarely significant; only when they rise up against oppression do they shape history. And no matter how much Critchfield's villagers tried to protect themselves from the changes associated with the modern era, they still came, and in ways that have made village ways increasingly difficult. Yet these ways remain the core of traditional agricultural societies, the preferred way of the majority of people in the world today.

The interesting—and unanswerable—question is what the next stage of cultural evolution will bring. How would a Sahlins or a Critchfield describe life two hundred years from now, or a thousand, or however long it takes for a new stability to be established? If cultural evolution is a useful guide, the new societies will almost certainly value stability and continuity as much as villagers do today, but beyond that little that can be said. Even though much modern technology is dependent on abundant energy, many of the most revolutionary ones could be sustained with renewable energy—medical care, communications, birth control, and the collection and preservation of knowledge. The ambiguous prospects for other technologies make predicting the future futile—especially given the even less predictable social changes that accompany changes in technology. Who knows what new taboos might appear—what elements of the modern will be suppressed as firmly as hunters and gatherers suppressed the knowledge of agriculture? Just as it would have been impossible for hunters and gatherers to predict what changes agriculture would bring, it is impossible for us to predict where cultural evolution will take us in the future. There will always be the hope that valued and familiar ways can be preserved, but we might be dismayed if we could read how our descendants will live in the future—just as hunters and gatherers would have been dismayed to learn how agriculture would change their lives.

One thing is likely: the quality of that future will be influenced by what we do now. All we can be concerned about is the initial stage of the process—the ones our actions will influence—but Americans have their eyes as closed to such matters as Critchfield's villagers do to matters outside their villages—although with less justification given the knowledge available to us. It is time to question the fine claims made for the modern consciousness when it puts us on such a high pedestal that we feel we can shape everything to our needs and have nothing to learn from the past; such arrogance could lead to the complete ascendancy of the aggressive genes our ancestors struggled so hard to overcome. The free-market economy may have been good to us, but this god, too, will fail as the Marxist god did, if for a different reason—because it produced too much rather than too little. What takes its place is the question we should be concerned with.

A truer faith would be in the evolutionary process, that it will again be able to overcome the aggressive ways that so darken our future. How the Earth will once again become a secure home for humankind cannot be known, but it will not be through the military heroes and empire builders that have so absorbed the West. They are a prescription for another dark age, especially in the crowded, angry circumstances their actions have created. If we are to avoid leaving this future to our children, we must regain the qualities that are the core of the human achievement—of living simply, peacefully, and in balance with the environment. Unfortunately, such ways are far from where we are now.

CHAPTER THREE
A Costly Wealth

The United States is wealthy, almost certainly the wealthiest nation the world has ever known. We live better than kings did in the past in terms of the comforts we enjoy, our medical care, our entertainments, and the information available to us. So little work is left for human muscles that keeping has become a major industry. Why, then, do we not seem to be enjoying it all that much?

Part of the answer may be suggested by the definition of abundance, which in most dictionaries includes words such as "a great plenty" and "wealth surplus to needs." With all the wealth in this country, how many of us feel we have a great plenty or more than we need? Rather few, I imagine. The economy, in fact, depends on just the opposite—on unsatisfied needs—to keep it strong and growing, and with the help of advertising it is doing this quite effectively. Dissatisfactions today do not stem from having too little but from being conditioned to want more regardless of how much we have. This continues right to the top, to the billionaires who want to have more billions than other billionaires. If there is a feeling of being on a treadmill these days, this is what keeps it going, the urge for more; growth only speeds up the treadmill. And the disturbing questions of why we don't seem to be enjoying our wealth very much can be put aside when the rest of the world is following our lead in the global economy. Imitation is the sincerest form of flattery, and it is telling us that we must be doing something right.

Still, there is less of the optimism that characterized the decades after World War II. Winning the war had generated a confidence in what the collective will of a good society could accomplish, and it was a welcome relief from the hardships of the war and the Depression before it. Regular paychecks permitted people to buy cars for the first time, homes away from the noise of the city, and to put their kids through college. Individual freedoms, opportunities, and civil rights were expanding, medical advances were coming one after another, and better transportation and communications were drawing the world closer together. Problems remained, of course, but it seemed they would fall away as the others were.

But while the economic lines have continued on their upward paths, the problems encountered have eroded the optimism about where they were taking us. The gains have begun to seem less important than the losses, the modern plagues of broken families, weakening communities, declining moral values, and the destruction of nature. The collective good will of the postwar era seems to have been replaced by a collective ill will, with people angry at someone, or threatened by them, or just plain dissatisfied with what things have come to. Our homes are larger and finer now but the quality of life in them has declined, and our technically superior cars crawl along congested freeways through graying cities, endless suburbs, and out into a world that has less of the beauty it once had. At times it seems that so many people are rude, angry, or on the make that even a small kindness makes one's spirits soar. Affluence, as it turned out, has come at a price, and the price has been high.

Social Selection for Dynamism

It should not be surprising that urban industrial society found its fullest expression in the United States. The abundance of land and resources here and the freedoms offered to immigrants attracted the vigorous and discontented from Europe (and later the rest of the world). Those who were comfortable with the restraints of the "old country" stayed there, a process of social selection that facilitated the passage of the U.S.

Constitution here and the freedoms it protected. The progress that resulted was so exhilarating that Americans molded their behavior—and the nation's—to the needs of the economy. But to produce a growing mountain of goods and services requires the hard-driving, competitive behavior that is making life stressful. Those who relish such ways are fortunate, but those who were satisfied with their lives on small farms and communities based on face-to-face relationships paid dearly for their attachments, with falling incomes, declining property values, and finally bankruptcy—all the ways by which economic forces drive people to conform to the requirements of an urban industrial way of life.

Societies through the ages have relied on markets for their proven capacity to allocate goods and services, but the markets were usually embedded in larger cultures that were organized around other, higher values. Market values might be fine for Saturday markets, but they were almost universally considered too base to be allowed to shape all of society. It was when the guardians of higher values in Europe, the nobility and the churches especially, grew oppressive that the movement to reject them gained force. This was the Enlightenment, and its two most influential spokesmen were Thomas Jefferson and Adam Smith. It is more than a coincidence that their most important writings, *The Declaration of Independence* and *The Wealth of Nations*, were both published in 1776, since both reflect the primacy of the individual—in democracy and free enterprise respectively. No longer would people be told what to do by the rich and powerful. The Constitution was the first fruit of this movement, and it is still among the most important, as evidenced by its longevity and worldwide influence. But *The Wealth of Nations* must be considered to have pushed ahead in importance as free-market ways shape the entire world, including undemocratic societies, such as China, that achieved some of the highest growth rates.

In the United States, the government's key role—the one most apt to get presidents reelected or voted out—is keeping the economy strong, which is done by maintaining the circumstances that permit the economy to function smoothly and efficiently. The freedom the market depends on for its efficiency meshed neatly with the yearning for freedom that brought immigrants here, but the Founding Fathers never expected that the economy would gain such momentum, that one freedom—economic freedom—would come to dominate others as much as it has. Jefferson's ideal of independent, self-governing communities still has wide appeal in this country, but such ways have inexorably been pushed aside by those individuals that capitalized on the economic freedom so firmly protected by the Constitution. Jefferson worried about this during his lifetime; he had been to England and seen the effects of the Industrial Revolution there and wanted to have nothing to do with it here. He pushed for policies to keep industry out of the U.S., by importing manufactured goods from Europe in exchange for the export of raw materials and foodstuffs. But Alexander Hamilton argued that this would leave the U.S. too vulnerable to the designs of European nations that still coveted this rich colonial prize, and he carried the day. But Jefferson was constrained by a dilemma he faced—his belief that "the best government is the least government." It did not permit the kind of laws that would be necessary to preserve the agrarian society he wanted. (Marx, 1964) His vision reflected the cultural landscape of Europe, a landscape that had been shaped by feudalism and the medieval church—institutions that Jefferson, and most Americans, had little taste for.

For a long time after the new nation was established the full expression of free-market behavior was constrained by the values immigrants brought with them to this country. The ways of the industrial barons in the nineteenth-century were remote from the daily lives of most people, but as the wealth they amassed became more public it was perhaps inevitable that the ways of the boardroom would spill out into Main Street. They now shape everyday life to the point that it is taken for granted that everyone, individuals and businesses alike, must employ whatever means they have to get what they want in an increasingly competitive environment. No longer can an agreement be based on a handshake, and no businessman can feel qualms about putting competitors out of business, moving jobs overseas, or using the environment in the most profitable way. It is not a matter of moral values but survival in the circumstances we live in. An industrialist who did the right thing by his workers, his community, and the environment would be rewarded for his conscientiousness by going broke, unable to compete with managers whose eyes are more clearly focused on the bottom line. Responsible firms become takeover targets for investors who feel they can increase profits and push stock values up; stockholders sometimes even sue managers to force them to do this. Media firms grow into conglomerates on the strength of sales of violent, sexually explicit materials and fall back on the defense of "if we didn't do it, someone else would." The same thing would be said about narcotics if they were legal, and it is only because they are still illegal that they are reserved for the budding entrepreneurs on the mean streets of inner city neighborhoods. Lawyers are blamed for the huge increase in litigation, but they are hired by those who hope to gain from a growing range of legal actions. Whatever works is right in the hard-headed struggle to get what is wanted today—the modern form of "take or be taken."

Still, the economy is strong; that's all that needs to be said to bring the issue back to reality—today's market-based reality. Everyone is exhorted to push ever harder to keep the nation competitive, and in ways that give the affluent society its sense of desperation. Hard-driving management and down-sizing are accepted as necessary to hold onto world markets, factory closures cannot be questioned, and rural areas can be left with mostly old people. Workers have no choice but to accept that they will have to retrain for new jobs several times in their working lives and move to where the jobs are. Reduced social welfare spending must be accepted as necessary to force people to work harder, and taxes on the wealthy must be reduced so they will invest more. The hard won gains of environmentalists are undermined as the need to create jobs becomes all important. Nothing can be allowed to stand in the way of the economy, no matter how noble or decent, and any talk of turning away from the hold the economy has on our lives is ridiculed as being out of touch with reality. Instead of the economy being embedded in culture, culture is embedded in the economy, a point Karl Polanyi makes in his account of the effects of the Industrial Revolution in England, *The Great Transformation.* (1944)

A tense, anxious society finds itself increasingly hostage to the economy, willing to put whatever is necessary into preserving its competitiveness, if only because there seems to be no alternative. The consequences of failure are too threatening to even think about. The economy is the solid core of society now, the place where one's investment of time and energy are most certain to be rewarded and success is most universally acknowledged. Personal relationships, in contrast, have grown prickly and contentious, especially when they get in the way of the freedom to do what society pulls us to do. Civic virtue, personal honor, and the good name of one's family have all receded into the background, as outside the economic nexus, as relics of a past discredited by its material poverty and lack of freedom.

There is overstatement in this, for which I apologize, but it does point to the direction things are moving in a society increasingly shaped by the self-interest demanded by the modern economy. Few will disagree that the tenor of life in this society changed as the market economy evolved. There are different opinions about whether such ways are desirable or not, with those defending them apt to be those prospering from them. Those who feel the loss of what are generally referred to as traditional values are thinking of the times before the market shaped behavior so much, a time when we were poorer but family and community were more important parts of day-to-day life. Wealth and economic freedom have enabled Americans to avoid the difficulties of living and working with others, but this has left them more isolated, and more dependent on the rewards of the marketplace for their sense of self-worth. No longer is the old saying heard, "It isn't who wins that's important but how the game is played." Now winning is everything, but this makes losing more painful, and more common, too, since there is little honor in playing the game well. Cheating becomes more common, too, and in everything from school work to corporate accounting methods.

But nothing is all good; we have hitched our ways to the free-market economy and there seems to be no choice but to go where it takes us. Or so it seems to us anyway, with our frontier heritage. European countries have followed a somewhat different path, as might be expected from those who were satisfied enough with the old ways to stay in Europe. Solidarity was more important to them, and they continue to work for it more than we do. They resist the great differences between the incomes of the wealthy and the poor tolerated in the U.S., and pay higher taxes to fund generous social services even if this reduces the incentive to work. Europeans have long found it unconscionable that we allow a large part of our population to have no health care, with the highest incidence among children—where poverty is also the highest. The biggest item in the budget of the European Union is for the Common Agricultural Policy, which provides subsidies to small farmers and helps to preserve the attractiveness of the European landscape while discouraging the movement of people to the cities. Europe has done things differently, but they pay for it, too, with higher unemployment, budget problems, and a growing difficulty competing with the U.S.

We have pulled out all the stops in order to drive economic advance as rapidly as possible, and whether described in positive ways—as providing incentives to work harder—or negative—as coercing people to do so, the result is the same— the strongest economy in the world. It means we have more billionaires but also more minimum wage jobs without benefits, more palatial estates but more poverty and homelessness. We may see our economy as vigorous and creative, but other countries see it as harsh and overbearing, as the bully on the block forcing others to act in the same way if they do not want to get run over. Imagine how leisurely the world might be if no country's economy was more productive than, say, Mexico's or Greece's. In putting ourselves on the economic treadmill, we are forcing other countries to do likewise; there would be a worldwide sigh of relief if we decided to move toward sustainable ways. By our actions we are making sure others do as we do, whether they want to or not. This is true for Americans, too, since there are few alternatives for making a living other than in the highly evolved urban industrial economy.

The Disappointments

It is interesting to go back to the optimistic times after World War II and compare what prosperity was expected to do for us with what the results actually have been. It is a useful exercise, too, since it should temper the blind support the economy enjoys in this society, especially the expectations of what continued economic growth will do for us in the future. The differences between what was expected from the affluent society and what was delivered are quite extraordinary.

Education. In the early years of the postwar era, education was expected to be one of the good things that would be more widely enjoyed as the new machines reduced the labor it took to produce goods. Through the wonderful concept of lifelong learning, education was to be a key part of the enrichment of life that would accompany affluence. No one— absolutely no one—predicted that by the end of the century education would have turned so heavily in the vocational direction, or that young people would face an almost desperate task of getting the right education if they want to get a job that paid enough to support a family. Even elementary school-children are being prepared for what will clearly be their main challenge ahead, conforming themselves to the needs of the economy, which means being proficient with computers. In an era when wealth and professional achievements have become synonymous with personal worth, students hardly need parents and advisers to tell them about the importance of getting the right education.

The liberal arts departments that were expected to thrive as the machines took over the work of human hands have instead been among the ones to decline the most. Nor is a liberal arts education still recommended as the best preparation for a rich and satisfying life—as well as prestigious work; by the late 1990s, unless liberal arts majors found work in professional, managerial, or technical areas, they had no more earning power than a high school graduate. Many of the departments offering courses in philosophy, literature, or the classics survive only because of the general education courses that students must take if they want to get the useful degrees—the ones that get them jobs. Students no longer have the luxury of being able to go into the fields they are most interested in and still find a job, while the business schools, which in the 1950s and 1960s were scrounging for students, are now fighting them off. Students able to handle math and science are told they would be foolish not to go into the technical fields that are the surest source of well-paid work. There is now a surplus of graduates in many fields, including law and medicine, and even in many of the sciences, especially with a Ph.D. (*Science*, 1998) The media speaks glowingly of the high salaries offered to graduates in some fields but little about the limited opportunities in other fields, while the rising costs of higher education mean that many students graduate heavily burdened with debts. Much attention is given the young Internet millionaires, but not the decline in real incomes of many workers since the 1970s.

Leisure. A common complaint about life today is the stress caused by having too much to do and too little time to do it in. What happened to all the leisure that was supposed to be created by the remarkable machines that were taking over the work human hands formerly did? Productivity has continued to rise; why hasn't leisure too?

The fall in the length of the workweek got off to a good start, declining from 48 hours at the end of World War II—working on Saturdays—to the 40 hours of the five-day week by 1950. It continued to decline, to 38 hours in the mid-1950s, leading to predictions that by the end of the century it would fall to 28 hours, with some predictions as low as 22. The steady growth in productivity would have permitted an even greater drop in the workweek if its benefits had been taken in increased leisure. But for whatever reasons—and they are complex—Americans chose to take their productivity gains in the form of more income and consumption rather than more leisure, because today the average workweek has climbed back up to 43 hours. There is a lively debate over this figure, but there is no question that many people are working overtime or taking second jobs. Such data can be collected quite accurately, but it is more difficult to determine how many unpaid hours salaried people work. The longer hours that entrepreneurs and professionals have always worked are spreading to other workers now, especially as competitive pressures increase, not only to get the promotions but also to avoid being laid off in a downturn. And just because jobs in manufacturing are declining doesn't mean that the hours worked are declining. In the course of a year, U.S. factory workers put in 320 more hours than their counterparts in Germany and France—the equivalent of two months.

Other research, however, suggests that there has been no increase in the time devoted to work, and the effort to reconcile these apparently conflicting figures led to what seems to be the logical explanation, that work is increasing primarily in the higher income groups, while at the other end of the spectrum are the part-timers and temps who would like to work more hours to buck up their low incomes. The fact that so many women are working now is the other important factor that creates time pressures, since the tasks that stay-at-home moms used to do must now be squeezed into after-work hours—something that also leaves less time for children. The stress caused by all this activity generates its own needs, such as for the physical activity that is so helpful in dissipating stress.

The changing forms of recreation in recent decades are another illustration of the influence of economic forces in our society. In the 1950s recreation departments were established in colleges and universities to plan for ways of using the growing amounts of leisure time that were confidently expected. Plans were made for new parks and recreation areas and bond issues prepared, but progress was slow. Not only did land for parks and recreation areas grow expensive, but fewer people were using them, especially in and around urban areas. The rising status consciousness of an increasingly affluent society made public facilities less attractive than private ones, causing people to vote down bond issues and put their money instead into private forms of recreation—condos at the beach, the lake, or ski areas, foreign travel, and all manner of mechanized recreational equipment. These investments evidently provided higher psychic returns, but the real estate investments were profitable, too. All of this reduced political support for public facilities, a pattern that was reinforced when public parks became places for disaffected youth to gather and were blighted by rowdyism and vandalism. When parks turned from neighborhood assets to liabilities—from places for children to play and weekend ball games to places to stay away from—the prospects for neighborhood parks turned negative. Few are being built now, with investments instead going into private recreational facilities and gated communities.

People frequently say that they are short of time because making a living takes more time now than it did in the past, when one income could usually support a family. But this is hard to square with the doubling of real incomes that has occurred since 1960, a time when fewer married women worked. The only explanation is the increase in what is deemed necessary now. The houses in the first Levittowns built in the 1950s averaged 750 square feet, while at the end of the century new houses averaged 2,300 square feet. They also contain more appliances and electronic devices than in the past, larger yards, and more cars in the garages, all of which need more time to maintain and use, as well as more money to pay for in the first place. The lower density caused by the larger lots of modern subdivisions means that things that once could be done on foot or on a bicycle must now be done by car but turning parents into chauffeurs for their children.

By taking the fruits of rising productivity in the form of higher consumption rather than more leisure, Americans are saying another thing—that they do not have things to do with their spare time that are as satisfying as what more income does for them. It is a disturbing thought, especially when so much time is spent watching television; the Nielsen rating people say this averages 28 hours a week, although other surveys put the figure at 22 hours. The Internet is now offering another opportunity for what is essentially a solitary way of using spare time. The use of leisure is thus following the larger trend, of private activities displacing the more social ones of the past.

Financial security. An important benefit of the rising productivity of the postwar economy was to be the relief it promised from debt and financial insecurity. This attractive thought seemed reasonable enough as incomes rose, but it remains only that, a thought, because debts have increased faster than incomes. As a percentage of after-tax income, personal (non-mortgage) debt is higher now than it has ever been. During the boom year of 1998, when rising incomes finally generated the tax revenues that balanced the federal budget, 1.4 million Americans declared bankruptcy, an all-time high, and leading to legislation to tighten the bankruptcy laws. In that year people spent more money than they earned after taxes, and when corporate spending is added, 4 percent more was spent than was earned, a level of debt accumulation that had not occurred since the Depression. If there is a nascent movement toward living simply today, and there is evidence for this, it is still buried by the fully evolved consumer society in which consumption is far more important than getting out of debt. Balancing budgets is something voters can demand of government but not of themselves, leading economists to warn that excessive debt could contribute to the possibility of a "hard landing" if it cannot be sustained. (*Economist*, 2000) The high levels of corporate debt could also trigger a wave of bankruptcies if demand weakened, something that was confirmed even in the first months of the recession in 2001. Rather than the financial security growth was expected to bring it has instead increased insecurity to record levels. Who could have predicted this?

In *The Overspent American* (1998), Juliet Schor reports that servicing their debts is the main reason Americans give for having to work so hard. A detailed survey she carried out in a large telecommunications firm with 80,000 mostly well-paid employees found that they carried an average non-mortgage debt of $13,700. Her research suggests that it is not keeping up with the proverbial Joneses that motivates spending now, mainly because few Americans have much contact with their neighbors. It is what she refers to as "reference groups" that establish the standard of living people aspire to, with debt caused when people choose reference groups with a higher social status. Television appears to be an important factor, since the more hours a week people watch television, the greater their spending and debt. But savings decline with higher education as well, evidently because college graduates are more status conscious than others. Those with the most savings are those who maintain their old reference groups as their incomes increase, the manager who goes back to drink coffee with his old co-workers, for example, or the millionaire who continues to live in the same house rather than moving to an upscale neighborhood.

Happiness. The polls taken since World War II that ask people how happy they are were mentioned in Chapter 1. Taken in many countries, they ask the disarming question: "Everything taken together, would you say that you are very happy, pretty happy, or not too happy?" It would seem that, if rising income was the good thing it is assumed to be, the percentage of people reporting themselves as very happy would rise along with incomes, and this was the case until the mid 1950s, as shown in Figure 6. (Easterlin, 1995, 1972; Smith, 1979; Oswald, 1997) But then it began to decline, and at the end of the 1960s it dropped abruptly to a level that, while continuing to fluctuate, remained below the level it was at the end of the war. Higher incomes have evidently not led to greater happiness; rather, it has been the other way around. Or the post-war optimism made people feel better than the greater wealth does now.

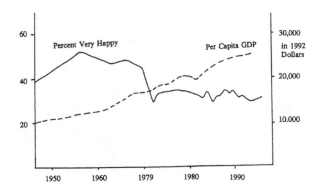

Figure 6. Percentage of Americans Reporting Themselves as Very Happy

:

A similar graph for Japan is even more striking. Between 1960 and 1987 when per capita incomes climbed fourfold—more than twice the rate of growth in the U.S.—there was no change in the level of happiness reported. Data collected in European countries between 1973 and 1980 (and reported in Easterlin) show almost random fluctuations from year to year but no clear trends. The differences between countries, however, are significant, varying from a low of 10 percent reporting themselves as being very happy to 55 percent. (At around 32 percent in recent years, the U.S. is close to the middle.) The countries reporting the highest levels of happiness, Denmark and the Netherlands, are the two countries that Schor reports as having the largest number of "postmaterialists," those who are least concerned about making money, getting ahead, or consuming heavily.

Is the economy really growing? Another way of looking at the matter is to ask if the economy really has been growing as much as suggested by measures such as Gross National Product (defined as the goods and services produced by the economy in the course of the year; it is not significantly different from the revised version now used, Gross Domestic Product, GDP). The question of whether these measures are flawed was addressed in an article in *The Atlantic Monthly* titled "If the GDP Is Up, Why Is America Down?" (Cobb, 1995) It argues that GDP includes many goods and services that are actually "bads," and should be deducted rather than added to any figure claiming to be a measure of the good things the economy produces. This includes the costs of crime, pollution, family breakdown, drug abuse, congestion, and so on. Other items are simply transfers from the home—to day care providers, for example, when mothers go to work, or to gardeners when fathers no longer have time to mow the lawn, or to the government when help formerly provided by friends and neighbors is provided by social welfare agencies instead. Other additions to GDP are actually the drawdown of assets, pure and simple, as when oil is pumped out of the ground.

When all of the costs are subtracted from GDP, the resulting measure is termed the Genuine Progress Indicator (GPI), as shown in Fig. 7. The GPI increased during the 1950s, but stabilized in the mid-1960s and 1970s before beginning a long, relatively steady decline to the early 1990s that accelerated in the late 1990s. The high point of the GPI can be thought of as when environmental resistance began to grow faster than the economy. GDP is a useful measure of economic activity since it determines how many jobs the economy will generate; with unemployment such an affliction, this is important. But it says little about the good life, or how well-off people feel. GPI does this better, at least as reflected in its better fit with the graph for happiness.

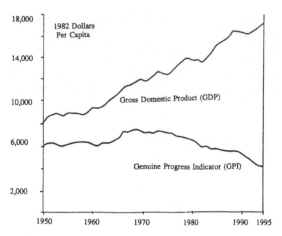

Figure 7. Gross Domestic Product (GDP) vs. Genuine Progress Indicator (GPI), used with the permission of Redefining Progress

Income inequality. Another way of understanding the disappointments of growth is that so many of its benefits have gone to upper income groups, especially in the 1980s and 1990s when all the stops were pulled out to speed growth. Between 1979 and 1995 only the upper 20 percent of male workers ended up with real increases (after correction for inflation). The rest experienced a fall in their purchasing power, with the largest drop being among the poorest. Women did better, with real incomes of the upper half rising, mainly as women began moving into better positions and closing the gap between their wages and those of men. Half of family incomes increased, mainly because of the increase of two-income families, but again it was the affluent who gained the most and the poorest who lost the most, the real income of the poorest fifth falling 20 percent. Only at the end of the century did the median family income reach the earlier 1972 peak, but again this reflects primarily the increase of two income families and the increased number of hours worked. In the world perspective, the inequalities in incomes have grown grotesque. Twenty percent of the world's six billion people live on one dollar a day or less, while the world's three richest individuals *each* have more assets than the *combined* GDPs of the world's 48 poorest nations.

Yet Americans do not like to hear that so many incomes in the U.S. are falling. Robert Reich, in his book, *Locked in the Cabinet* (1998), describing his four years as Secretary of Labor in the first Clinton administration, reported that the polls President Clinton relied on to find out what Americans wanted consistently showed that they did not want to hear about the downside of the economy—only that it was the strongest economy in the world. This must have been the right strategy, since Clinton's approval ratings remained high, even as Republicans and the media had a field day over his personal problems. Americans did not want to hear about the less attractive parts of the economy, only that it was the longest boom in U.S. history. Winning has clearly become important in this society, and if individual Americans do not feel much like winners, they can at least be proud that the nation as a whole is a winner.

Increasing inequalities between rich and poor have historically been dangerous since it created a class of people with less stake in the social order—people who could be drawn into a rebellion since they had little to lose. There is no danger of this happening here since everyone is so dependent on a job and the smooth functioning of the economy. What is different now is that the whole country is vulnerable to economic setbacks. It is interesting, too, that it is the well-to-do who express most discontent with government and push for measures they benefit the most from, such as a flat tax and cuts in capital gains and inheritance taxes, plus further cuts in spending for the poor. The larger number of people with falling incomes are saying little, even as programs to assist them are cut back. It is an interesting phenomenon, and an unflattering reflection on the effects of wealth on the people at the top of such a rich country.

The relative income hypothesis. This is a way of reaching an even more disturbing conclusion about the value of economic growth—that it does nothing except heighten status consciousness. It turns out that it is the increase in one's income relative to others that brings happiness, not a general rise in everyone's income. Rather than keeping up with the Joneses, it is getting ahead of them that is important, to stand out in some way in an increasingly amorphous urban crowd. This explains why debt has increased with incomes, since consumption is increasingly important as a way of displaying to others what one has achieved in an urban society in which few people know each other. But it is also a zero-sum game, since what one person gains in status someone else loses. This suggests that all the time, energy, and resources that have gone into economic growth could just as well have been saved with no loss of overall happiness; perhaps happiness would even have increased if people were less apt to compare what they had with others, or used their time in more genuine ways, by enjoying friends, for instance, recreation, or social activities. But Americans seem to have a hard time enjoying such things, at least compared to "getting and spending." The older pleasures are the ones our society has drifted away from, perhaps because they do not carry the status that can be flouted before others.

Conspicuous consumption is the subject of a book by Robert Frank titled *Luxury Fever*. (1999) It points to the absurd levels the super-rich have gone to out-spend others, buying $200,000 Ferraris, $1,000 bottles of wine, snifters of brandy for $200, and premium cigars that sell for $50 each. He points to the great increase in cosmetic surgeries, ever fancier kitchens and vacation condos, and the three-ton sport utility vehicles that get eight miles a gallon. Frank argues that the growing incomes of the affluent only mean they have more money to push the quest for status to ever more ostentatious levels. He compares this to the gaudy tails of peacocks and the five-foot spread of elk antlers, both of which reduce their survival prospects but still drive other males to outdo them if they are to attract females. Income earning potential is now the most important quality women look for in choosing a husband, and it is the second most important thing that men seek in women, after physical appearance—the ultimate way for males to display their superiority.

The so-called progress of modern society has only served to move us back toward the ways of the animals that our ancestors worked so hard to move away from—in large measure by avoiding the effort wasted in competing over mating.

There is, however, a bright side to the relative income hypothesis. If it is correct that increased per capita income does nothing for happiness, then it may also be true that the decline in income associated with a move toward the sustainable economy may not cause a drop in happiness. Perhaps happiness will even be improved as the treadmill slows down toward the level of the 1950s, for example, when people reported themselves to be happier even though poorer. Perhaps it might be higher yet if the treadmill stopped altogether—in a community in which no one wanted to humiliate others by having more than them. That would be fortunate, but there is no data to prove that the thesis works in reverse. All that can be said now is that competitive consumerism requires a good deal of time, energy, money, and resources in a zero-sum game.

The Downside of Rising Markets

Property owners cheered when real estate prices rose rapidly during the 1980s. Fortunes were made, and developers, builders, and real estate people all patted themselves on the back for doing things right. It was all a lot of free money—except for the young couples who found they could not afford to get into the market for homes, at least not without working for years to get a down payment together. Such buyers should have been the foundation of the higher prices, but as they were forced out of the housing market, prices began to weaken. It was a classic bubble, and as bubbles usually do, it finally burst, or at least developed a major leak. Prices didn't fall as much as they had risen, so long-term homeowners remained ahead, but for the young couples who had struggled to get a down payment together, it was disheartening to find their property worth less than their mortgages. As with so many things in this time toward the end of the era of growth, it is the young who are finding things most difficult, especially given the exaggerated expectations they have grown up with—that the economy would be as generous to them as it had been to their parents. But overall, the problem was manageable. Real estate and construction were just one part of a large, complex economy, and even though the savings and loan industry had to be bailed out, the nation had the resources to do that. People grumbled about the cost, but there was no collapse.

The rising stock market at the end of the century generated much of the same euphoria, but far more money was made since the rise in values was not just in one industry but all across the economy, and overseas too. Even though the rising stock prices were sometimes referred to as paper profits, they could be used to purchase real things, including investments in everything from retail spaces in the U.S. to manufacturing plants overseas. There was little concern about the possibility of over-investment, in large part because of the confidence of the times, and the feeling that the nation had finally learned how to manage the economy for sustained growth. All during the post-war era, the investors who had been most successful were those who counted on growth to justify risky investments, and this pattern had become firmly established by the 1990s. If there was excess supply, demand would grow along with the economy and turn the new facilities into good, solid investments. The confidence in continued growth was so strong that the majority of stocks did not even pay dividends but were purchased only for the growth in share prices. (*Economist,* 1999) Even the fear of inflation drifted away as steady economic growth generated the tax revenues that balanced the budget. Miracle of miracles! It seemed that if we carefully tailored our ways to the needs of the economy we could do anything.

All of this optimism, however, assumed that a steady growth in demand would make the new investments profitable. The Asian crisis that emerged in the 1990s jeopardized this, and to a much larger degree than the earlier crisis in Mexico. Asia had become a much larger part of world demand, and as its stock markets and currencies fell, its imports fell, too. Instead of contributing to worldwide demand, Asian countries flooded world markets with goods made cheap by the fall in their currencies. The International Monetary Fund and other agencies arranged the huge loans to halt the fall of these economies, and finally to turn them around so falling demand would not undermine other economies—the domino effect which, if left unchecked, could undermine the world economy. Far broader than the real estate bust of the 1980s, the fear was that a worldwide slowdown could turn into a worldwide depression.

The threat of such a slowdown in demand is also what made OPEC's oil price increases in the late 1970s so worrisome. As money was diverted from the purchase of consumer goods to paying for newly expensive oil, a decline in jobs occurred, especially in industries that were heavily dependent on oil, such as autos and airlines. This led to downward pressure on wages and a growing federal deficit because of reduced tax revenues and the increased need for unemployment and welfare assistance. There was a collective sigh of relief when OPEC was defeated by its own greed, its high prices triggering an expansion in both oil exploration and energy conservation that together led to the oil surpluses that held for decades. This was the market working as it was supposed to, and it contributed to the optimism that the market could solve any problem.

Perhaps it created too much optimism, including the belief that the market could be expected to deal with any problems in the future. People were told from every direction that they should hold onto their stocks, since any fall would be only temporary. Such optimism could well have been a part of the mind set that led to the overinvestment that meant bankruptcies later. The market has proven itself an impressive institution, but to put such complete faith in its benevolence would be to set the stage for the ultimate bust.

The Last Bubble?

Predicting how the economy will behave is notoriously difficult, but still, to push growth so uncritically reflects the unspoken belief that the economy can grow forever. The spokespeople for growth brush aside talk of environmental limits by saying that the doomsayers were wrong in the past and they will be wrong in the future, too. Most agree that there are risks ahead, but none that we need to worry about for "the foreseeable future"—a term that is rarely defined.

In the late 1960s, one of the pioneers of computer modeling, Jay Forester of MIT, put together a model of what he called the world system. It charted the interplay of population, industrial production, resource use, and pollution to see where they would move in the future. Forester felt that this was the kind of problem computers were best suited for, problems so complex that the human mind by itself was unable to deal with them adequately. His efforts generated such interest that a larger study was funded by the Club of Rome, an international group of primarily European industrialists, with the results published as *The Limits to Growth* in 1972. The standard run of the world model—the one most likely to occur—is shown in Figure 8. It has growth continuing until around 2010, when industrial production peaks and then declines, mainly because of the depletion of natural resources, especially oil.

Anticipating objections to the bleak prospects for the twenty-first-century, the study team doubled the estimate of resources, but this only delayed the peak of industrial production by two decades. One of the purposes of the study was to show that the interdependent nature of the world system made it necessary to solve all of its problems before stabilization was achieved. Even if natural resources turned out to be unlimited, the growth of population and pollution would still bring things down; it would just take longer. If population growth was halted, the depletion of resources would be delayed, but not halted unless industrial production was controlled too.

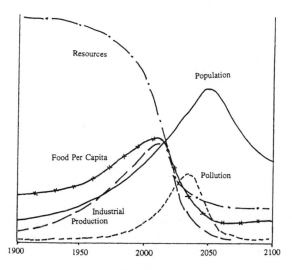

Figure 8. The World Model, Standard Run

Environmentalists were excited about the study. They felt people would finally pay attention to what they had been saying for years when it was said by industrialists backed up by the most sophisticated computer technology of the time. The initial media response to *Limits to Growth* was tentative but positive, seeing the study as a responsible, important effort. But then a number of powerful business and economic groups opened up on the report, criticizing its methods and estimates to the point that it became difficult even to discuss without generating a hostile response. The report was effectively discredited and ceased to be mentioned.

Were the estimates off? This was the focus of most of the report's critics, with special attention given to the issue of the remaining supplies of oil, since transportation is so heavily dependent on it. The mode of analysis used was developed in 1956 by M. King Hubbert, a petroleum engineer for Shell, who used it to successfully predict the peaking of U.S. oil production in 1970—a time when most geologists were suggesting many decades, even centuries, of continued oil production. Hubbert's technique was based on the declining rate at which new oil deposits were discovered per foot of exploratory well, with the assumption being that a declining rate of discovery meant that oil was growing scarcer. This led to a prediction that was uncannily accurate; he hit the exact year that U.S. oil production peaked, and since 1970 it has fallen by a third. Hubbert's method was used in all the studies of when world oil production would peak mentioned in Chapter 1, and given the fact that the Club of Rome study was done decades earlier, its projections have been remarkably on track so far. Figure 8 has half of the world's resources consumed by 2012, right in the middle of the range of 2003 and 2018 of the recent studies. Nor have there been major energy break-throughs since 1972—a matter that will be returned to in Chapter 5.

So, does this mean that the overshoot/collapse pattern projected by the Club of Rome report will turn out to be correct? Of the many reviews of *The Limits to Growth* at the time it was published, only one reflected a feeling for the process of cultural evolution. It was by Kenneth Boulding, the distinguished Quaker economist whose long career included being elected president of both the American Economic Association and the American Association for the Advancement of Science. One of the outstanding thinkers of the postwar era, he was also the author of one of the most celebrated articles of the environmental era, "The Economics of the Coming Spaceship Earth," so his credentials as an environmentalist are beyond dispute as well. Boulding's criticism of the Club of Rome report was that the model was made of "glass" rather than "rubber." The software could predict where current trends were taking us, but not how these trends might change behavior as people responded to the changing circumstances—thus taking the model straight over the precipice toward collapse. This may be what happens in nature, where instincts are immutable, but not necessarily with humans who have the capacity to change in response to changing circumstances.

In other words, Boulding argued that the optimists and the pessimists were both wrong, the optimists because they saw growth as going on forever and the pessimists because they saw it as leading straight to collapse. Both are extremes, and both are wrong for essentially the same reason—the unwillingness to accept that circumstances change, and people with them. As with so many things, it is the middle path that is most likely, the path between utopia and oblivion.

The Benefits of Barriers

It is of course possible that we will follow our present path to overshoot and collapse; the unwillingness to think about matters such as the peaking of world oil production suggests that we are doing this now, and we could continue to press blindly on this way. It is interesting that such matters could be discussed in the 1970s, not only in response to *The Limits to Growth* study but in the widely quoted words of Pogo: "We have met the enemy and he is us." But that was at a time when there was less dependency on the global economy than there is now, when there is the fear that any mention of the possible peaking world oil production could weaken the stock market and cause a recession that could spiral down into a worldwide depression. We are now so heavily dependent on the ways of the economy that we cannot permit anything that could weaken confidence in it, and this leads both politicians and the media to tell Americans what they want to hear.

If this continues it will only be the barriers encountered that will slow the economy down, and for these we should be profoundly thankful. They may be all that keep us from the excesses we might otherwise plow into if there was nothing to stop us from doing so. Nor are the declining oil supplies and rising pollution levels of *Limits to Growth* the only things that could end growth; there could be military conflict, social decay, political breakdown, or other barriers we cannot foresee now— or a combination of several of them. All would be telling us the same thing in different ways, that we have taken growth beyond the stage where it was constructive and beneficial.

In one sense it is fortunate that Democrats and Republicans both agree on the goal of keeping the economy strong and growing. Regardless of all the rhetoric over the differences between the two parties, they are differences in degree only, and mainly over how extensive the government's role should be. This means there will be little basis for one side blaming the other when growth falters. There will always be those on the fringes who will never accept that growth cannot go on forever—those on the left who see it as a plot to benefit big corporations and on the right as a way to weaken America. But most people are more sensible, and the process of moving toward a new understanding of reality will get under way, hopefully with broad public support.

It will be a major transition, there is no question of that, but delaying it will only make it more difficult. Even if done under the best of circumstances and with plenty of time, it will still involve changes on the scale of the Industrial Revolution. Yet the hardest part may not be the economy, since we have the analytic skills to guide the process of moving toward sustainability once the need for doing so is accepted. The hardest part is apt to be what goes on within each of us, since all of us have been shaped by the economy. This is especially true if sustainable ways are to be seen as worth striving for, rather than the sullen endurance of defeat. It is the ways that the urban industrial economy has conditioned us to think and act that may be most difficult to change—the matter we now turn to.

CHAPTER FOUR

Human Relationships
In a Market-Based Society

Many of the changes of the modern era are seen as desirable, but none more so than the expansion of individual freedom that enables people to pursue the goals that are most important to them. The Declaration of Independence promises "life, liberty, and the pursuit of happiness," and the free-market economy has become the main outlet for this; indeed, it is required if one is to do well. The economy effectively organizes the pursuit of individual achievement, freedom, and other Enlightenment ideals that are at the heart of the differences between our society and traditional societies. The freedom we see as essential is seen in traditional societies as selfishness, while the creativity that source of progress they see as challenging the ways of the ancestors.

Americans may look back nostalgically on the times when the bonds of family and community were stronger, but not to the point where they take precedence over individual interests and personal growth. Concerns about social security, for example, could be resolved easily if grandparents lived with their children and grandchildren, as was common until recent times. But even thinking about such things today sends shivers down our backs. We find it hard enough to keep marriages together and children on track without adding grandparents to the volatile mix. It is not realistic, we tell ourselves; we have moved beyond all that. Family and community are fine when they add to our lives, but not when they place too many demands on us. For decades we have been establishing institutions to take care of what were once family obligations—day care centers for children, welfare programs for the poor, retirement homes for the aged, and institutions for the mentally ill. With our actions we are saying that we want to follow our own stars and arrange for others to take care of the problems as they come up. Often this is the government, even when it is grossly unsuited for the tasks, but others simply get lost in the busy shuffle of life. One result is the aloneness that afflicts so many people, especially the most vulnerable—the young, the old, and the poor.

Now the focus is on the self, and it seems straightforward that once we determine what is right for us we should go for it. Only we know what is best for us, and what we do with out lives is our business; others can do what is right for them. But in pursuing what we deem to be in our best interests, others fear that what is good for me may be at their expense. Whether true or not, the natural tendency is to become wary, and to draw back. It is not necessary to be taken advantage of too many times before we put up protective barriers around ourselves, but these barriers create distance between people and cause social life to grow cool. This is especially true in urban areas, where there are so many superficial encounters and rip-off artists can disappear so easily into the crowd. The work environment provides many such opportunities, even if under a facade of civility, but even friends and family members can be hurtful, even if unintentionally, when focusing on their own needs. Whether the drive for self-fulfillment has created the satisfactions promised undoubtedly varies among individuals, but it clearly has altered the character of human relationships since it undermines the trust that warm human relationships depend on. Intimacy is not characteristic of aggressive societies; think of the Mongol horsemen trusting their horses more than their kin—and people today who feel closer to their pets than other people.

The weakening of the cooperative institutions means

there is little left but the individual quest, with the economy loudly proclaimed to be the great outlet for this. This is what works in our society, especially when reinforced by the honor accorded individual achievement. But it is a lonely quest—so aloneness is renamed independence and honored, while dependency is named "neediness" and made into a sickness, a reason to see a therapist. With failure always possible, it is a threatening quest, so strength becomes all-important. The ability to capitalize on one's assets is essential important, to be outstanding in some way, even if this contradicts the goals people tell pollsters are important to them—security, emotional warmth, spirituality, and joy. (Yankelovich) Some individuals undoubtedly thrive in the ways market-based society deems to be fulfilling, but the broader reality is reflected in high divorce rates, growing numbers of people living alone, more hours spent in front of television sets and computers, and a good deal of work for counselors and therapists. The selfish genes are clearly in the ascendancy now—whether we like it or not. But the costs of frustrating the peaceful genes are clear, if we choose to see them. It leaves open the question of whether there is an increase in satisfactions today—or ever more ways of trying to convince ourselves that we are the winners. The poet may be closest to the mark: "Free, free, free, like little boats lost at sea."

The Ties That Bind

In a real sense, the economy is functioning as religions did in the past. The Latin root of the word religion is *religare*, meaning "to bind," and it is something that all societies must have if they are to hold together and survive. An often obstreperous human nature must somehow be bound into a productive unit, and through most of human history this has been the role of religion. It was never an easy task, since what must be accomplished is, at its core, the integration of a society. To do this it is first necessary that people be bound together effectively by an ethical system; let us call this horizontal integration, of people to people. But human nature seems to require answers to the ultimate questions of life, answers that sustain people and give them heart so they will not to be pulled down by feelings of meaninglessness or the futility of going on. Let us see these answers as providing vertical integration, between people and ultimate reality. To accomplish these two quite different forms of integration in one religious system might seem to be a difficult task, and many religions have failed in it. But those which accomplished it most successfully gathered millions, even billions, of followers to them to form the great world faiths. We, in our idealization of freedom and the new, tend to look down on these cultural achievements, in part because they are the source of the restraints we no longer see as necessary or desirable. But this is only possible because of the new religious system that is holing our society together, the one that functions through the invisible hand of the marketplace.

In the deepest sense, the economy is binding our society together now, a case that is increasingly heard, (Loy, 2000; Cox, 1999), and the integration it provides is impressive. It is especially strong in the horizontal integration it provides, since the free-market economy is almost magical in the way it keeps this huge, complex society functioning. It pulls everyone toward contributing to it as usefully as they can, in order to earn the best living. Not only is the economy organizing day-to-day activities, it is providing a form of vertical integration as well, even if the salvation it promises, success, is earthly in many ways. Whatever one's feelings may be about the economy, few would not agree that it is what makes this nation work, and does so with values that are widely shared.

One of the reasons for the triumph of the market faith is that its tenets are clear and the ways of meeting them straightforward. Much of this stems from the workings of Adam Smith's brilliant metaphor for the market's capacity to draw people toward profit and repel them from loss, the invisible hand. Think of how the needs of a city with millions of people are met, and the profusion of goods and services that appear spontaneously because providing them is rewarded with income. The magnitude of the task is reflected in the massive bureaucracy required by non-market systems, such as the former Soviet Union with its abject failure in providing even a meager standard of living. Because the market functions so efficiently, it is not surprising that allegiance to the market faith is strong. And the salvation it promises is not only in the things money can buy but in the respect that comes with them. To be economically successful means to be someone of worth in this society, while to be poor is to be of little worth, or even of negative value if government assistance is needed. To be poor is the contemporary version of hell, not only because of having to scrimp to get by but to work in dull, low-wage jobs, or worse, be unemployed, on welfare, or homeless. The market also provides a clear vision of heaven, the powerful individuals with beautiful people all around them, the infinite variety of things they have, and the freedom to do whatever they want. Right from the beginning, during the Renaissance, but especially with the Industrial Revolution, the market faith was justified by the wealth it created, and this is a large part of what keeps it strong today.

On its surface, then, the market faith could be said to be a materialistic one, but at its core it is still a personal faith; material things are important mainly as a way of communicating to others what we have achieved, that we are persons of worth, especially compared to others. And since it is always possible to move upward relative to others, a solid basis for growth is created. It is not surprising that growth came to be the golden calf of the market religion since it brings forth everything that is good—jobs, higher incomes, profits, tax revenues, and new opportunities. Government, in contrast, is a negative force, at least to the degree that it discourages growth with taxation, regulations, and welfare programs. The heretics are those who refuse to work, but they exist only because the government makes this possible, one reason for the hostility toward welfare. The market also encourages the major engine of growth of our times, science and technology, since new products can be so profitable. The market faith makes it possible to disregard problems such as over-population, resource depletion, and environmental degradation, since the market can be expected to bring forth the technology to deal with them—as it has in the past. All that is necessary is for government to keep its hands off and let people respond to market signals, since they are what bring forth the intelligence, discipline, and hard work that solves problems. The proven success of the market is the best evidence of its divine power. And if hunger or urban unrest in the Third World lead to violence in which many die, that is the process by which balance is restored.

This may seem like a caricature of both religion and economics, but there are important truths in it. The most important one, however, is that the economy is ordering our lives now, and doing so quite effectively. So strong is the faith in it that we can block out its unintended side effects, or blame them on the devil—the government, or the devil on the left, big corporations. In fact, there is no longer any separation of church and state in this country since every elected official must work to strengthen the market faith if they are to stay in office. Other, more conventional religions can continue, and they provide important comforts, one of the age-old functions of religion, but their role is increasingly restricted to the private realm. What is left is the quest for spirituality, but in a market-based society this often becomes another way of achieving a private benefit. The "spiritual marketplace" is alive and well, as reflected in the large sections in the bookstores devoted to it. But the rare mention of restraints or obligations suggests that it a search for a good "spiritual investment," one with a high "benefit/cost" ratio.

The market faith is buttressed by the most aggressive proselytization any faith has ever enjoyed, with billions of dollars going into promoting it worldwide in order to win converts and keep demand strong. It is an impressive faith, but it is young and its longevity is yet to be proven. To be optimistic is good, but it is equally important that the optimism be based on solid foundations. Historically, it has been the emotional bonds between people that held a society together, not impersonal market forces, especially when they turn people into competitors defending their own interests. The question is whether the market could provide the basis for an enduring society (even disregarding environmental limits), or if the competitiveness it depends on would work ever more effectively against trust, solidarity, and cooperation, to the point where aloneness was all that remained.

But then biology would be a problem, since all societies depend on the most intimate of relationships for reproduction and the raising of healthy children.

Marriage and the Family Under Pressure

It is hard to imagine how any society that makes marriage and the raising of children so difficult can be on a solid evolutionary footing. One of the essential requirements of any society is that children be raised with the capacity to carry that society on into the future, hopefully to improve it but at a minimum to preserve its good qualities. Yet our society draws energy away from the family so insistently that less is left for the activities that still go on in the home. The family had important economic functions in traditional societies, but they were ones that strengthened the family rather than drawing energy from it as ours does.

A good marriage must be one of life's greatest blessings, for rich or for poor, but few will disagree that it is not easy to find today. The movement toward self-fulfillment has worked against love in general, at least as reflected in the rapidly growing number of people living alone. This is the opposite of what was expected at the start of the modern era, a time when marriages were often arranged on the basis of practical needs. It seemed reasonable to expect that marriage would be stronger when they could be based on mutual attraction and love rather than economic need, but instead it has led to one of the greatest of modern failings. It is striking how often two people who are attracted to each other enough to get married end up in the most hostile of circumstances—divorce proceedings. Divorce is one of the three sources of greatest stress in our society, along with long-term unemployment and the death of an immediate family member. Divorce is clearly associated with modern society, since not only are divorce rates the highest in the U.S. but they have risen with modernization all over the world, while in traditional societies they remain low to non-existent. The same phenomenon is reflected in love poetry, which has gone from lyrical praises of love to sad ruminations of the problems that afflict it now or despair over its loss—regardless of the ecstasy new love creates. Whatever the advantages of modern economic society, and there are many, it must be conceded that it works against love and marriage.

A good part of the reason for this stems from the mode of thinking that drives market exchanges and is known as *quid pro quo*, or something given for something received. It is one of the most attractive aspects of the market since all exchanges are voluntary. No one is compelled to give up their money to obtain a product or a service; they do so willingly because what they receive is deemed of greater value than what they give for it. If both sides of a trade do not end up being better off, the trade would not occur. But when applied to personal relationships, things quickly get tangled because it is so much harder to value what is being exchanged. The natural tendency is for each spouse to see things from their own perspective and to value their own contributions more highly than their partner's, leading both to feel they are giving more than they receive—that they are being taken advantage of. Resentments build up, and when they explode into an argument both sides feel they are being treated unfairly, that their contributions are not valued. The marriage begins to feel like a "bad investment," and when efforts to increase its "rate of return" fail, there is a tendency to turn away and seek a "more profitable" marriage. But the search is unlikely to be successful if it continues to be based on the *quid pro quo* of the marketplace.

Friendship is moving in the same direction, continuing as long as it pays off for both parties but being dropped if difficulties appear or one party finds a more profitable friendship. The result is the superficial friendliness of today, with many acquaintances but few friendships with the staying power that friendship once had—much as marriage lost its staying power. It becomes increasingly acceptable to say, "If what I do is hard for you, that's your problem; I have to do what's right for me." It doesn't take long for others to get the idea: "Take care of yourself; no one else will." Hence the spreading aloneness—even in marriage—that leads people to turn to careers, diversions, or even pets for the loyalty that has grown scarce between humans. The marriages that work now are often those between busy professionals who come together for meals and other activities but can still focus their energies on their own pursuits.

The deepest, most satisfying love now is often of parents for their children, in large part because the roles are clear and parents can offer their love freely, and without being concerned with *quid pro quo* or the fear of rejection. It is ironic that such love is only possible because of the requirements of human reproduction; biology, in effect, has barred us from destroying this last great treasure. Yet children grow up in this society, and Mary Pipher argues in *The Shelter of Each Other: Rebuilding Our Families* that young people today feel almost honor bound to revolt against their parents as proof that they have become independent, autonomous individuals. Pipher's books, about girls growing up, families, and seniors, sympathetically explore families today, the good things they offer and the problems they face. (1995, 1997)

Divorce rates in the U.S. were almost insignificant at the start of the twentieth-century. They took an initial jump after World War I and then exploded in the 1960s and 1970s. Even if one partner finds divorce liberating, the other one often does not, and children are almost always hurt by it. And there are many children being hurt this way; 45 percent of children experience divorce before the age of 18. This is *The Divorce Culture* that Barbara Dafoe Whitehead writes about, (1997) and she presents evidence that children are not only hurt by the harsh words that precede divorce but also by the traumatic experience of a family breaking up, of being separated from one parent, and the continuing tensions between the parents, often over the children. Divorce usually means that children live in reduced economic circumstances, and since both parents must work, it usually means less time spent with parents. If remarriage occurs, the children face the added hurdle of melding with a new parent and siblings, the difficulties of which are the main reason for the failure of second marriages. Whitehead reports that five years after divorce, a third of the children still suffer from depression, and that the chances of a girl from an advantaged home becoming a teenage mother are five times higher if her parents do not live together, while her chances of dropping out of high school before finishing are three times higher. Other sources report that the children of divorce suffer from lower self-esteem, are more apt to look back on their childhood as the unhappiest time of their lives, and have a greater likelihood of divorce when they marry than children from intact families.

In other words, there is no basis for the oft-heard claim that children are better off when fighting parents divorce than when they stay together. It would be far better if spouses could overcome their differences, or at least recover enough of what led them to marry in the first place to avoid injuring their children. But making human relations work is not something this society does well, while affluence makes going it alone possible. Many of the marriage customs around the world, even ones that on the surface seem arbitrary or even strange, can be understood as helping to overcome the innate difficulties between mean and women so the important task of raising children can be accomplished. We are moving in the opposite direction, toward ever more effective ways of making marriage difficult and leaving children insecure and less able to get along with others. Marriage rates have fallen by a fifth since 1980, and the Census reports that for every three married women there are now two single ones, twice as many as in 1970, while the number of single men has tripled. Although the stigma of divorce has largely disappeared and the singles life has gained acceptance, this should not be taken to mean that people prefer to be alone. Marcelle Clements, in *The Improvised Woman: Single Women Reinventing Single Life*, (1998) found in her survey of single women that most saw themselves in a default position, as wanting to be with someone but preferring to be alone rather than in an unhappy relationship. Single women tend to see the life of married women as cozy, warm, and safe, but married women envy the excitement of being independent and free from the demands of family life. Neither alternative is working well, with pulls in different directions making balance hard to find. No one disagrees that to be happily married is a great blessing or that it is best for children, but there are other benefits as well, as Linda White points out in *The Case for Marriage: Why Married People Are Happier, Healthier, and Better Off Financially.* (2000) Many good selfless things are going on in families, but they are declining with the rise of the modern self-absorbed consciousness.

Much stress today comes from simple overload, especially for working parents who want to do what is best for their children. It is probably just as well when those who are most oriented toward careers decide not to have children, since they would be the ones most apt to resent the time and emotional energy raising children requires. It is not just the need to earn money that draws mothers to take jobs; staying at home is isolating in suburban neighborhoods and there are few opportunities for casual interactions with other people. Taking a job not only provides human contacts but additional income, too, which, even if not essential is still nice to have in a society so oriented to having things. Jobs also help women avoid the stigma of being "only" a housewife, one of the most glaring prejudices against the "uneconomic" activity that goes on in the home. Two full-time jobs also help justify putting aside the gender roles that women find so unfair, replacing them with a greater equality in household chores, the unrewarding tasks compared to those outside the home. Then there is talk of "quality time," of somehow making the bits and pieces of time left for children into something intensely valuable and productive—the same kind of thinking that made divorce beneficial for children.

The pervasive role of culture in shaping the behavior of men and women is strikingly reflected in the dynamics of marriage. The spectacular advances of the modern era increased the prestige of masculine roles all across the board, in economic activity, politics, science and technology, even warfare. Women's roles, in contrast, were diminished as less work was done in the home, families grew smaller, children spent more time in schools, and women became isolated in suburban neighborhoods. It was inevitable that women would want to move into the more exciting and remunerative roles in the economy, but the costs have been high as our society moved in the ever more masculine ways demanded by the economy—and away from the softer, more supportive ways of the home. The demands the economy placed on men are reflected in the fact that they now die six years younger than women, a difference that was only two years in 1900 and is not found in traditional societies. The difference here reached a maximum of eight years in the early 1980s, a time when the women who were dying had not been as active in the economy as those who are dying now. It will be interesting to see if the life spans continue to move together as women become more involved in the economy—if it becomes more a source of their self-worth. But even as it stands now, the difference in life spans suggest that the competitiveness demanded by the economy is toxic to people who evolved as hunters and gatherers.

Children and Young People

Since children are the easiest ones to love and benefit so much from being loved, it is sad to think of them spending so much time in child care centers, on sidewalks, home alone, or in front of television sets. As they spend less time actively involved with their parents they are more apt to be shaped by the experiences and values received from others, with the result being tension with their parents and rebellion against them. Parents tend to blame this on everything except their own values and how they use their time. This does not mean that children are not still valued and enjoyed; they usually are, but that there are powerful pulls on parents' time and energy in other directions.

Virtually all research supports the conclusion that the home is the major influence on the way children grow up—for good or for ill. Still, the search goes on for someone else to blame, and often it is the young themselves, that they have become lazy, spoiled, and disrespectful, or revel in all manner of anti-social or self-indulgent behavior. The young could, with more justification, blame their parents for taking care of them-selves first and blaming economic necessity, rather than admitting that there were things to do that were more exciting than staying home with the kids. We also had all sorts of things we wanted the government to do, such as proving our military superiority and building more freeways, but at the cost of a national debt which will likely burden future generations. Many of the ways used to balance the budget came at the expense of the young; now it is programs for seniors that are exploding in cost—Medicare and Social Security especially. They are paid for with the higher taxes young workers are paying now compared to the low ones seniors paid during most of their working lifetime. This is a massive transfer of benefits from the younger generations to the older, from today's least fortunate age group to those who could well be the most fortunate generation that ever lived. When the market economy took off after World War II, everything was inexpensive, including homes and college educations, while at the end of the century the poverty rate for children was the highest of any age group in the nation, 23 OPEC—compared to 3 percent in the Scandinavian countries. At the same time, the poverty rates for those over 65 in the U.S. had declined to 8.6 percent, the lowest in the nation except for the 45-54 age bracket—those at the peak of their earning power. So much for criticizing the young for being self-indulgent. They are, all too much, our children.

The younger generations do not say much about this, to their credit, and it is true that they were not done with evil intent toward the young. The Americans who enjoyed the post-war boom felt they were creating the prosperous way of life that following generations would inherit. But the economy has grown tighter than it was during the easy decades after the war, with good jobs harder to find, houses harder to pay for, and higher education more expensive, more necessary, and more time-consuming as graduate degrees become more important. Young people are less likely to enjoy the rising standards of living the older generations did, the appreciating value of homes and stocks, or get more out of Social Security than they put in, all the things that most of today's retirees have enjoyed.

It is in this light that we must try to understand young people today. There are many ways of doing this, but for our purpose here, of seeing how the economy has shaped behavior, it can be said that the young were useful more as consumers than workers. With unemployment an ever-present concern, the young were discovered as a new market, a potentially large one, and advertisers went to work convincing youngsters that the new consumer items were things they needed. They were so successful in this that polls now report adults overwhelmingly feel kids are too materialistic and consumer-oriented. But we are stuck with their consumerism since it supports important Industries, such as clothing, music, films, electronics, and recreational activities. These industries provide jobs that are important for adults, but not for youngsters, who are left with few opportunities for work, especially in jobs where they can learn useful skills and the ways of the world. Self-esteem has been found to be strongest in young people who, from an early age, did tasks in the home, tasks by which they could demonstrate, to themselves and to others, what they were capable of. But the labor-saving devices that made things easier for parents also reduced the need for children's help, and the changing economy left only a handful of niches for the first paying jobs other than the proverbial flipping burgers.

Passive consumption is rarely satisfying, so it should not be surprising that many young people are troubled by boredom, lassitude, and low self-esteem, or that some gravitate toward alcohol or drugs to create excitement out of the emptiness they feel. Those with the capacity to do well in academics, sports, or social activities at least have outlets for their energies, and useful ones, too, since they prepare them for the competitive society they are moving into. But balance is hard to find when many of the young are pushed so hard to achieve by their parents, teachers, or counselors. There is economic logic in this, but it means putting youngsters on the treadmill at ever earlier ages rather than letting them enjoy youth as a time free of adult pressures. Even social life has become status-conscious, separating the smart, the beautiful, and the successful from the rest, those who get invited to private parties from those who go to the high school dances, or stay home to avoid the invidious comparisons that can be so hurtful. It was in the upscale high schools where the worst shootings occurred, and it turned out that these supposedly ideal settings for preparing for successful lives were rife with cliques and hostilities. It is a troubling indication of what could be ahead in an ever more competitive society. (Powers)

Even in more settled circumstances, the high achievers our society is so focused on make it hard for those with average capacities and face declining job prospects when they finish school. All kids are bombarded by the same messages, about how important it is to set their sights high and get the right education if they want to have the good things our society offers. But there are few slots for doctors, lawyers, or start-up companies, so for the majority of youngsters, aiming high will only mean disappointment, perhaps the first of many. It is interesting how our society tends to focus on the high flyers in the economy, almost as if it is trying to buck up the faith in the market economy as the source of everything that is good. The declining real incomes of most workers is the more realistic view.

With young people facing such daunting prospects, it is not surprising that many decide that the way to avoid failure is to refuse to compete—to cut classes, hang out with other kids, and salvage their self-esteem by looking down on straight society and getting their highs from alcohol and drugs. This is understandable, but sad too, both for the youngsters, who will suffer the consequences of limited education all their lives, and for society because of the antisocial ways some will fall into. But it is not just the losers who are disaffected and cynical. Two Stanford sociologists compared the attitudes of recent generations of graduates and found that 35 percent of the students in the 1990s were cynical about institutions, bleak about the future, and generally dissatisfied with their lives, compared to 25 percent in the 1980s and 20 percent in the 1970s. (*Stanford Today*) The scarcity of good work could well be the greatest deprivation the young face, since it means limited opportunities to use their minds and bodies in constructive ways. Many feel inadequate to the demands of the high-tech economy but see few niches elsewhere in which they can use their energy and abilities in constructive ways. It may have made sense for their busy parents to hire a gardener or a handyman to leave more "quality time" with their kids, but it would have been healthier if they had worked side by side on tasks that not only helped them learn the meaning of family but also building skills and self-confidence.

Community in Retreat

There may be no word embodying greater incongruities in our society than community, between the longing for the warmth and emotional comfort it promises and the flight from it that is actually going on, and has been for a long time. The reality is that it has become difficult for people to work together, especially when there are so many incentives to do the easier thing, to pursue one's own interests.

It is unlikely that it was ever easy for people to work together. They did so in the past largely because they had to, since many of the good things in life could only be enjoyed collectively. There was rarely enough wealth to have them individually, and the novels about the wealthy suggest they were afflicted with similar jealousies and antagonisms our society is. The importance of community in traditional societies is reflected in how close houses were built together, often with common walls, something that was true even in agricultural villages which required farmers to walk to their fields. This is in contrast with the efficiency—and the loneliness—of the isolated farmstead that the abundant land in the U.S. made possible. In suburbia, the large lots we aspire to reflect the urge to be separate from our neighbors, partly for privacy but also to demonstrate what we have accomplished and our individual tastes. There is little effort to hold to a community standard in order to remain in good standing within it, or to wear traditional clothing that reduces competitiveness over appearance. Such ways were the rule in much of Europe in the past, and in this country, too, as reflected in the architectural unity of old villages and towns. Our individualism is the opposite of the quest for unity of traditional societies. All such differences reflect the primacy of the individual over the community, and all contributed to the decline of community.

There are still rewards for working for community, and many people still do so, and generously. As with family, there are pulls both ways, but the pulls toward community are much weaker than those toward family. Part of this is because working in a community can be slow and frustrating, and at times can involve a good deal of jockeying for credit for what is done. It can mean the politics that turn many people away—and can be avoided by the independent that is more comfortable. At times it is only when property values are threatened that people can be counted on to come together and act. With other problems, the tendency is to complain about them but hope someone else will do something. If no one does and a problem worsens, the government can be called on: "That's what we pay taxes for." Or left to fester, especially in the inner cities where problems seem intractable, with drug dealers, gangs, and physical decay.

Robert Putnam of Harvard's Center for International Affairs has assembled a mass of data about the decline of what he calls social capital in America—the connections between individuals and the communities they are a part of. (2000) He presents a disturbing view of the direction of change in our society, since participation rates in civic activities have declined significantly. Membership in the PTA dropped from 12 million in 1964 to 7 million now, a fall of 42 percent (after falling to 5 million at one point). The League of Women Voters has experienced a similar drop, and volunteers with the Boy Scouts are off by 26 percent and the Red Cross by 61 percent. Membership in fraternal organizations such as the Elks, Lions, and Rotary Clubs fell in the past two decades by amounts that vary from 12 to 39 percent, and with this came drops in the public service projects they did. Church attendance fell by a sixth between the late 1950s and the early 1970s, with some polls showing the drop continuing while others see it stabilizing. Socially, things have changed too. Dinner parties, once a social staple, declined 60 percent in the last 20 years, and card playing declined by the same amount in 15 years. Participation in bowling leagues was off by 44 percent between 1980 and 1993, even while the number of bowlers increased 10 percent. (Putnam's book is provocatively titled *Bowling Alone: The Collapse and Revival of American Community.*) Even with the decline in these activities, however, the number of Americans who reported themselves as always feeling rushed increased by half since 1962.

Trust is also declining in the U.S. The percentage of Americans who feel most people can be trusted fell by more than a third, from 58 percent in 1960 to 37 percent in 1993. The most trusting Americans were born before World War II, and they also did more volunteer work in community projects, were more tolerant of minorities, and readier to vote and serve on juries. Those born in the 1920s are twice as trusting as those born in the 1960s, belong to twice as many civic associations, are three times as likely to vote and read newspapers. Married people are a third more trusting than those who are single, divorced, or separated, and also belong to 25 percent more groups. The fall in trust was most striking in government, with those feeling they could trust Washington to do the right thing most of the time falling from 70 percent in 1966 to 25 percent in 1992. At the same time, the core measure of civic involvement—voting—fell by a quarter in national elections. The organizations that are growing today are those which require only the writing of a check once a year. Many are charitable organizations, but the largest one, the American Association of Retired Persons, reflects the political nature of many—the shaping of public policies in ways that benefit its members. Also growing are support groups such as Alcoholics Anonymous, which was the pioneer in the twelve step movement. They are important organizations for the individuals they serve, but not ones that can be enjoyed by the community as a whole.

In trying to explain the falling rates of community involvement, Putnam looked at a number of possible causes: the pressures of time and money, increased mobility, divorce, suburbanization, women joining the work force, the changing economy, the revolt against authority, and television, but none could clearly be correlated with declining civic capital. Even education, which increased dramatically after the war and is associated with greater civic involvement, did not halt the decline. The only significant relationship found was when the respondents were born, which determined the values they encountered while growing up, especially the Depression and World War II. Difficult times made trust and cooperation important, while prosperity led to their decline—yet another consequence of a strong economy that no one could have predicted.

At times community works, even spectacularly, as when responding to emergencies, and the satisfactions people feel in such efforts should remind us of what we have lost. But the trends now are clearly in the other direction. The mobility demanded by the job market not only cuts into family ties but also separates people from their friends in the old neighborhoods. The multitude of shops in the malls with their plentiful parking have put neighborhood shops out of business and reduced the chances of meeting friends and neighbors when shopping. The low-density residential areas people overwhelmingly prefer depend on cars, meaning less chance of meeting friends on sidewalks, and less reason to build front porches since no one is walking by. With less chance of meeting friends in eating places, parks, ball fields, or at civic activities, the television set is always there and so easy to turn on, and now the Internet, too. The economic segregation of cities isolated the poor and minorities in their cast-off neighborhoods, and the cold bureaucratic help they receive from the government is a far cry from the more personal help formerly received from neighbors, churches, and civic groups.

The Warmth Grows Cold

The changes in our society tell us that something profound is going on, something that will probably be understood only with the benefit of hindsight. It does seem, however, that it must stem from the spreading influence of the economy in shaping our society, and especially the movement toward the primacy of the self at the expense of the more collective ways of the past. The only real way of learning about something is to try it, but it does seem perverse the way something so universally seen as desirable has instead taken us in such troubling directions.

One body of research may shed light on what has been going on inside of people as the pace of modernization accelerated. It was carried out by a cardiologist, Meyer Friedman, who first identified what is known as Type A behavior. The first book describing his research sold spectacularly, and Friedman feels this was because people bought copies to give to friends and relatives—in effect suggesting they had the hard-driving, aggressive ways that increased the likelihood of heart attack. The medical implications of this work led to substantial amounts of research money to develop a fuller understanding of Type A behavior, including large scale psychological research projects to determine what causes it. The conclusions reached, however, were not ones Americans wanted to hear, and Friedman's second—and far more important—book, *Treating Type A Behavior and Your Heart*, published in 1984, sold poorly and has gone out of print.

Many Americans are familiar with Type A behavior, but few know the unsavory forces that drive it—status insecurity and hostility. Nor is it just the super-achievers who are afflicted by it; it is common throughout our society. As with many personality characteristics, Type A behavior is formed in the earliest years of life and relates to the universal need for love. Infants and children who do not receive unconditional love from their parents are left feeling defective in some way, as if they do not qualify for their parents' love for some reason. Without love they do not gain the security and acceptance that would allow them to venture out into the world in an untroubled way and open to its wonders. Instead, they are left anxious and striving for their parents' love, even by misbehaving if necessary. As they grow older, the unsatisfied need for acceptance shifts to society as a whole and comes out in the drive to succeed. But without the confidence to know who they really are or what is important to them, they strive to succeed in ways society honors—through acquiring wealth and influence. The intensity of this drive is what produces the impatience characteristic of Type A people— the "hurry sickness" in Friedman's apt phrase. The hostility comes from seeing others as vying for the same attainments they so desperately need, and is expressed by seeing the worst in others, envying their successes, an easily aroused anger even over trivial things, a fixed and angry defense of positions, the frequent use of obscenities, and the urge to control others. It can come out against anyone but it usually falls on those who are the closest and most convenient outlets for it—spouses, children, coworkers, and neighbors.

Most Americans are afflicted with Type A behavior in varying degrees. It is hard not to be in a society in which winning is so important and family life is thin enough that children often do not receive enough love and warmth. But it has to be seen as an emotional injury since it takes away from the pleasures of life. It causes the world to be seen as something to be conquered and controlled, rather than enjoyed and savored. Not only do the insecurity and hostility eat into us, the anger they cause gives pain to those we come in contact with, while the impatience makes it difficult to relax and enjoy the good things we have. And the senseless, ungovernable drive to succeed leads nowhere since it is insatiable; the wealthier people get the harder it drives them. The pain associated with Type A behavior means that people afflicted with it are more apt to commit suicide. Some analysts see cynicism as the defining characteristic of Type A individuals, as a way of pulling others down to build oneself up.

The saddest part of Type A behavior, however, as well as the most alarming for the future, is that those who are not loved as children find it difficult to love others when they grow up. Love is not something they had much experience with when they were young, so they have little feeling for it or its supreme role in human relationships. They often express skepticism about love, suspecting it of being manipulative, which of course it can be. The inability to love causes their marriages to be unsatisfactory and, worst of all, they pass their affliction on to their children. The growth of Type A behavior could already be a self-sustaining process since it is being encouraged at all stages, from the cold modern family to the hot modern economy. There is little question that the economy benefits from hard-driving Type A individuals, since they are the ones who keep the U.S.

competitive in world markets, but the pain that drives them must leave one wondering just who should be envied in our society. Perhaps the super-achievers should be pitied for the insecurity that drives them so insistently and denies them the joy of loving others. Can anyone say that a society that makes love so difficult is on the right trace?

It may be that the mother who is happy taking care of those she loves could be the one most to be envied. She would be more Type B. (Pure Type As or Bs are rare; most people are somewhere on a continuum between the two.) Type Bs are comfordable with themselves, cooperative, flexible, and forgiving. They are happy when others do well, and have no need to tear others down to build themselves up. Since they are not trying to impress others, they sometimes seem almost dull compared to Type As, who cultivate all manner of sparkling qualities to gain the regard of others. But it is the Type Bs who are easy to be with and can enjoy other people. And, most importantly, they are able to love their spouses and their children, to accept them as they are, and to forgive their failings and misdeeds. Many traditional virtues have a Type B quality about them, as reflected in an Arab proverb:

> A friend is someone you can pour out the contents of your heart to, chaff and grain together, knowing that the gentlest of hands will take and sift it, keeping what is worth keeping and, with a breath of kindness, blow the rest away.

Another more modest piece of research leads to a similar conclusion. Conducted by Bernard Rimland of the Institute for Child Behavior Research and published in *Psychological Reports*, it is titled "The Altruism Paradox." (1982) It involved a simple classroom experiment in which college students were asked to list the ten friends they knew best (using their initials) and then record whether they were happy or unhappy. The students were then asked to go through the list again noting which were selfish or unselfish, with selfishness defined as a stable tendency to devote one's time and resources to one's own interests and welfare. The students were then asked to group them in four combinations of happy/unhappy and selfish/unselfish, with the instructor totaling the results on the blackboard. Besides being a useful exercise in empirical research, the results were an impressive lesson to the students. Of the happy subjects, ten times more were unselfish than selfish, a conclusion that persisted through many years of repeating the project in classes (although since the data was collected in the late 1950s, it must be wondered if the exercise would be as useful now that cultural change has made self-interest so necessary).

Rimland speaks of this as a paradox because it would seem that those who devote their energies toward making themselves happy would be the ones who would be the most happy, but the effect is just the opposite. The same paradox is reflected in the phenomenon of the spoiled child, since it would seem that the children who are given the most would be the happiest, rather than the whiny, insecure children they often are. The implications for our society are staggering: the self-centered behavior so powerfully encouraged may be just what is causing so much unhappiness, insecurity, and dissatisfaction.

The Other Way

The selflessness asked for by all the great faiths is the polar opposite of the ways called for by the market faith. All see liberation, enlightenment, salvation, or redemption—however it is defined—as coming from selflessness, whether in ceasing to desire, bringing honor to family and nation, surrendering to the will of Allah, or loving others as ourselves. Whatever the form of selflessness asked for, however, the result was societies that were different from ours shaped by the market faith and the goals of success, power, influence, or self-fulfillment—however it is defined.

The ideal of selflessness was never fully realized in any of the cultures built around it, but the ethical systems they led to still created a setting where life could unfold with greater security and emotional comfort—and thus, many philosophers would argue, truer freedom. A multitude of obligations were established to preserve the family and the community that together shaped life and provided many of its satisfactions. Economic motivations were subsumed under ethical requirements that encouraged the well-being of all. It did not mean that happiness was assured or conflict eliminated; human nature remained the same, with different genes pulling in different directions. But it did mean that life could move forward in a way that encouraged involvement in a community and the individuals it was composed of. This provided a security and a concern for others that is in deep contrast with the insecurity and aloneness so often behind the bright facade of our society.

The selflessness asked for by the great faiths sustained traditional societies for most of recorded history, but this order has been breaking down in a long and complex historical process, and it is now rapidly being replaced by a market-based order. Constitutional democracy is still important, but because government is vulnerable to waste and corruption, its role is being displaced by the more autonomous functioning of the market. Those who are uncomfortable with these currents, for whatever reason, are left with the task of deciding how to make life as comfortable as possible in such circumstances. There is wisdom in what a Roman philosopher once said: "No man is happy who does not think himself so," and this is especially so when there are so many good things to enjoy: books, music, study, travel, entertainments of all sorts, and a myriad of diversions—enough to allow all of us to find ones to our liking.

Americans thrive on correcting wrongs, but through the ages people have accepted what they could not change, and this is pretty much what we are doing now. What made past societies different was their greater stability compared to the present, with its explosive growth of population, technology, and economic activity. Still, even if the need for change was accepted now, there would be little agreement on what changes would be best. The only way of dealing with such circumstances is the evolutionary one. It calls for accepting what is and making the most of it while also keeping an eye on what seems to be ahead, and taking steps to avoid being caught in a trap from which there is no way out. It is both an acceptance of things as they are and a seeking of better ways, and requires not only knowledge and wisdom but the good sense to balance idealism and pragmatism. It is to know that nothing is all good, just as nothing is all bad, and that perfection is the enemy of the good—the most that can reasonably be hoped for. Let us proceed with this in mind.

CHAPTER FIVE

Environmental Resistance to the Global Economy

It is easy—and correct—to say that a growing world economy will inevitably encounter the environmental resistance that slows it down and brings it to a halt. It is not easy, however, to know when this will occur or which forms will be most important in bringing the economy to a halt. This is true for both the alarmists, who see things as all set to collapse, and the cornucopianists, who see technical bravado as holding off the end of growth for centuries. There is clarity in the overall picture—nothing can grow forever—but murkiness in the specifics, and unfortunately, the specifics are all we have to go on. And they can be confusing, especially the economy with its booms—and excessive optimism—and its busts—and excessive pessimism. Still, the decisions we make could leave our descendants either on their way to a secure future or trapped in the inexorable working of things that is the essence of tragedy.

Complexity is the stumbling block, not only the complexity of nature, but of human nature, too, as well as the interplay of the two—in short, everything. The first Earth Day in 1970 brought to a wider audience problems that had been growing for a long time, and since then several have been reduced, some have gotten worse, and new ones have appeared. But none are clear enough to weaken the overwhelming support economic growth continues to enjoy. Perhaps more correctly, no other visions have the power to draw our society away from its growth track—regardless of the concerns people have about where it is taking us. Since all societies tend to stay with things as long as they can, all that can be done now is to sift through the consequences of our actions for ones that appear solid enough to force change—at some point. Hopefully this will be before the environment is so over-exploited that our descendants have only degradation and ugliness to live with.

We are of course fighting environmental resistance with everything we have, and gains have been made: new mineral deposits have been discovered, the chlorofluorocarbon (CFC) refrigerants that created the ozone hole are being phased out, air and water pollution are being reduced (in the developed countries at least), and genetic engineering is finding improved ways of feeding people. At the same time, a consensus is emerging among scientists around the two problems with the most potential for derailing industrial society. One is the heavy dependence on fossil fuels and the climate changes associated with using them, and the other is the declining biodiversity that is an inevitable consequence of growing levels of population and economic activity. Modern agriculture will be used as an example to introduce both of them.

Farming with Oil

The phrase, "farming with oil" sounds, exaggerated. Surely everyone knows that plants grow in soil with sunlight and water—a natural process. This is true, but the use of fossil fuels in the process has multiplied agricultural productivity many times over, far more than is commonly realized—perhaps six or eight times. It is important to understand how fossil fuels do this, since they not only feed the world's population but also power most of the activities that keep urban industrial society functioning.

Chemical Fertilizers. This is the most important factor, since chemical fertilizers literally flood the soil with the nutrients required by all plants for growth. They increase yields many times over what is possible with traditional farming methods, where fertility is limited by the small amounts of nutrients naturally found in the soil or returned to it in the form of manure and composted wastes. Rarely are such materials sufficient to replace those that are lost, regardless of how carefully erosion is kept to a minimum and wastes are recycled. The main way of replacing lost nutrients is to periodically rest the land, to leave it fallow while organic matter breaks down, soil organisms fix nitrogen, and the parent geological materials in the soil break down to add small amounts of minerals. But resting land this way means it is not producing crops, and when it is cropped again there are still only small amounts of nutrients in the soil, so yields are low. With chemical fertilizers, however, not only are crops far heavier but they can be taken off the land every year without having to rest it. They also make infertile soils productive, such as sandy ones that do not hold nutrients well but are otherwise easy to work and for plant roots to grow through. Chemical fertilizers are at the heart of the Green Revolution, since the miracle strains of wheat and rice were developed to take advantage of the abundance of nutrients chemical fertilizers make available. Without them their yields would be lower than traditional varieties.

The three main components of chemical fertilizers are nitrogen, phosphorous, and potassium—the N, P, and K whose percentages are printed on all bags of fertilizer and are essential for all plant growth. Phosphorous and potassium are mined, which requires only a modest amount of energy to exploit the large reserves of both minerals that are available and to ship them worldwide. Nitrogen, however, is a different story. It is abundant, since air is 80 percent nitrogen, but plants cannot use it in this gaseous form, and the energy costs of converting it into a solid chemical form are high. This can be done with electricity, but it is more efficient to use natural gas. Nitrogen is also fixed by the roots of certain plants, especially legumes, and one of the first projects undertaken by genetic engineers was to add this nitrogen-fixing capacity to the main grain crops—wheat, corn, and rice. But not only did this effort encounter technical difficulties, interest faded when it became apparent that the energy to fix the nitrogen would come from the photosynthesis of the plant, thus reducing crop yields. This early goal of genetic engineering is no longer mentioned among current projects, which are focused on projects that are profitable in the advanced countries that can pay for them, such as producing tomatoes with a longer shelf life or plants that are resistant to herbicides.

Irrigation. The deserts can be made to bloom, but only if water is taken to them. There is a long history of this using gravity to move water, but the opportunities to do this are limited, and close to fully exploited. The modern contribution has been to build larger dams and more extensive distribution systems, both of which take some energy. But most energy goes into the most widespread form of irrigation, pumping from wells to fields or through pipelines to higher areas. The results have been impressive, putting large amounts of land into production and getting higher yields elsewhere when water is supplied just when needed and in optimum amounts. Semi-arid regions, such as the Great Plains, which formerly were limited to winter grain crops harvested in the spring, can now produce irrigated summer crops as well. Turning the deserts green is only the most conspicuous example of what irrigation can do to increase food supplies; increasing yields on other lands is equally as important. But all require energy, and higher costs for electricity are already reducing the irrigation of marginal lands, such as those used for grazing. As the cost of energy continues to rise, other uses of pumped water will decline, and with it food production.

Farm Machinery. Land that formerly had to be left in pasture to feed horses, oxen, and other draft animals can now be plowed up to produce food for humans instead. Diesel fuel has replaced hay and oats to power farm work, freeing up significant amounts of land for the production of crops for human consumption. Modern farm machines are truly impressive, but without fossil fuels to move them they would be useless hulks with weeds growing up around them.

Cooking and Heating. In the same way, the woodlots

that used to exist all across the U.S. and Europe became unnecessary as coal made its way to rural areas, later to be supplemented by oil, propane, and electricity. As this change took place, land could be released for raising crops.

Transportation. Efficient transportation allows land to be used for its most productive crops, with the products shipped to wherever they are needed. North Dakota raises wheat; California fruits and vegetables; and Florida oranges, all with the high yields possible when crops are grown under ideal conditions. If transportation was not available, however, or became prohibitively expensive, then each region would have to produce a larger array of crops, including ones not so well suited to local conditions, with the result being lower yields and less diverse diets. In the U.S., transportation of food uses as much energy as growing it in the first place. Inexpensive sea borne transportation makes it possible to ship food to food-deficit countries around the world, but with the downside of allowing populations to grow beyond the capacities of their lands, and thus increasing the probabilities of food shortages and famine in the future.

Food Processing. Refrigerating, canning, and freezing all allow crops to be grown on optimum sites and times of the year and preserved for consumption later and far from where they were grown. As with transportation, food processing permits the most efficient use of available land and diversifies diets, but it too uses as much energy as growing the food.

Pesticides. Insecticides reduce losses from insects, while herbicides reduce the weeds that compete with crops for nutrients and sunlight. Both permit higher yields, but both are petrochemicals made from oil or natural gas. Both are good energy investments, as their supporters argue, herbicides because they reduce the need for tractors to cultivate weeds and insecticides because they reduce crop losses. But both have significant ecological consequences, including ones beyond the immediate effects of poisons on target insects and weeds—bringing us to the matter of biodiversity.

Declining Biodiversity and a Rising Human Monoculture

At this time when oil and food are abundant, the use of chemicals in agriculture bothers people more than the energy used, partly because of the health implications of the chemicals but also because of their effects on other forms of life in the environment. These matters trouble people today, but the implications of declining biodiversity are much broader and potentially more severe.

When grasslands and forests are turned into fields, the diversity of the original ecosystems is radically reduced to what is called a monoculture—the culturing of one species, the crop. When land is cleared of its native vegetation, it is also cleared of the birds, insects, and the other forms of life that were sustained by the capacity of plants to fix solar energy and draw nutrients from the soil. In the original plant community it was unlikely that any one insect would become a problem since most feed on only one plant or group of plants, and there were many predatory insects and birds to keep their numbers in check. The result was both ecosystem diversity and stability. When the land is cleared, however, and a single crop is planted, an insect that relishes that plant finds itself in "bug heaven," its food supply everywhere. Given the capacity of insects to reproduce rapidly, their numbers overwhelm the few predatory insects and birds left, so the farmer has little choice but to spray the field with an insecticide to save his crop. Initially this works; only a few insects survive, but they do so because of an innate resistance to the poison, and this resistance is passed on to their offspring. Each time the insecticide is applied, this "unnatural selection" occurs, and it is not long before the insecticide becomes ineffective. The farmer must then find another spray to use, but over time insects develop resistance to whole classes of insecticides. Stronger ones have to be developed, but they often cannot be used because they adversely affect beneficial species far from the fields, killing birds and insects and reducing ecosystem diversity even more. The result is that agricultural losses from insects in the U.S. are greater today than during World War II when DDT was first used.

Only part of these losses are due to the greater resistance to insecticides. Others are due to the decline of crop diversity as farms became larger and more focused on one crop. Economic pressures forced farmers to choose from among the few crops that grow best in a region. Often only one could be grown at a profit, with the result being the emergence of a number of agricultural regions in which only one crop is grown. Naturalists and biologists long ago noticed that environments with low diversity like this tended to be unstable, with frequent population explosions and die-offs. This was first observed on oceanic islands and in the Arctic where diversity was low and populations fluctuated in ways totally unlike areas with higher diversity, such as tropical forests and temperate grasslands, which were quite stable. Loss of diversity also resulted from the introduction of plants, insects, and animals, both intentionally or inadvertently, that exploded in the environments suitable to them and squeezed out native species.

The dilemma we face is that population growth is virtually requiring that natural areas be cleared to produce food needed by humans. It is not just big corporations that cut down rain forests; most is done by people who need land to farm and have no other choice but to use the rain forests, even though their soils are heavily leached and can only be worked using slash and burn methods. Historical forces are leading inexorably toward an increasingly humanized environment—and more of the problems associated with declining biodiversity. No one disagrees that biodiversity should be preserved, but neither can anyone deny that biodiversity will decline with rising populations and standards of living. A few highly valued species can be preserved in protected environments, but this is a far cry from the huge loss of biodiversity that has occurred in the last century and is occurring faster all the time.

Economic diversity is similarly being reduced as the small-scale enterprises of a century ago are being displaced with the large national and international operations that are so efficient that small operations cannot compete with them. There are significant advantages in this (as will be noted in the following chapter), but they are obtained at the cost of greater dependency on a highly integrated global economy that, if it stumbled, would have global consequences. With so many eggs in one basket, if that basket broke it would mean many eggs would be broken. Many countries would be effected, not just one, as was the case in the past. Loss of diversity afflicts modern cities, too, since they are being driven toward dependency on the industries they are most competitive in. It has long been observed that cities heavily involved in one industry, such as Detroit with its autos, are more vulnerable to recessions than cities with greater diversity, such as Los Angeles. A highly competitive global economy has driven entire nations toward dependency on one or a few industries, especially as transportation costs fell. Television sets are no longer produced in the U.S., for instance, while other countries find it hard to compete with Japanese cars or American films and music.

But the loss of diversity—economic as well as eco-logical—has other consequences that could be even more important. One of the most significant is the return of diseases once thought to be conquered and the appearance of new ones. Part of this is analogous to the problems farmers faced with insects that developed resistance to insecticides. There are strains of pneumonia now that are resistant to almost all anti-biotics, creating the fear that it could once again become the disease that kills babies and old people. Tuberculosis is growing rapidly in the U.S., and explosively in places like Russia, as the drugs that formerly controlled it no longer work well and people with the disease are no longer isolated in sanatoriums. Malaria is spreading as DDT becomes less effective in controlling mosquitoes and the quinine based drugs no longer control the disease. New diseases are also introduced as human activity spreads into formerly isolated areas, such as rain forests, bringing humans into contact with diseases such as AIDS, which evidently had existed in remote parts of the Congo basin for a long time before human contact brought it out. As the numbers of domestic animals grow, diseases they carry, such as mad cow disease and avian viruses, are making the genetically difficult jump to humans. Rapid transportation has facilitated the spread of diseases worldwide, with those with long incubation periods, such as AIDS, spreading widely before their symptoms first appear. Even diseases that are easily controlled can cause epidemics in Third World countries, as when primitive sewage systems are overloaded and spread cholera. In the U.S., global warming is a factor that helps explain the increase of tropical diseases such as dengue, encephalitis, and malaria. If diseases become unmanageable, the U.S. could be forced to pull back from the world economy, or at least limit the movement of people and goods in highly restrictive ways—ones determined by national security needs of a different sort than ones we are familiar with. (White, 2000)

It is easier to control diseases in plants than in humans since plants can be crossed with varieties selected for resistance to disease. This is done regularly because genetic materials have long been collected in seed banks, and we should be thankful for the scientists who had the insight to establish them many years ago. Historically, farmers used their own seeds or traded with neighbors, a process that led to the great genetic diversity that is so valuable now; it is what enables plant breeders to produce a steady stream of new seeds to keep ahead of plant diseases. This is especially important with the high yielding Green Revolution seeds, since they are genetically identical and thus highly vulnerable to diseases. Traditional farmers also preserved crop diversity in meeting their own needs, but they could not achieve the high yields of the modern methods that are necessary to feed the world's population. We are moving toward a human monoculture—one dominated by humans and their activities—and as this process continues problems will appear that did not exist in the past when growth was easy and environmental resistance had not been encountered.

For human diseases, we have less choice but to turn to the genetic engineers to control diseases. This has significant potential, but it is most apt to be pursued in the affluent countries that have the skills and the economic means to do so. Much of the effort has been focused on the diseases that end lives, but if this is successful it will lead to the kind of problems our society finds hard to deal with, including larger elderly populations and greatly increased demands on retirement programs. And unless the degenerative process that weakens minds and bodies can be overcome, too—which is more difficult than conquering specific diseases—the result may be more time spent passively, even vegetatively, in nursing homes. Increasing life spans also adds to the dilemmas already being encountered, of whether failing bodies or minds should be helped to die. If humans play god in keeping people alive, it may become necessary to play god in their deaths, too, something no one could relish.

At times in the past death has been seen as an angel of mercy. Famines and epidemics were one way excess populations were reduced so the survivors were left below the carrying capacity again. This could be the way epidemics are seen in the future, as bringing populations back into a balance with the environment. The major advantage of diseases as a limiting factor, assuming one is needed, is that epidemics preserve culture better than other limiting factors, such as wars, anarchy, and social decay. Culture is the critical factor, since it provides the organized basis for learning from setbacks and moving toward more sustainable ways. It is when cultures fail that violence is let loose and the dangers of a downward spiral grow. It is not a pleasant vision, of disease being the form of environmental resistance that is important in the future, but it reminds us that death is as much a part of life as birth. It is not possible to have more births than deaths, not for long anyway.

Global Warming and Climate Change

Global warming is primarily a consequence of the burning of fossil fuels, and thus should be a part of the energy section that follows. It is dealt with here because it is such a complex issue and one that is often obscured by the media's coverage. It is not correct, for example, to blame global warming on the burning of rain forests. Such burning does convert biomass to carbon dioxide, but as the forest grows back the carbon dioxide is converted back into biomass by photosynthesis. This is the cycling of carbon that occurs in all life processes. The burning of fossil fuels, in contrast, is a one-way process, with hydrocarbons removed from deep in the ground and left as carbon dioxide in the atmosphere after burning. It is because plants use carbon dioxide and give off oxygen in the process of photosynthesis that over billions of years they were able to convert the Earth's atmosphere from being rich in carbon dioxide and hot, to rich in oxygen and cool. Most of the carbon dioxide that plants removed from the atmosphere in this way was left bound up in the Earth's mantle, most of it as limestone formed when plankton in the ocean died and settled to the bottom, their skeletons accumulating as sediment. But a small amount of organic matter was left in the form of fossil fuels, and this is the part going back into the atmosphere now as it is burned. In the two centuries since industrialization began, carbon dioxide in the air has increased 25 percent, from 275 parts per million to 360. This is still a small amount, but it is the highest it has been in the last 400,000 years, with the increase surpassing the decrease during the ice ages.

The process by which carbon dioxide causes warming is well established, both by theory and experiment. In a greenhouse, the air warmed by the sun is kept from escaping by the glass; in the atmosphere, carbon dioxide and other greenhouse gases function like the glass, keeping the heat from escaping into space and thus leaving the atmosphere warmer. As long as carbon is cycled in natural processes there is no carbon dioxide buildup; the carbon dioxide released by decay or burning is taken back up by plants as they grow. When tropical rain forests are logged and the wood is used in items such as furniture that last many years, the carbon is tied up in a solid form so carbon dioxide in the atmosphere is reduced, at least until the items are burned or decay. Slash and burn farming recycles carbon, but the cycle takes twenty years or so, the time it takes for the trees to regrow and collect the nutrients necessary to repeat the farming cycle. Still, the amounts of carbon left in the atmosphere are small compared to those left by the billions of barrels of oil and tons of coal burned each year.

That much is agreed upon. It is the task of predicting the consequences of the increasing amounts of carbon dioxide and other greenhouse gases into the atmosphere that is so difficult. First, there is a great deal of buffering going on, mostly by the oceans, which absorb both carbon dioxide and heat from the atmosphere. The increasing amounts of dust and moisture in the atmosphere also reflect incoming solar energy back out into space, thus reducing the rate of warming, but other types of clouds, moisture, and pollutants hold heat in. For a number of years between the 1940s and the 1980s there was no clear evidence of the rising temperatures that both theory and research predicted would accompany rising carbon dioxide levels. But then it was found that sulfur dioxide released during the burning of coal was reflecting sunlight back into space. Unlike carbon dioxide, however, sulfur dioxide does not stay in the atmosphere permanently, and when this was factored into the computer models, the temperature pattern was explained, including the rapidly rising temperatures in the 1990s. The increase of almost one degree Fahrenheit was more than was originally predicted by the National Academy of Sciences when it first brought the issue of global warming to public attention in the 1980s. Made up of the nation's top scientists, the Academy's predictions also did not include the instability in the weather that has increased storm and drought losses so greatly.

The United Nations conference in Kyoto in 1997 led to

strong proposals to reduce the buildup of carbon dioxide worldwide, but the U.S. opposed these measures, almost alone among the industrial nations. This was due, in large part, to the efforts of the fossil fuel industries, which spent a good deal of money to argue that global warming had not been proven. While technically correct, this was misleading, since such a complex phenomenon will never be fully understood. Other matters are not completely understood, such as how photosynthesis works and the source of the gravitational force, but this does not mean that their effects are not well established and effectively utilized. There is little question that global warming is occurring now, and even if the process is not fully understood and the effects hard to predict, it does not mean the matter can be ignored. Even scientists who were initially skeptical about human activity being able to influence something as powerful as the world's climate have been converted by a growing mass of evidence. Often this was because of the growing number of what are called bio-indicators of rising temperatures, not just possibly misleading temperature readings. Spring now comes earlier in much of the U.S., sea ice is diminishing in the Arctic, and recently it has been established that ocean temperatures have risen. Several changes are potentially unstable, making them especially dangerous. One is the increasing rate of decay of the peat that reaches great thicknesses in the far north. The carbon dioxide released by this decay contributes to warming, which then increases the rate of decay, causing more warming, faster decay, and so on in an accelerating process. The potential is significant since as much carbon is tied up in peat as in all the world's fossil fuels.

This is another form of unstable equilibrium like those introduced in Chapter 2, one in nature rather than culture but just as dangerous, perhaps more so, since once triggered the change could continue for centuries. There are similar potentially unstable equilibriums with polar ice. The Arctic ice is less worrisome since it is floating, so if it melts it would not raise the ocean level. Still, if the area of white ice, which reflects sunlight, were replaced with dark water, which absorbs sunlight as heat, the warming of the oceans would accelerate, at least until the ice was gone. The Antarctic is more important, since most of its vast amount of ice is supported by land. If it melted, the level of the oceans would rise, possibly enough to submerge the deltas of the great rivers such as the Nile, Tigris and Euphrates, Ganges, Yangtze, and Yellow, which are among the most densely populated parts of the world as well as the most productive agriculturally.

Because the oceans are the major buffers of global warming, they are the focus of much research. One fear is that some currents may be in a delicate equilibrium and easily diverted in different directions with massive consequences. The Gulf Stream, for example, brings warm water past Europe and keeps it much warmer than other regions at the same latitudes. If it was diverted elsewhere, Europe could find its weather more like that of the northern U.S., Canada, and Alaska that are on the same latitudes as Europe. Scientists have also found that the monsoons, which bring rain to virtually all of Asia during the all-important summer growing season, weaken when water temperatures in the Indian Ocean diverge from the norm. Yet so complex are these matters that even the largest super-computers would not be able to handle the relevant data, even if it could be collected.

It is unfortunate when an issue is so complex that it leaves all statements open to the charge of being unproven—and thus alarmist. It was only when insurance losses from storms increased so dramatically that the insurance industry demanded the government do something—which then generated the opposition of the more powerful fossil fuel industries. If the questions were not so complex, it would be easier to know what to do. As it is, action is discouraged by the hope that changes will not be necessary, especially ones as draconian as reducing the use of fossil fuels. Action is also discouraged by the difficulty of getting all countries to participate, and especially to agree on the distribution of the cutbacks between the wealthy and poor countries.

Scientists agree that any actions that risks disturbing something as basic to the Earth's weather system should be approached with great caution. A fundamental rule of science is the conservative principle, that any action for which the results are unknown should be avoided, or at least undertaken with great care. It is thus ironic—again—that the supposedly conservative elements of our society, particularly business interests, are the ones trying to deny the significance of human activity in causing climate change. Their campaign against the Kyoto global warming treaty garnered a good deal of public support, probably because it told people what they wanted to hear—that global warming was not a problem—or even had advantages, such as making cool areas warmer and the higher carbon dioxide levels causing plants to grow faster. One wonders how many of the supposed benefits of modernization reflect the same kind of rationalizations.

The actions of the fossil fuel industry reflect the behavior of a society shaped by the values of the market economy—that everyone has the right, even the obligation, to take care of themselves, regardless of the consequences for society as a whole. And since the industry can find scientists to say what it wants said, science, too, is tarred with the same self-serving image. The tobacco companies contributed to this when they found scientists who would argue that the adverse health effects of smoking had not been proven. But the huge legal judgments against them can be seen as characteristic of a legal system that encourages the search for "deep pockets" to get into by legal means, even when the health effects of smoking were well known to smokers at the time. Will the fossil fuel industries be sued the same way in the future for the consequences of global warming? This is what things have come to in a society in which everyone has the incentive to get what they can out of it— and then sees so much cynicism in its political institutions.

Fossil Fuels and Their Alternatives

Modern industrial society transformed the world by tapping into the huge source of concentrated energy in the fossil fuels, in coal first and then oil and natural gas. These fuels received their name because they are the fossilized remains of plants and animals that lived millions of years ago but were kept from decaying by the absence of oxygen, usually under water and sediment. They were then slowly "cooked" by high temperatures and pressures into the fossil fuels. In a real sense they are fossilized sunlight, but they are much more concentrated than the solar energy that falls on the Earth each day. Think of what one gallon of gasoline can do for us in our cars, taking a ton or more of steel some twenty or thirty miles along a highway, up hills easily, even pulling a trailer or boat if that is what we want. Imagine pushing a car that far ourselves, or pulling it with a horse. That's the concentrated power that oil has, and the U.S. consumes over 250 billion gallons of it each year, 940 gallons per person. Coal and natural gas together provide an even larger amount of energy, and taken together the fossil fuels provide 87 percent of the energy the U.S. uses. This is the kind of energy it takes to keep industrial society going. It is also why it is significant to our future that oil production in the U.S. has fallen steadily since peaking in 1970, down 40 percent by 1996, with imports exceeding production since 1993. Even though the efficiency with which energy is used is improving, the use of fossil fuels still increased an average of 1.5 percent per year in the last two decades of the twentieth-century. Most of this increase is due to economic growth, but it was the easy availability of inexpensive fossil fuels that powered such growth in the first place. They give us the power to do almost anything we want, but this is also what makes the depletion of U.S. oil deposits so threatening. The average American oil well now produces only 11.3 barrels a day, while the average Saudi well produces 5,800 barrels.

Fossil fuels are non-renewable; they cannot be recycled

as materials can. This alone makes energy a different matter than materials, since they can be recycled—although this takes energy, as does pollution control. As energy becomes more expensive, we will find that there is less we can do—and less reason for being so pleased with ourselves and feeling superior to other peoples. Three decades of intensive research into alternative forms of energy following the first energy crisis found none with potentials even close to those of the fossil fuels. Renewable forms of energy could keep a sustainable economy going, although it is hard to say at what standard of living or population level. And even though the renewable resources are significant, they have more limits than the impression given in the media. The following is a brief summary of the potentials and limitations of the main fuels we have: fossil fuels, nuclear energy, and renewable energy.

Fossil Fuels. As mentioned in Chapter 1, world oil production is expected to peak sometime during the first two decades of the new millennium and then decline to 20 percent of peak levels some 50 years after peaking. The figure often heard today, of proven reserves adequate for 50 years, is misleading because of the phrase that usually follows, "at current rates of consumption." This suggests we can continue consuming oil as we are today for 50 years, but the actual process is apt to be much different, with consumption increasing until it peaks and is followed by a long decline in consumption driven either by rising prices or declining GDP. The less essential uses will be squeezed out first, from gas-guzzling cars to excessive heating and cooling of homes and businesses, after which the cuts will hurt more. Oil exploration will continue, with greater skills in locating and tapping smaller fields being important in slowing the decline in production. But even though a new field with a hundred million barrels sounds impressive, it is still equivalent to only six days of current U.S. consumption. The oil estimated to be in the Arctic National Wildlife Reserve might provide about a year's supply, but it could be left in the ground—and for our children—if the fuel efficiency of cars was improved by one mile per gallon. Many of the remaining fields will be expensive to develop, such as those in remote locations that necessitate the building of long pipelines, or in difficult places such as the far north, under deep water, or deep in the Earth. Some may never be developed if the costs of developing them are greater than the value of the oil produced. There is still hope that ways will be found to get additional oil from depleted fields, where over half of the oil is usually left, but success in this to date has been limited; the task is akin to trying to clean crankcase oil out of the ground it has spilled into. The largest remaining oil reserves are in the Middle East, especially in Saudi Arabia, leading to the problem of huge amounts of money going to a country with a small population, and leaving the question of how to get the money back into circulation to keep the world economy going.

Of the other fossil fuels, natural gas is by far the best since it burns cleanly and there is no danger of gas "spills"—unless they catch fire explosively. U.S. gas reserves are somewhat larger than those for oil, but much of it is in deep, tight deposits that will make removal slow and expensive. The rapid increase in natural gas prices in 2000 was not expected, but probably reflected the economic boom at the time. Natural gas has one significant disadvantage compared to oil: it is bulkier. This makes it difficult to use in transportation, since fuel tanks must be large; buses can have them on their roofs but they would fill the trunks of cars. Moving natural gas by pipeline is more expensive than oil since the pipelines must be larger in diameter and frequent compressors are needed to keep the gas moving. Natural gas can be liquified to move by tanker, but this requires that the gas be cooled to minus 273 degrees Fahrenheit before it condenses to a liquid, so it is expensive. Europe's air quality is improving as it shifts from coal to natural gas, much of it from the North Sea, but most of the world's gas reserves are in unstable regions, Russia first and secondly the Middle East, where most is presently being used in petrochemical industries. This avoids the flaring of gas which is the fate of the gas that comes up with oil in places where there are no nearby uses for it.

Natural gas is less likely to be helpful to poorer countries because of the difficulties of transporting and distributing it.

Coal is the fossil fuel that is available in greatest abundance and most widely distributed, at least in the Northern Hemisphere. (The Southern Hemisphere is poorly supplied with fossil fuels in general, which explains at least part of its relative poverty.) The U.S. has used only some ten percent of its coal, so it is a significant resource. Coal's problems stem mainly from the fact that it is a solid, which means it must be mined rather than pumped out of the ground, transported by truck or train rather than through pipelines, and is more polluting when burned because solid fuels do not burn evenly and impurities are harder to remove. Burning coal also produces more carbon dioxide than oil and natural gas. So even though coal is the most abundant form of energy, and thus the cheapest, it has problems that limit its use in the U.S., where most is used to generate electricity. Its use is growing most rapidly in developing countries to avoid the cost of importing oil, with both India and China having significant resources.

Until global warming emerged as a problem, coal was seen as the wave of the future, mainly by making it into synthetic oil and gas. This is relatively expensive because hydrogen must be made first, which uses a significant portion of the coal and increases carbon dioxide. These two disadvantages caused coal to be placed on the back burner. Interest in oil shales has declined, too, partly because of environmental problems associated with mining and processing it but mainly because so much energy is needed to mine oil shale and convert it into a liquid fuel that there is little energy gain. Canadian tar sands are being utilized now and are a significant resource, as are the heavy oils of Venezuela, helping the global economy but not the U.S.'s.

Nuclear Power. If the nuclear age is still ahead, it will only be because nuclear power does not produce carbon dioxide. Otherwise, the prospects for nuclear power are bleak, and for a number of reasons. Safety is most important for the public but for utilities it is the high cost of building nuclear power plants, far higher than coal-fired plants. These high construction costs are the reason that no nuclear plants have been started since 1976, so the 7 percent of our energy that now comes from nuclear power will decline as old plants are closed down—a process that has already begun. Even with its high construction costs, several important costs of nuclear power are still not being paid, especially the processing of spent fuel and decommissioning of old plants. Even the scarcity of the rare forms of nuclear fuel that conventional nuclear power plants use would keep it from ever being a significant source of energy in the future. Maintenance costs have been high, too, and the operating lives of nuclear plants have been shorter than expected, both for the same reason: the high energy particles that come off the nuclear reaction weaken the metals in and around the reactor, especially the heat exchangers that transfer heat from the reactor core to the steam that drives the turbines. Work on the breeder reactor that uses a more common type of Uranium has stopped all around the world because of its far higher costs and much greater safety hazards than current reactors, including a more rapid rate of metal decay.

The problem of metal decay also seems to be dooming what is still regularly described as the ultimate form of nuclear energy, fusion. It employs the same reaction as the sun, but on Earth uses a type of hydrogen for fuel, deuterium, that is common, inexpensive, and safe. One of fusion's main assets is that the reaction has no chance of getting out of control as in conventional nuclear plants; rather than a runaway reaction, the process would simply stop. In fact, keeping the reaction going is the main problem facing fusion. The reactors built so far have not reached break-even, the point at which more energy is produced than goes into generating it; there is no energy gain yet. The huge investment needed to build the next generation test reactor has not been forthcoming, primarily because of its cost. But behind this reluctance is undoubtedly the material problem, since the materials in the reactors would deteriorate much more rapidly than in conventional reactors. Particles come off the fusion reaction at close to the speed of light, meaning that even though much more energy is produced than in conventional nuclear plants, the metals in the reactor break down much faster too. As it stands now, fusion reactors would deteriorate much too quickly to justify their huge costs—even if fusion's other technical challenges could be overcome.

Renewable Resources. The temperament of the times clearly favors renewable resources, and for good reason—they employ natural processes. Almost all are based on solar energy in one form or another. Hydroelectric energy is powered by water evaporated into the atmosphere by the sun and collected behind dams; winds are driven by air that has been heated by the sun (as well as the rotation of the Earth); firewood is solar energy fixed by photosynthesis; and ethanol is grain alcohol made from the photosynthesis of corn. Only geothermal energy comes from a different source, the decay of radioactive materials in the core of the Earth. But all are available in an unending supply, with no radioactivity, exotic pollutants, or buildup of carbon dioxide in the atmosphere.

The potential of solar energy is huge, far greater than that of the fossil fuels, but it has two major limitations compared to fossil fuels. One is that solar energy is not concentrated, which means large areas of collectors must be built to collect it. Secondly, it is intermittent, meaning that it must be stored for times when the sun is behind clouds, behind the Earth at night, or diminished in winter. Both make solar energy expensive, and point to the reasons why the fossil fuels are so dominant today: they are highly concentrated forms of energy that can be easily stored and converted into the many forms of energy we now take for granted. Solar energy, in contrast, is most easily collected in the form of heat, which has limited uses. It can be collected as electricity using photo-voltaic cells, but this must be stored in batteries that are expensive, have limited capacities, and must be replaced regularly. In other words, it takes a lot of costly hardware to collect, store, and put solar energy into a few useful forms, and so far this does not include a liquid form that would be useful in transportation. Even in the uses for which solar energy is best suited, for space heating and hot water, it is abundant in the summer, when less is needed, and scarce in the winter, when more is needed, necessitating expensive backup systems. The bottom line is that solar energy is expensive, and close to cost-effective only in its simplest applications—the passive heating of houses and water that do not use pumps, fans, or supplemental storage devices.

Great hope is still held for the photovoltaic cells that convert solar energy into electricity. Also known as solar cells, their price dropped for a number of years, to the point where they are widely used in remote locations not reached by commercial power lines. But the drop in price bottomed out in the early 1990s, and the lack of breakthroughs after so much research effort caused corporate interest to fade. This was compounded by an even more discouraging lack of progress in developing more efficient batteries—something almost everyone confidently expected would happen. The large solar electric plants in the deserts avoided this storage problem by being connected directly to the power grid, but most of these have closed down or survive on subsidies. It remains to be seen how high fossil fuel prices will have to go before solar electric plants becomes competitive, but higher fuel prices would increase the cost of solar cells, too, since it takes a good deal of energy to produce them; solar cells must be operated for as much as five years before the energy produced is equal to the energy costs of making them—before net energy gain is reached. Carbon taxes would help all renewable energy sources, but there are still major questions about whether deserts will ever be covered with solar collectors.

One problem after another has beleaguered every new form of renewable energy investigated. Hydroelectric energy remains by far the most useful, its greatest advantage being that energy can be stored in the form of water behind dams and dropped through turbines when electricity is needed. But even though it is heavily utilized now, it produces only 3.1 percent of our energy, and producing more would require flooding broader, lower valleys, flooding more land to generate ever smaller amounts of electricity. Wind energy is superior to solar energy in the few places where wind speeds are high and steady, but such sites are rare, and slow winds that blow intermittently do not justify the cost of building wind generators. Hydrogen has many advantages, but it is not found in nature and is presently made using fossil fuels; in effect, it is a costly way of reducing air pollution. If fuel cells become a practical way of powering cars, it would mean vehicles made clean by moving the emissions to the plants that produce the hydrogen—just as electrical cars moved it to electrical generating plants. The main hope for hydrogen is if it could be made from water using solar energy, but even though some progress has been made in this, the technology is still at the laboratory stage—the one so many hopeful ideas did not get past. Firewood is an efficient way of using solar energy since nature does the work of collecting and storing it, and it could be expanded significantly if fast-growing trees were planted on sites not useful for other purposes. It is a solid resource, but burning wood creates too much air pollution to be used in urban areas and transporting it is expensive. Garbage is burned in European and Japanese cities to produce hot water for space heating and sometimes electricity, but there is resistance to this in the U.S. because of the air pollution caused—even though it is a fraction of what cars produce.

Gasohol was adopted quickly in the U.S. since we had the land to grow more corn and a strong farm lobby pushing for it. Made up of 10 percent ethanol (grain alcohol) and 90 percent gasoline, gasohol was promoted as a way of growing our own fuel so we could tell OPEC where to go. But it ended up taking as much fossil fuel energy to grow the corn and convert it into alcohol as there was in the resulting alcohol; the energy gain was zero. It is still produced only because of the power of the farm lobby to preserve a subsidy in the form of reduced gas taxes. And it is a large subsidy, since one gallon of ethanol makes ten gallons of gasohol, all of them without federal tax. It survives only because of the power of the farming states and the corporation that operates most of the ethanol plants.

Geothermal energy has a solid energy gain, but it has encountered limits, too, either because the water found was not hot enough to generate electricity profitably or it contained so many impurities that the heat exchangers become fouled. The one commercially successful site north of San Francisco was overexploited, causing temperatures and pressures to fall off; if it is to be operated in a sustainable way, it will have to be at a lower power output. Trying to capture the energy in ocean waves turned out to be very difficult, mainly because of the corrosive nature of the salt water but also because of storm damages and the difficulty of getting the energy ashore in a useful form.

Conservation. It seems perverse how difficult it has been to find alternatives to the fossil fuels, especially when it seems we can do anything with electronics, computers, and communication technologies. If there is one thing that has been learned during the last several decades, it is that conservation— saving energy—is far more cost-effective than developing new sources. The only thing holding back conservation, and some renewables as well, is the low prices for fossil fuels. When OPEC increased oil prices abruptly in the late 1970s, it led to a 17 percent drop in oil consumption in the U.S. compared to where it would have been if oil prices had remained low. This was an impressive achievement; it would not be until the mid 1990s that consumption regained the level of 1979. This suggests that the potential of conservation is high, dwarfing all new sources. Still, unless public attitudes change, it will be necessary to wait until scarcity drives oil prices up before learning what the mix of energy conservation and alternative sources will be in the times ahead.

Expanding and Consuming the
Niche of Industrial Society

The ecological niche occupied by industrial society expands every time new technologies are found to use formerly unused elements in the environment. But the niche shrinks when fossil fuels are consumed or the productivity of the environment is reduced. The interplay of such matters is what *The Limits to Growth* study addressed, and it concluded that much of the new century will be occupied with the dreaded grinding-down process. The more constructive—and evolutionarily correct—response by Kenneth Boulding was that the potential for adaptation to the new circumstances was significant. And even though it is not possible to know how long the age of affluence will last, it does leave the interesting question of whether it will be looked back on as a golden age of freedom and opportunity or a dark age of competitiveness, self-centeredness, and stress, or—as is more apt to be the case—some combination of the two.

Even if we are driven toward sustainability in wrenching ways, Americans can still feel blessed with the abundance of land and renewable resources we have. This does not justify the standard response, that everyone will have to move to rural areas to grow their food; only the dark age scenarios suggest that. Those who want to live in rural areas should once again be able to do so, but urban areas will continue to exist, even if in different forms than today—smaller, more compact, and more dispersed to reduce the need for transportation and make recycling easier. Urban and rural areas both have their forms of monotony today, and both will move in more interesting directions as sustainability comes to be based on local resources and environments. Technology will remain important, but unlike the heroic age that split the atom and took astronauts to the moon, technology's role will be more down to earth, of making simpler ways better and more secure. There will be enough challenges in the process to satisfy even the most pioneering, trailblazing types, and there will be no shortage of work to be done, if for no other reason than the physical plant of urban industrial society will have to be rebuilt in sustainable ways.

Americans have always relished such challenges, and there is no reason to assume that this will not continue to be the case. Even for those who see the changing circumstances as the failure of a dream, there will be compensations, significant ones, too, especially if the evolutionary process proceeds in ways that embody reasonably good sense. In the same way, it is difficult to know how the environment will pull through when it is so painfully true that, when our interests are at stake, we readily sacrifice nature, perhaps with a few of the necessary obeisances, but also with the feeling that we have little choice in the matter: "We must be practical about these things, you know." If there are losses in the beauty and productivity of nature, that is unfortunate, but we figure we will get by; we always have. When the Greeks first said "Man is the measure of all things," it may have been a brave assertion, but now it is a measure of our lack of courage in accepting the consequences of our actions. From the evolutionary perspective, it the denial of reality, and that is never a healthy thing.

Still, in the end, as they say, nature bats last, but it has marvelous recuperative powers. Nature will survive the human onslaught, as the poet Robinson Jeffers expressed so well in 1954:

> It [nature] has all time. It knows that people are a tide
> That swells and in time will ebb, and all
> Their works dissolve. Meanwhile the image of
>   the pristine beauty
> Lives in the very grain of the granite,
> Safe as the endless ocean that climbs our cliff.

Joseph Wood Krutch made a similar argument in *The Modern Temper*, published earlier yet, in 1929. He saw humanity as too smart for its own good, compared to the ants, for example, which are protected from dangerous excesses by instincts honed fine by millions of years of existence.

There is no shortage of visions of the future, good and bad, and even though they may stimulate useful thinking, in the end the future will be determined by the process of cultural evolution—of people taking steps to make things better, for themselves and their descendants. And for this, self knowledge is essential. How well we rise to this challenge will be the test of our species—and whether we are as smart as we think we are.

CHAPTER SIX

The Failure Of International Success

The rise of the global economy has been one of the most important developments of the postwar era. It has led to higher standards of living worldwide, improved diets, and lowered birth rates, all while encouraging peaceful relations between nations. These are real achievements, and even though elements of coercion have been involved—just as in the modernization of the West—it is still true that more people are living better now than ever before.

But—always the but—a smoothly functioning global economy will also lead to the faster depletion of the world's resources while enabling population to grow further beyond what ultimately can be sustained. It could well be that all the global economy will succeed in doing is to propel countries that were close to their limits in the first place well beyond them. And if something interrupts trade, few countries will have the room to maneuver the U.S. has, with its abundance of land and wide range of resources. The U.S. is one of the few net exporters of food today (along with Canada, Australia, and Argentina), and even though other countries could become self-sufficient if forced to, others are heavily dependent on imported food—including a number of affluent ones in Europe and Asia.

For the time being, however, there is a surplus of most commodities, including food, as reflected in the low prices for virtually all raw materials traded in the global economy. Labor is the expensive item in modern societies, but this is only another way of saying that incomes are high, and thus standards of living. Indeed, low raw material prices were an important part of the rapid economic expansion in much of the twentieth-century. But these low prices were hard on the people who produce the materials. It was low prices that drove farmers, ranchers, miners, and loggers off the land in the U.S., and a similar process is going on worldwide as commodity prices fall. This is especially true of countries in tropical regions, since crops such as bananas and coffee have been badly hurt by over-production. Yet most tropical countries have few other choices, and food exports made good sense, both ecologically and economically. As tree crops, they fit into the forest ecosystem much better than growing grains, especially when slash and burn methods were the only alternative, and tropical crops have good markets in the temperate regions where grains grow well. Exchanging them paid off well for quite a while—until over-production appeared, much of it from large plantations established by foreign firms. As surpluses drove prices down, national incomes fell, reducing the ability of countries to buy imported grains. Grains may still be inexpensive in dollar terms, but when coffee and banana prices fell by half, grain prices doubled in terms of the exports needed to pay for them. The result was not only falling incomes but rising malnutrition as well, especially in Africa.

This leads to a dilemma Americans may have to face some day. Would we be willing to send ever larger amounts of grains to such countries, even as their capacity to pay for them declines? If the answer is the hard-headed one—no money, no food—it would mean having to watch people starve on the evening news while the U.S. had large stocks on hand. But if the answer was the generous one—yes, give them food—it would mean sending ever larger amounts of food to more and more countries, perhaps indefinitely. This leads to Kenneth Boulding's "utterly dismal theorem," that anything done to reduce suffering without changing underlying circumstances only increases the magnitude of the suffering later. Who would want to be a member of Congress facing such a decision? It would be easier to vote no if the federal budget was in bad shape, with huge holes opening up in the social safety net, but even a yes vote would be a far cry from the modern vision of what trade was supposed to do for poor people around the world.

Or is this just the way we tend to see it, we who have grown so accustomed to our abundance and comforts that we have lost the tenacity that enabled peasants to endure famines and epidemics through the millennia? Nobody has a crystal ball, but we may be the ones left at a disadvantage if prices rise or incomes fall, especially since we have so little experience dealing with them—and such a tendency to find someone to get angry at when thing so wrong.

One thing seems likely: at some point each country will have to come to terms with its own resources. Trade may have many advantages, but it is too vulnerable to depend on, at least for long. And in terms of receiving help from more fortunate countries, there is already little willingness, in the U.S., anyway, to help poor countries with nothing to offer in return. The phrase increasingly heard in the political process is "in our national interest"—a euphemism for self-interest. The percentage of our GDP that goes to the economic development of Third World countries is the lowest of all the industrialized nations, and most of our aid goes to countries that offer us something in return. So much for wealth leading to generosity. It seems to be the just the other way around, the hardness associated with success in a market-based society reflected in our relations with the rest of the world.

But even in terms of immediate self-interest, most of the world has a stake in making the global economy work. The U.S., as its main architect, took the first steps toward it by reducing trade barriers, and the trade that resulted contributed to the longest boom in U.S. history. The inexpensive goods that flooded into this country raised standards of living here, but they also led to the trade deficits that could only be reduced by getting other countries to open their markets to American goods. The groups opposed to the World Trade Organization (WTO) have good points to make, but they tend to ignore the powerful momentum trade already has; it is essential to the economies of many countries, even to their survival in terms of importing food, oil, and other essential items. For our purposes here, of seeking ways of moving toward sustainability, the present role of trade must be accepted—its benefits as well as its dangers. Still, the whole issue of trade provides what may be the clearest illustration of the workings of a cultural trap—especially how easy it is for nations to be drawn into it, especially when it offers so many benefits.

The Pros and Cons of World Trade

The key advantage of trade is that it permits the fullest use of the world's resources, in much the way that transportation permits the fullest use of U.S. agriculture resources. Rather than letting most countries struggle without oil, for example, while Middle Eastern countries sit on a huge pool of it, all countries have access to the oil they need, at least as much as they can pay for. In the same way, American grain farmers have export markets for their surplus stocks of wheat, corn, and rice so Third World farmers do not have to farm ever steeper hillsides or clear remaining forests to grow the food they need. Instead, they can use their labor more profitably to make products that can be sold on world markets. That's the theory, anyway, but there is much truth in it, as demonstrated by the rising incomes of many countries. Visitors to Mexico, for example, are often surprised to see how prosperous Mexico City is compared to what they expected.

The character of much of this development is reflected in an article in *The New York Times* in 1997 about the need for more sweatshops overseas. (1997) The jobs they provide are important for the growing number of people who have been forced off the land and into burgeoning Third World cities seeking work. If leftist critics are quiet now, it is because those who provide the jobs are the new heroes for those who need them. Japan began its rise to a world power this way, producing cheap plastic goods for export out of its postwar devastation, and other countries have followed its lead, especially in Asia—Hong Kong, Taiwan, Korea, Singapore, and Malaysia. The U.S. didn't much like it when Japanese workers displaced American labor in the steel, auto, and television industries, but American retailers—and consumers—loved the inexpensive consumer goods that flooded in from overseas. Selling them was profitable when they could be purchased so inexpensively, and their availability contributed to the veritable explosion of retailing space in the U.S.—up six fold during the last two decades of the twentieth-century, much of it in the "big boxes" along freeways. Such changes contributed to the dominance of the service sector in the U.S. economy, which now provides 80 percent of the jobs, including most of the high paid ones but millions of low paid ones, too. Manufacturing has slipped to 16 percent of employment, and food and raw materials to less than 4 percent. This is the fully evolved urban industrial society, and world trade is at its core. At one time there were fears of a shortage of the low-cost labor needed to keep the cheap goods coming in, but then China came into the picture with its almost limitless supply of industrious labor. Strong export markets have been a blessing to the poorest, most crowded countries, such as Bangladesh and Haiti, since their wages are the lowest.

But from the beginning of the Industrial Age the limiting factor has not been workers to produce the goods but consumers with the money to buy them. This is why it was important for the U.S. and other advanced countries to encourage higher incomes overseas, since they enable foreigners to purchase the products the U.S. and other developed nations export. This is a source of danger, too, since the U.S. cannot sustain its huge trade deficits indefinitely, not without undermining the value of the dollar anyway.

Economists use the concept of comparative advantage to

explain how trade works to the benefit of all countries involved in it. The market draws each country to produce what it has a comparative advantage in, whether in low-cost labor, high-tech skills, or abundant natural resources. All nations benefit from the assets each country brings to the global economy, but this does not mean that everyone in all counties are better off, as we know from the loss of blue-collar jobs in the U.S. Environmentalists are unhappy, too, when Third World countries keep their costs down by using their environments in ways not allowed in the U.S., leaving American companies at a competitive disadvantage—and pressuring politicians to loosen environmental regulations. We hear about such issues because they affect us, but we do not hear about the one issue that is having the most unfortunate impact on Third World countries—U.S. agricultural exports.

In trade negotiations, the U.S. pressures countries to open their markets to American farm products in exchange for allowing them to import their products here. Food exports benefit the U.S. by increasing farm income and reducing the trade deficit, but they also drive Third World peoples from local self-sufficiency in their villages to the global economy of the cities. Imported food has been instrumental in the modernization process ever since the Industrial Revolution in Europe; this was the only way to feed the large numbers of workers needed to build factories, canals, railroads, and mines. European labor would not have been available for this if farmers had to continue working the small fields that had been cropped for centuries and were barely able to meet Europe's food needs, let alone the needs of a large industrial labor force. It was only the abundant grains that poured in from the virgin soils of North America and southern Russia that released labor for the Industrial Revolution, but it was not a pleasant process for those caught up in it. Europe's villagers had hoped to stay with the ways they had held to through the tumult of the Reformation and the Enlightenment. In *The Great Transformation*, Karl Polanyi describes the effects of the markets being created at the time, especially for labor.

(pp.70-76) Markets for wheat and oxen were one thing, but a market for the labor of human beings was a denial of the sacredness of human life in the medieval worldview. But the availability of cheap imported grains made it possible to drive farmers out of their villages to the cities to create the labor market that was so useful for the makers of the Industrial Revolution. The stage was set for the degradation of the early industrial cities that Dickens wrote about and contrasted so starkly with what people remembered from rural England.

The same process is going on around the world today, except now it is being driven by pressures originating in the U.S. to open markets for its farm exports. One of the most powerful lobbies in Congress is made up of representatives of farming states, farm organizations, and agribusinesses, in large part because there is no opposition to their efforts; no Americans are hurt by increased food exports while many benefit from them. The lobbyists focus on what is euphemistically referred to as "developing markets" for food exports, much of which is done with "food credits"—loans that can be translated directly into food shipments, often at low interest rates and with the long payback times that make them irresistible to poor countries. This is also a good way of getting rid of the food surpluses that the government accumulates when supporting crop prices, while agricultural interests can claim that food is being sold overseas— even with loans at such favorable terms that they are unlikely to be repaid. Europe and Japan have been strong enough to resist such lures, but when poorer countries bite, they are expected to open their markets to other American imports and join the global economy. The imported food impoverishes farmers, just as it did during the Industrial Revolution, and drives them into the cities where they can play their designated role in the global economy.

Mexico provides a good example of the process. In negotiations over North American Free Trade Agreement (NAFTA), the U.S. demanded that Mexico open its markets to American corn. The Mexican government resisted, since it had long supported the price of corn to keep historically rebellious peasants on the side of the ruling party. It finally gave in to U.S. pressures because of the benefits of increased trade with the U.S, but as price supports for corn were removed many peasants were hit hard. The poorest were usually Indians living in marginal areas, mostly in the mountains; they only wanted to continue growing their beloved corn, which had religious significance for them. Working small plots of often poor land, they had never been prosperous, but it was the life they knew and wanted to continue. But they had little hope of competing with the hybrid corn grown on the rich black soils of Iowa, heavily fertilized, and with machines that allow one farmer to work a thousand acres. One American farmer benefits from the misfortune of who knows how many of Mexico's poorest ones. The U.S. gains, too, when farmers move to the cities to produce the export items U.S. retailers and consumers like—and later to be consumers of American high-tech products. That this has worked for the U.S. is reflected in the rapid growth of trade between Mexico and the U.S. In the present political climate, this is all that needs to be said; NAFTA has been good for us.

There are problems with trade today, as reflected in the disputes that go on within the WTO and the street demonstrations outside its meetings. But overall, so many countries, rich and poor, depend on it that it must be considered unstoppable; it is analogous to the power that economic growth has in the U.S. The new wealth is distributed unevenly, as in the U.S., but this is what draws effort to the more "productive" economic activities and away from "unproductive" ones, such as farming. Our contacts are mostly with the newly well-off in the cities, not the impoverished farmers of the countryside whose way of life is so alien to ours, so all we hear about is the new opportunities being created. An *urban* industrial way of life is evolving, and since we are the winners in this process, it is a source of pride to us, and wealth, too, not problems. The income gap between rich and poor countries continues to widen; the incomes of the richest 20 percent of nations are now 74 times higher than the poorest 20 percent, up from 30 times higher in

1960, with some sources putting the figure at 150 times higher. (Coward, 2000) This leaves the wealthy countries with huge amounts of capital to invest overseas—the capital that gives the global economy its momentum. This may be success from the perspective of the winners, but it is also what makes a job in a sweatshop a good thing for those not so favored by global markets.

One advantage of trade is harder to question: it has encouraged peace in recent decades. The growing dependence on the global economy makes it dangerous for countries to under-take military activities that could disrupt their economies. Ever since the Vietnam War, when international trade began to grow in earnest, there have been none of the major conflicts that so marred the first two-thirds of the twentieth-century. The one large-scale conflict, the Gulf War, was a brief one and was fought mainly to remove a threat to the one commodity—oil—that is essential to all trade; it was perhaps the only commodity that could unify the world against Iraq. One of the major incentives for Europe to move toward integration in the European Union was to overcome the causes of the two world wars earlier in the century.

The stability the global economy has achieved so far is a major asset, but—there's that but again—the growing depen-dency on trade is likely to lead to the tougher economic circumstances that make military ventures more worth the risks, no matter how dangerous. The bombing of the World Trade Center may have been an early indication of the anger associated with trade, but shocking as it was, it may have been modest compared to other potential problems. If, for example, Saudi Arabia fell under an Islamic regime that threatened to cut off oil exports to the U.S., would we feel we had no choice but to occupy the region in order to assure our access to oil? We could probably pull this off, especially with Europe's assistance, but what if China backed new Saudi leaders in a move to challenge U.S. dominance of the region? That would change things significantly. How would the U.S. respond? Would such a war be seen as a way of crushing this new challenger while securing control of Middle Eastern oil? Pushing on in this way could lead to devastating consequences, especially considering how easy it would be to sabotage the oil handling facilities. It is when oil supplies are cut off that transportation is disrupted, factories come to a halt, and food grows scarce. It is when such desperate actions begin to make sense that it can be said we are reaching the dark end of a cultural trap.

Fortunately, this is not a place we should ever have to be, if only because of our location between two oceans and our abundant land and resources. We will always have the alternative of pulling back to our own shores and beginning the process of living within our own means. Pulling away from heroic military efforts is in keeping with the evolutionary process, especially when there are alternatives that do not jeopardize the nation's survival. The good fortune of this country is that we have this choice, rather than the more desperate choices of countries heavily dependent on imported food, energy, or raw materials.

Changing Terms of Trade

For the time being, the value of trade and the global economy will continue to be shaped by what economists call terms of trade. Europe needed Russian natural gas in the 1980s and was willing to pay a good price for it, while the Soviets desperately needed the hard currencies that exporting gas would earn. The terms of trade were excellent for both sides—it was a "deal made in heaven" so President Reagan was unsuccessful in his efforts to block construction of the pipeline that would deliver the gas. The terms of trade for coffee and bananas have improved for the industrialized countries but have deteriorated for the tropical countries that depend on them for the export earnings to buy needed imports. Such deteriorating terms of trade make growing yams or cassava look better, even if it means returning to slash and burn agriculture. If the terms of trade of tropical countries decline to the point where more countries do this, it will hurt U.S. exports since there will be less money to pay for them. The Asian economic crisis caused a drop in U.S. food exports, a fall in farm incomes, increased federal assistance to farmers, plus huge government loans to prop up economies half way around the world. International assistance helped overcome the Asian crisis, but it suggests how global trade is apt to peak and then begin its long decline—when countries run out of money to purchase imports.

Every country will try to resist this by keeping the prices and quantities of their exports up. The U.S. has a greater capacity to do this than most countries, but this capacity is not unlimited; subsidizing crop prices for American farmers and loans to pay for exports can get expensive. It can be argued that the global economy would be better of if the prices of U.S. grains were allowed to fall so poor countries could afford to buy them, but this would create difficulties for American farmers and their already fragile rural bankers. Higher oil prices would hurt everyone's terms of trade, since they would drive all prices up at a time when countries were sending more of their money to OPEC—the only countries whose terms of trade would be improving. But even the price OPEC could sell its oil for would be limited by how much money countries elsewhere had to pay for it.

When countries reach the point where there are no trades that leave them better off, the movement away from the global economy would be underway. Some of the poorest countries are already in this position, but as time passes more countries will find themselves in similar circumstances. When there are no trades left that leave countries better off, they will have little choice but to move toward getting by on their own resources. It is an understatement to say that this will be painful; there is an element of heartlessness in the evolutionary process as natural forces correct imbalances that have built up but cannot be sustained. It will at least mean that countries will move toward sustainable ways, but it would have been less painful if this had begun sooner—before trade had permitted populations to double a few more times, cities to grow so large, and the ways of village self-sufficiency to erode so much. Outsiders may be able to help in such a forced return to sustainability, but even if free of self-interest—a big if—foreigners would not be able to put themselves into the shoes of the people themselves and experience the effects of their history, culture, and environment. Effective adaptation is something that only the people themselves can carry off, and in their own ways.

The terms of trade for the U.S. have been favorable for a long time. Our most important exports—financial services, entertainments, computer software—bring good prices, while imports have been generally inexpensive. The less advanced industrial countries have been less fortunate since many of the products they produce—steel, textiles, chemicals—are produced in many countries and plagued with overproduction and low prices. They would love to move into the newer, more profitable industries, but this is not easy when it means competing against a powerhouse like the U.S.; even with subsidies, European countries find it hard to produce films that can compete with American ones. Countries dependent on the export of raw materials have faced perhaps the harshest markets in recent decades, since sophisticated methods of exploring for minerals have led to the discovery of high-grade deposits that quickly turn older mining operations into money losers. The efforts of countries to protect less efficient industries is what makes the disputes handled by the World Trade Organization so bitter—but also so important. Such disputes have soured relations between the U.S. and Europe, mainly over Europe's efforts to protect its smaller farmers. The U.S. often wins these decisions, but they could be pyrrhic victories if in winning everywhere we impoverish the countries that otherwise would have bought U.S. goods. We would be like the predator that was so successful in taking its prey that it ended up starving to death itself.

Trade could decline for other than economic reasons. The U.S. does not like to be dependent on imported oil; think of how we would feel if we were dependent on imported food, too, especially if food prices were rising along with oil prices, as seems likely. We would probably want to move toward food self-sufficiency by restricting food imports, but if many countries did this the power of the WTO to control trade could collapse. Also, many of the U.S. exports that earn the most money are not exactly essentials; countries could bar imports of television shows, computer games, and compact discs with little adverse effects on their efforts to move toward self-sufficiency. This would make trade disputes nastier, and could spill out into trade wars that accelerated the decline of the global economy.

The smoothest evolutionary process would be one in which trade declined slowly but steadily over a long period of time, finally to the point where it was sustained by renewable resources. This could still be significant, since sailing vessels were moving goods worldwide before steam powered vessels appeared in the nineteenth-century. Many of these ships were quite impressive; think of the fast, beautiful Clipper Ships, and how their performance could be improved with newer materials and computers. It could also be that a breakdown in trade could result in the abrupt end to the dangers of overgrowth and a movements toward sustainable ways. About the only thing that can be said with any confidence is that international trade cannot continue at its present level, when a billion tons of exports and imports pass through U.S. ports each year—four tons per person. The largest single item is oil, and it is the one that is most apt to decline, whether from peaking oil production, global warming, or deteriorating terms of trade.

During the Asian economic crisis of the late 1990s there were palpable fears that a global recession was being held off only by strong U.S. demand for imports. Equally important was that rising stock prices made Wall Street a good place for foreigners to invest the huge number of dollars left in their hands by our trade deficits. If these deficits continued and countries started turning in their T-bills instead of buying CDs and computer software, the value of the dollar could fall, causing a global recession by itself, one that could spiral down into a global depression. It is also possible that the global economy could restart spontaneously when oil prices fell. But all such matters are speculative; all we know now is that it is dangerous to have so many economic eggs in one global basket, since if that basket broke many eggs would be broken. If countries fell into a depression they could not get out of, they would quickly come to the conclusion that they would have been better off to have stayed with their own resources and cultures rather than joining the global consumer culture with its ephemeral demands for gym shoes, electronic organizers, and stuffed animals.

Population Growth

Population growth no longer receives the attention it once did. It is still regarded as a problem, but two things have worked against devoting more effort to it. First, birth control programs were rarely effective, especially in Third World countries where the need was the greatest. And secondly, birth rates fell almost automatically as economic development moved forward. The result is the general view held today, that development will continue to cause birth rates to fall until population stabilizes sometime later in the century. This is what happened in the West as it developed, so it is not surprising that the same thing is happening in the Third World now. It is an optimistic scenario, but it seems reasonable enough, especially as birth rates fall along with economic development.

Unfortunately, there is a flaw in this scenario, a major one. The solution—urban industrial society—requires far more energy and raw materials for its metabolism than the traditional agricultural way of life being replaced. Villagers get by largely on renewable resources, in the crops they grow, the vegetation they feed their animals, and the firewood and dung they burn for fuel. They buy some machine-made goods, such as cloth, cooking utensils, tools, and increasing amounts of chemical fertilizer, but their energy needs are few compared to cities, where fossil fuels are needed for everything—to bring in food and materials, manufacture goods, export them to world markets, move people around, and process wastes. If Third World countries modernized enough to bring population growth to a halt, the world's resources would be depleted much faster than now projected. And even though a good deal of modernization has occurred and birth rates have fallen, the annual net increase in world population has declined only slightly, from a peak of 84 million in 1990 to 79 million in 1999. Most of the increase continues to be in the poorest countries—those with farthest to go if modernization is to stabilize world population.

One part of the scenario, however, cannot be questioned: modernization is the surest form of birth control. When villagers move to cities they begin using the contraceptives they did not use in the villages. Not immediately, since they bring their village ways with them, but soon they realize that a large family is not the asset it was in their village. Many children become a burden for mothers who need to earn money to help support their families. Children function as a form of social security for parents in Third World societies, but in cities this is best achieved by educating children so they can get the jobs that will enable them to support their parents when they grow old. Cities also offer better access to medical care and food supplies, so fewer children are necessary to insure that at least one survives to care for the parents in their old age.

The change from the high birth and death rates of traditional agricultural societies to the low birth and death rates of urban industrial societies has been so clear that it has been given a name, the demographic transition. In many developed societies birth rates have fallen so low that growth would have stopped, even turned negative, if immigrants had not been allowed in to help meet manpower needs. In Europe, birth rates have fallen as low as 1.4 children per couple, well below the replacement level of 2.1. This occurred even in formerly quite conservative Catholic countries, such as Spain and Portugal after they rejected autocratic governments and joined the European Union. Countries as traditional as India have enjoyed slowing birth rates as economic development draws people to cities in hopes of joining the middle class. Such changes form the basis of the projections that world population growth will continue to slow and come to a halt later in the century.

The problem is in the Third World villages where so many people still live. We find it hard to understand why they continue to have so many children when surely they can see how scarce land is and how bleak the prospects for their many children are. They are undoubtedly troubled by this, but their behavior mimics ours when we act as if unending economic growth is possible. In both cases, people are making do as best they can in the circumstances they live in. We know what economic growth does for us, just as people in poor countries know what children do for them; both are the source of the best things in their quite different lives. For villagers, children are the one source of pleasure they can still afford, with the ideal being to be surrounded by children and grandchildren. Those who followed the advice of birth control workers often ended up alone, especially if they also followed the advice to educate sons—who then went off to the cities and neglected the parents whose sacrifices enabled them to get their educations. The middle classes in Third World countries do not just pick up what is good about the West; they also pick up the self-centered drive that is as necessary to get ahead there as it is here.

In other words, the high value placed on large families in traditional agricultural societies has a logic to it; it cannot simply be blamed on ignorance, lack of birth control, men trying to prove their virility, or women's pride in being able to bear many children. All may be part of the story, but not the main part—that children simply make life better.

In the past, large families did not mean population growth, since death rates were high, too. Population will be stable when birth rates equal death rates, and this can happen in two ways, with high birth and death rates, as in the past, or the low birth and death rates of modern societies. These are the two ends of the demographic transition, and they lead to an interesting question: Which would you prefer, to live in a society with many children and few old people, or one with many old people and few children? The general preference would be for more children than old people, but this is the high birth and death rates of traditional societies. We have not experienced the full impact of the low birth and death rate society yet, since we still have several workers supporting each retired person. A stable population in the U.S. could mean as few as two workers supporting each retired person and require much higher deductions from paychecks to support the retired population. The only real alternative is requiring people to work longer before retiring, but this leaves fewer jobs for young people.

This leads to a related question: Would you enjoy each day more if death was an ever-present possibility, as in the past, or if you could count on living into your eighties, perhaps longer, but often alone or in a nursing home with body or mind failing? Although simplified, these are the choices if population is to be stable.

We have a hard time imagining how people in the past managed to get by without modern medical care, enduring sicknesses that were not understood, pain without anesthetics, watching children sicken and die, or orphans left when their parents die. Yet people lived with such circumstances throughout human history and they were accepted as part of the human condition. Did their capacity to endure enhance their relish for life? With all the poverty and limited opportunities of the past, people still created the poems and love songs that have come down to us, and the dances, festivals, and feasts which are such treasures, while existential nausea is a modern phenomenon. Why should this be?

Even with all our knowledge, experiences, and comforts, much of life still remains mysterious. To protect ourselves we tend to see the worst in the past and in Third World societies today, with photos of people pawing through garbage piles for food or children's faces covered with flies. Travelers to India and Africa find less of this than expected from the media here, but much of what there is a consequence of rapid population growth. When population doubles every 30 years, as has often been the case, everything else must be doubled too, houses, jobs, food supplies, and schools—a tremendous burden. With the relatively stable populations of the past, only maintenance would have been necessary, so houses and religious buildings could be decorated, elaborate clothes sewn for special days, and fields interspersed with woodlots—all the things shown in the sketches made by early travelers. There is evidence that India had a higher standard of living than Europe until the Industrial Revolution two centuries ago.

Still, the only way of life we can really know is our own, the one we are living; there is no way of experiencing lives in the past or other cultures. It is probably true that all peoples tend to see what is good in their own ways, and this would be fine if such ways were sustainable. As it is, however, we are forced to cope with rapid changes with no ideas of where they are taking us.

How Stable is the World Trading System?

The instabilities of world financial markets in recent years have confirmed long-held feelings that the financial system is the most unstable part of the world economy. Trade itself is relatively solid, at least as long as two parties benefit from an exchange, even if to varying degrees. This is what led to the formation of the World Trade Organization as a watchdog over trade, to insure that it is carried out as fairly as possible and to avoid the downward spiral of trade wars. But there is no such organization to regulate international financial matters. It is interesting that, even though financial markets are the part of the global economy that functions most like a truly free market, it is also the most unstable part, and the focus of most concern.

Financial activities have been creative, there is no question of that. They now respond quickly and efficiently not only to new opportunities but also to problems—real or imagined—all around the world. Rumors are often all it takes to trigger a run on a nation's currency, yet there is no global equivalent of the Securities and Exchange Commission and the Federal Reserve System to regulate the process. Nor is there likely to be. Even the World Trade Organization is regularly attacked as giving away too much of our sovereignty, while the United Nations has been given little real power. How well the world financial systems perform will have an important bearing on the future—and the survival of the market faith.

Warnings about the dangers of financial markets have come from every direction, including major players in international finance. One of the most interesting is George Soros, who was extraordinarily successful in accumulating a huge fortune by speculating in the changing value of currencies. He then devoted a major portion of his winnings to helping Eastern Europe make the transition from communism to democratic ways. Writing in *The Atlantic Monthly* in 1997, he decried "democratic but sovereign states pursuing their self-interest to the detriment of the common interest. The international open society may be its own worst enemy. . . I blame the prevailing attitude, which holds that the unhampered pursuit of self-interest will bring about an eventual international equilibrium. I believe this confidence is misplaced." He goes on to ask for "generally agreed-upon standards" that are higher than markets are apt to exhibit when functioning on their own. Later, during the height of the boom in 2000, he pulled out of the financial markets altogether when he felt they no longer had any relationship to underlying economic realities.

John Maynard Keynes was not only the father of modern economics but he was also a successful speculator and member of the Bloomsbury group of artists and intellectuals in London during the 1930s. He expressed skepticism about both international finances and trade:

> I sympathize therefore, with those who would minimize, rather than those who would maximize,

economic entanglement between nations. Ideas, knowledge, art, hospitality, travel—these are the things
which should of their nature be international. But let
goods be homespun whenever it is reasonably and
conveniently possible: and above all, let finance be
primarily national. (Quoted in Daly, 1996)

It would be interesting to hear what Keynes would say about
global finances today and the onslaught of American popular
culture overseas, the movies, music, clothes, fast foods, and
advertising. Would this fall under the definition of ideas and art?
The Internet provides even greater dilemmas for countries. A
number have tried to restrict it, mainly because of its prurient
content, but found this virtually impossible if they still wanted to
have access to the information it contains. Perhaps these are
areas where the charge of imperialism is still valid—cultural
imperialism, perhaps, but still imperialism, and driven by the
same economic motivations of earlier forms.

Still, it is undoubtedly true that most Americans would
be pleased if there was something this nation could do for poor
countries that would unquestionably help them. But as time
passes, this seems harder to find. Even medical assistance, which
seemed the surest gift the developed countries could offer the
rest of the world, may turn out to be a mixed blessing: perhaps it
could be the most destructive of all if it means a greater number
of people going through the agonies of over-shoot and collapse
later, with the survivors left to cope with their cultures decimated
and their environments damaged. What if improvements in
communications only serve to break down age-old restraints with
visions of the self-indulgent behavior? What if Western
investments only succeed in driving billions of people into cities
that cannot be sustained, or into the deviant behavior already
being seen in less developed countries, of kidnapping as an
economic enterprise, the production of cocaine and heroin, the
sex trade, or training impoverished kids in the use of M-16 rifles
by warlords who promise to take care of them in return? The
worst scenario of all could well have economic development

continuing until all the world's cultures were converted to the market faith, but just as the resources to sustain that way of life were depleted, leaving people with nothing to fall back on.

Such concerns are not new. One of the darkest expressions was written in 1921 by Yeats in his poem "The Second Coming:"

> Things fall apart: the center cannot hold;
> Mere anarchy is loosed upon the world,
> The blood-dimmed tide is loosed, and everywhere
> The ceremony of innocence is drowned;
> The best lack all conviction, while the worst
> Are full of passionate intensity.

Such fears may always have haunted people, even if the specifics were different—of crops failing rather than oil supplies, and mounted warriors pillaging and killing rather than nuclear or biological weapons raining down. What is different now is the scale of the potential disasters, especially with so much interconnectedness. This, too, was well put by a poet, Robinson Jeffers, in "The Purse Seine":

> I thought, We have geared the machines and locked all
> together into interdependence;
> we have built the great cities: now
> There is no escape. We have gathered vast populations
> incapable of free survival, insulated
> From the strong earth, each person in himself helpless,
> on all dependent. The circle is closed, and the net
> Is being hauled in. They hardly feel the cords drawing,
> yet they shine already. The inevitable
> mass-disasters
> Will not come in our time nor in our children's, but we
> and our children
> Must watch the net draw narrower, government take all
> powers—or revolution, and the new government

> Take more than all, add to kept bodies kept souls—or
> anarchy, the mass disasters.

These words were written in 1937 when it seemed that the rise of Hitler's Germany and Stalin's Russia meant totalitarianism was the way of the future. That fear is gone now, thankfully, but in its place is the equally troubling vision of the journalist Robert Kaplan, who, after traveling widely overseas, felt that governments were losing control of their countries—to ethnic minorities, rebels in mountain strongholds, gangs in cities, international drug cartels, fanatics of all kinds, or mafias, militias, and private security forces. (1994, 1996)

There is no question that there are things to be feared, for certainly there have been dark episodes throughout history. Nor is there any basis for denying that such things could happen again. But just as important is the fact that such setbacks have usually been temporary; the killers did tend to kill each other off, even if it took time, leaving the survivors ready to do anything in their power to replace the violence with goodwill toward others. Only culture can accomplish this, or forestall the violence in the first place. Its record is far from perfect, but it is still good. It is times such as ours that create the greatest challenges to be overcome.

The evolutionary process is most effective when it occurs in an orderly process, and in the U.S. this means the political process. One of its roles is regulating the economy, so politics is where we must begin, daunting as that may seem. It brings us to the question of what can be expected from the American political process.

CHAPTER SEVEN

Politics and Policies of Sustainabilty

Politics in this country has come to function much as the economy does, favoring those vigorous enough—or aggressive enough—to gain its benefits. Those who used government effectively did well, at least until others discovered that the squeaky wheel was getting the oil. Then there was a cacophony of squeaky wheels as all groups pushed their interests as loudly as they could. They had to; if they didn't they would lose out. Then in the 1980s the taxpayers joined in, demanding their taxes be cut without any specific ideas about where spending should be cut—except that it be from someone else's benefits. Politicians knew that cutting any spending would lose them votes, so the deficits grew, and with them the outrage toward politicians—for doing what was necessary to stay in office. The search began in earnest to find ways of cutting spending with the least voter backlash, with the deepest cuts ending up in programs for those least able to defend them, mainly the poor and the young.

The tax revenues generated by the rapid growth of the 1990s relieved politicians of the onerous task of making further spending cuts, and even permitted some tax reductions. Surpluses also cooled the overheated rhetoric of the Contract with America, but the distrust of politicians remained. The media are sometimes blamed for this, but they are only following the market here, with its insatiable appetite for anything that reflects badly on politicians. Money clearly influences the process, one reason why the well-off have done inordinately well in recent years. But it is also true that the biggest contributors—corporations, producer associations, and labor unions—speak for large numbers of ordinary wage earners and low-level employees—not just corporate chiefs and millionaires; in a democratic society they should be heard. The political process is essentially a group process, and Americans join groups to have their voices heard more effectively. This is as true of advocates for the environment, children, education, and the arts as it is for those speaking for tobacco, alcohol, gambling, and assault rifles.

If money distorts the political process as much as people believe it does, there should be legislation that clearly goes against the will of the majority. Which ones would they be? The most glaring examples are probably those that help local industries, such as tobacco in Kentucky, coal in Appalachia, or autos in Detroit, but such help is what people expect from their representatives in Congress. Similarly, money is spent building unnecessary freeways and keeping military bases open, but this does not make the process undemocratic; if anything, it is too democratic—too responsive to the will of the people who elect their representatives. At times politicians can find ways of benefiting campaign contributors, but if their political opponents find out about this it can produce devastating publicity. If, however, as is more often the case, the benefits help a local industry, there will be no adverse publicity—only the sense that legislators are taking care of their districts. Bills that threaten jobs can count on opposition, often a hornet's nest of it, while spending on the anti-ballistic missile system continued even as the threat of missile attack was reduced to weak countries such as North Korea and Iraq.

It is not correct that the broad middle class loses out in the process; there are too many of them, and they vote. Politicians fall all over each other making promises to the middle class, and if they cannot deliver on some of them it is usually because of budget constraints, opposition by other groups, or the complexities that do not fit into thirty second television pitches. Farm legislation is regularly described as helping the family farm, but crop supports go to big farmers, too, and they get the big checks since they can produce so much more, and at lower prices. If there is a food policy in this country, it is a cheap food policy, since that is what most voters want—even if it drives small farmers out of business. In the same way, any effort to cut Social Security benefits immediately results in media stories of struggling widows trying to get by on a small check—not the majority of seniors whose checks are frosting on the cake of larger retirement checks.

As with the economy, self-interest is the name of the political game now. It may always have been a large part of the political process, but now it is more blatant—and more acceptable. Moral arguments against this are rarely heard; people are expected to vote for the candidate who offers them the most. As winning becomes more important, the calls for non-partisanship rarely get far, especially when supporters threaten to pull out if a compromise is proposed. Presidential candidates must prove they are tough enough for the job, but driving away candidates with less taste for the harsh infighting that politics increasingly requires. Politicians must endure all manner of unsavory attacks, be the butt of jokes, and face being thrown out of office *en masse* by term limits. Special prosecutors function almost like inquisitors, and on matters that in the past were considered private and not appropriate for public discussion. The terrorist bombings in New York and Washington at least had the benevolent effect of pulling the nation together—or directing the anger toward enemies outside the country. Before that, however, it was the attack mode against political opponents that seemed to work best, and this is likely to return. Even if politicians are the favorite target, there are many others, from bureaucrats to welfare cheaters, environmentalists to corporate raiders, rednecks to immigrants, or anyone on the wrong side of issues such as abortion, school prayers, and gun control. We seem to thrive on such hostilities, but even when they are transferred to terrorists they still threaten the prospects of our children more than anything politicians can do on their own.

Finding an outlet for our anger may make us feel better, a salve for our fears and insecurities, but as with other spurious medications, it only makes the disease worse. Nor can prosperity be the answer, since partisanship rose to new heights during the boom years at the end of the twentieth-century. It is when winning takes precedence over principles that we should worry about the future of this country, since its heritages is one of deciding issues in reasonably effective ways. After all, it accomplished what was most important to Americans—keeping the economy strong and growing. It is disturbing when there seems so little appreciation of a political system that has provided this country with so much. Perhaps it is necessary to travel overseas to see how bad governments can before Americans will appreciate what we have here. Or it may be that the rising partisanship of recent decades only confirms old ideas about the pernicious influence of wealth, that it leads to hard-heartedness. If true, however, it is a hopeful thought since it would mean that a decline in wealth would pull people back together.

I will assume that the political heritage that has served this country well for over two centuries will survive this age of excess. If it doesn't, there would be little reason to continue with this book, since political stability is essential for the evolutionary process to function in productive ways. One thing, however, can be counted on: Politicians will change along with the voters, if for no other reason than to get elected. Hopefully, voters will ask them for wisdom and good sense—rather than to be winners, come what may.

What Do We Want From Politicians?

Even with all the discontent with politics today, there is little tendency to look beneath the surface for what troubles us, probably because the reasons are too close to the core values of this country. The dynamism that made this the wealthiest, most powerful nation the world has ever known did not come from limiting farms to 160 acres, shops to the size of family operations, labor mobility to what kept families together for Sunday dinners, or banning the violent, sexually explicit films that attract large audiences. Urban industrial society grew out of the rejection of all such limitations, and our values reflect this as clearly as traditional agricultural societies reflect the ethics of the great faiths. There was no plan to do this, no evil forces to blame; it is just how things worked out in the context of an abundant landscape and the freedoms that attracted immigrants to this country. Many good things came with the vigorous growth of the new nation, but there have been losses, too, including the ways that made simpler lives satisfying. Nothing is all good, just as nothing is all bad; it is not possible to have the benefits of a way of life without its costs.

Rather than accepting that there are deep contradictions between the traditional and the modern, we ask politicians to make them disappear—and then blame them when this cannot be done. The surveys asking people what they want from government vary with the times, but with the threat of nuclear war and crime reduced, the most important concerns, after the economy, are those associated with the breakdown of traditional values. Yet no aspiring politician is going to get elected by telling voters that the modern economy was built by those who rejected traditional values. They have little choice but to try and convince voters that they can provide the best of the traditional and the modern. Who, then, is to blame when this doesn't work? No one? Or everyone?

It is strange to be defending politicians when I find their actions as frustrating as most Americans do. Still, the logic that drives them is clear—the need to get elected in a representative democracy. If a substantial amount of money is wasted, that is one of the costs of maintaining grassroots support in our political system. If it means a government grown huge and bureaucratic, that is what it takes to keep a complex industrial society functioning, just as big corporations are necessary to keep the economy competitive. If lobbyists have inordinate influence in the political system, much of this is because legislatures need information from lobbyists about the consequences of legislation being considered in a diverse nation approaching 300 million people. Complexity forces politicians to act cautiously if they are to remain in office, and this makes compromise an essential part of the political process. Measures usually have to be watered down in order to gain wide enough acceptance to be passed, leading to the saying that the perfect compromise is one in which all sides are equally unhappy. This alone could explain much of the anger toward politicians when winning is so important. President Clinton figured out that offering what the polls told him Americans wanted led to high approval ratings, so now presidential candidates all promise much the same things, but making it harder for voters to chose between them. Voters may be unhappy with what presidents actually deliver, but presidents end up being disappointed with what they were able to accomplish while in office. The voters who are most angry with the political process are those farthest from the center, since their measures have little chance of passage, and third party candidates have little to offer other than outlets for anger toward politicians big business. All of this tells us that there is actually a good deal of unity in this country—the unity provided by a free-market economy under rules determined by representative democracy.

Several of the tasks politicians have to do are almost guaranteed to make them unpopular. One is to be the rule-maker among Americans who have a tendency to use their freedoms without regard to how they affect others. When problems arise, people get upset and demand that government do something, but the resulting rules only stimulate efforts to avoid them, necessitating the elaboration of rules that so maddens everyone. This brings to mind the words of Edmund Burke over two hundred years ago:

> Men are qualified for civil liberty in exact proportion to their disposition to put moral chains upon their own appetites. Society cannot exist unless a controlling power upon . . . appetite be placed somewhere, and the less of it there is within, the more there must be without.

Another important but thankless task of government is to level taxes to do what the market does not do, at least not effectively; especially the provision of the infrastructure on which so much of modern life depends. This includes not only physical facilities—roads, sewer systems, dams, airports—but institutional supports as well—defense, public health, justice, social welfare, and so on. All have grown steadily as the scale and complexity of modern society have increased, and all cost money, often quite a bit of it, especially given the bureaucratic inefficiencies that seem to be an inevitable part of all governments. Yet the provision of infrastructure, just as with rule making, is essential for the ongoing functioning of modern society. And even though greater efficiency is always possible, the U.S. seems to accomplish these tasks about as well as other industrial nations. Plato had it right almost two and a half millennia ago when he said that democracy is "a charming form of government, full of variety and disorder, and dispensing a sort of equality to equals and unequals alike." It may be a messy system, but nothing better has been found. And no matter how hard our society tries to keep government to a minimum, matters regularly appear that require its attention.

One of the main advantages of economics in ordering a society is that it works in impersonal ways, the result of millions of individual decisions taken in an ongoing process. No bureaucrats, for example, could have driven small farmers off the land, closed down small shops, or forced people from small towns into huge cities, not without a revolt anyway. But the market did all this quietly, efficiently, and remorselessly. The nation moved in the same direction under both Republican and Democratic administrations. The currents may have shifted left and right in the broad channel of American political life, to favor decisions by the market or government, but no administration changed the overall direction of flow. None worked to slow the rate of economic growth, for instance, or urbanization, technological advance, or restrict economic freedom—any of the dominant characteristics of urban industrial society.

What Can We Expect From Government?

In the overall sense, the workings of the American political system can be said to be clear, even transparent: politicians will try to do what keeps their constituents happy and gets them reelected. It would be an easy job if everyone wanted the same thing, but that isn't the case, and for some issues there are no good solutions. In such circumstances the conservative nature of the political process takes over—the natural tendency of legislators to avoid making a hard choice while hoping that something will happen to make it less of a no-win decision. The process is conservative in the truest sense, of not jeopardizing what we have in the process of trying to move ahead. Incremental changes are most apt to be taken, the small steps which, if they work, can be expanded, while if they don't can be altered or pulled back before major damage is done. Radical steps are not in the cards. They are simply too risky, both for the country and the legislators, who, if they turn out to be wrong, will be held accountable for in next election. At times the right and the left have their day in the sun, during the Great Society, for example, and the Contract with America, but this doesn't last long; the middle usually reestablishes itself. Politicians in this country have been called middle-of-the-road-hogs, the usual derisive term for something that is actually the greatest achievement of the American political system—its continuity for over two centuries.

Still, would this political system, with its slow, cautious ways, be able to respond effectively to a major threat to its economic security? The answer has to be yes, at least as reflected in the response to the first energy crisis. With the return of cheap oil there is a tendency to forget the problems high oil prices caused—the huge outflow of dollars into OPEC bank accounts, interest rates and unemployment both in double digits, and the dark shadows of bankruptcies. Yet government, business, and individuals all responded effectively. Government passed tax credits to encourage conservation and renewable energy, and the Energy Development Corporation was established to speed the development of the low-grade fossil fuels the nation had in abundance. With the hindsight we now enjoy, it could even be said that the country over-responded to the crisis, since in the end most of the programs were eliminated and President Carter was hurt in his reelection campaign by his vigorous efforts to establish them. But corporations over-responded, too; Exxon walked away from a two billion dollar investment in oil shales when falling oil prices made the venture uneconomic. In retrospect, the mistakes made were due mainly to the abruptness of the price rises, pointing to the value of slow, steady— evolutionary—change.

There are other lessons to be learned from the response to the first oil crisis. The oil companies, being the bearers of the bad news of rising OPEC prices, were blamed for them, or at least pictured as capitalizing on the higher prices to make windfall profits at the expense of consumers. Any politician who argued that higher gas prices were part of the solution was charged with being in the pocket of the oil companies, so price controls were passed and soon the gas lines began to form—and with them the anger of consumers. Suggestions that price controls were the problem were met with incredulity; prices, it was said, would go through the roof without them. But as the problems with price controls grew tiresome, removing them began to look better, and when they were finally lifted, sure enough, the lines disappeared and prices, rather than exploding, settled down as people found ways to use less.

Rationing was also proposed as a fairer way of cutting consumption than letting higher prices squeeze out the poor who couldn't afford them. (It is remarkable how much sympathy there is for the poor when the issue is the higher prices everyone pays.) But congressional debates on rationing led to difficulties, enough to make market-based solutions look better. Representatives from states like California said they needed more coupons per driver because of the longer commutes, and they were followed by legislators from thinly populated regions, such as in the Great Basin, where jobs and shopping facilities were often many miles away. Obviously, gasoline rationing would not be as straightforward as it had been during World War II. The constructive idea that came out of the rationing debate was the establishment of a "white market" in which ration coupons could be bought and sold, providing compensation to those who did not use theirs, including the poor, while the affluent could still get the coupons to buy additional gasoline. Even in the debates it fostered, the response to the oil crisis was constructive.

Oil prices came down, and as they did many nascent movements toward sustainability slowed and then ended. Cars became bigger and more powerful again, and thermostats were turned up in winter and down in summer. The suburbs resumed their expansion, reversing the movement toward the cities to reduce commutes, while the flicker of a renaissance in rural areas dimmed and went out as jobs in the cities drew people back to them. Could there be any greater demonstration of the importance of oil than the setbacks caused by high OPEC prices compared to the long boom caused by the low oil prices that followed?

Is there any reason to expect that the response to the second energy crunch—the real one this time, the one caused by peaking of world oil production rather than a cartel—will be any less vigorous than during the first one? Perhaps it can be said we are learning about the process of cultural evolution in our own times, including the circumstances that lead to change and those that impede it. If there had been less oil in the ground at the time of the first energy crisis, the movement toward sustainability would have been well under way by now. And if there was an excess of optimism during the 1990s, during the energy crisis years there was an excess of pessimism. Such swings are characteristic of the stock market, too; this is the conclusion James Grant reached in *The Trouble With Prosperity* (1998) after studying its long-term swings. It was striking, too, how quickly the Asian economic crisis led to questions about the viability of the world trading system—yet stopped just as quickly as the crisis passed.

With this rather extended introduction, let us consider the prospects for the sustainable economy and the policies that could enable it to evolve in parallel with the mainstream economy. It is based on the assumption that politicians will do what-ever they can to meet public needs to get elected, but only in ways that do not threaten the stability of the mainstream economy.

Policies For Sustainability

The workings of the political process may be clear in its day-to-day activities, and even in its response to obvious problems, such as the oil crisis. But it is not at all clear how it will respond to the ambiguous times we live in when it is so hard to know whether to prepare for growth or slowdown. The idea of sustainability itself is apt to receive support, given the pressures generated by the economy and the concerns about where it is taking us. Sustainability is not a radical idea, not unless the Jeffersonian ideal is radical. Suggesting simpler, more decentralized ways, wider choices of work, and stronger community, it has much in common with our past. Even those with no interest in the sustainable economy may see it as something that may be of value to their children, especially if finding a decent job in a good location becomes difficult.

Yet so powerful is the present economic reality that even thinking about moving away from growth brings forth feelings of a dream or a fantasy—responses that reflect how improbable it seems. But things change, often in unexpected ways, and as the prospects for growth become clouded, sustainability will begin to look better. It is the kind of thing the sensitive antennae of politicians pick up quickly in trying to be all things to all people. But sustainability will be seen as a good thing only if it is encouraged in ways that do not threaten the mainstream economy; people are too dependent on it to jeopardize it by encouraging "uneconomic" activity in the sustainable economy. The idea of the sustainable economy may not even be considered until it becomes a way of contributing to the health of the mainstream economy, by reducing the use of oil, for example, or the need for new jobs. But even legislators sympathetic to the sustainable economy will immediately turn against it if policies to encourage it threaten the mainstream economy in any way; that would make sustainability radical, and that's not the American way. It is also important that measures chosen be ones that can be introduced incrementally, and withdrawn if they do not work.

What follows is quite preliminary; if even a fraction of the high-powered talent now going into maintaining growth were diverted toward finding ways to allow it to slow down gracefully, better ideas would undoubtedly come forth. From the cultural evolutionary perspective, the key is to find ways of beginning the movement toward sustainability as soon as possible, and in ways that add to the stability of the mainstream economy, not an easy task. Identifying its main thrusts is probably the easiest part. There would seem to be three:

a) use less fossil fuels and more renewable forms of energy;
b) encourage work of a more sustainable nature, and

c) preserve biological productivity and diversity while
   supporting modest but adequate standards of living.

Interestingly, some of the most straightforward measures may be the most difficult to pass, at least for the present.

Taxes to Reduce the Use of Fossil Fuels. Taxes on fossil fuels have long been proposed as an effective way of reducing their use. Such taxes would also encourage the use of renewable forms of energy since, not being taxed, they would become relatively less expensive. A carbon tax is a variation of this, with the target being the reduction of carbon dioxide instead of energy. Some analysts argue that either tax would create solid, long-term investment opportunities for renewable forms of energy, but others are more skeptical, pointing to the limited effects of the subsidies provided for renewable energy during the energy crisis.

No one questions the overall logic of taxing fossil fuels, but just as clearly, such taxes would adversely affect consumers as well as a number of existing industries, such as autos and airlines, the fossil fuel industries, plus the states they are located in. The oil companies themselves are in an ambiguous situation, facing the depletion of their main product and interested in expanding into alternatives, but not to the point of cutting into the use of oil so much that their profitability is jeopardized; the profits of oil companies are what permitted them to invest in renewable energies as much as they have. Conservation groups are in an equally ambiguous position, wanting to reduce the use of fossil fuels but fearful of losing support if they support higher taxes on them.

The last time a higher tax on gasoline was proposed was when the senior President Bush included a modest increase as a part of his energy program. The representatives of the oil-producing states led the attack against it, but they had an easy time of it because of the pervasive resistance to increased taxes of any kind. Most legislators had promised voters they would cut taxes, not increase them, and President Bush, having promised this too, was hurt in his reelection campaign by his effort to reduce the federal deficit in this relatively constructive way. Gasoline taxes had long been seen as a way of raising a good deal of revenue, since every cent of tax generates a billion dollars, and it is easy to collect. But even though the tax proposed was a tiny fraction of the dollars per gallon Europeans pay, it still generated a groundswell of righteous indignation. The U.S. is not Europe, and in the end the tax increase approved was insignificant, a token of what was left of the energy crisis.

This could remain the case, given the cynicism about government and the resistance of oil-producing states, the oil industry, and consumers. The unfortunate thing is that once scarcity begins to drive oil prices up, it would be much harder to add taxes on top of the increases, certainly compared to the 1990s when prices were at historic lows. Such a tax does not seem to be in the cards, especially in a political climate in which all taxes are pictured as the government getting into people's pockets so it can waste more money. The response has all the earmarks of what politics has come to in recent years, of people demanding what is in their self-interest regardless of the broader national interest. But since this is part of a political system that has worked in this country, there is nothing to be gained by railing at it.

The problems with placing a tax directly on oil led to the search for other ways to use taxes to bias the market toward conservation in more politically acceptable ways, several of which turned out to be quite ingenious. They shed light on the often tortuous process of searching for politically acceptable policies.

A Rebated Tax. One way of reducing the aversion to higher taxes on energy would be by returning the revenue generated later, at income tax time, but on a per capita basis that left the conservers better off and the wastrels worse off. In this scheme, a tax would be placed on gasoline, and possibly other fuels, at rates judged most appropriate for the needs of the times. The entire amount collected would then be returned at income tax time on a per capita basis, by being deducted from income taxes as other credits are deducted. There would be no net increase in taxes, so the government could not be accused of getting into people's pockets again, but there would still be an incentive to use less fossil fuels, since individuals who consumed less than the average would receive more back than they paid in taxes. Such a proposal also would be good in terms of equity, since energy use rises with income; those who fly a lot, drive big cars, and heat large houses would pay more in taxes, while the poor would receive back more than they paid in and have more money to live on. Collecting and returning the taxes would be simple and inexpensive, and the higher prices for fossil fuels would still function to discourage their use, while also encouraging renewable forms of energy, which would not be taxed.

Still, many Americans would not like the idea of such a tax, especially the well-off, who would be most apt to pay more and have a greater capacity to influence the political process. Others would not trust the government to return all of the tax, or might even resent that it had the use of their money until it was returned. But the most serious problem would be if the tax was effective in reducing the use of fossil fuels, since this would adversely effect energy intensive industries, leading to lower sales, profits, and, most important of all, layoffs. It is easy enough to argue that the industries hit by the tax would be ones that energy scarcity will squeeze down anyway, while the industries benefiting would be those with better long-term prospects. But today's industries are the ones with clout, not those that might be large someday, and the new jobs are apt to be in different regions and benefit different workers. It is even risky for industries to start up in response to government incentives or tax policies, as illustrated by the rapid decline of the solar industry after federal incentives were removed in the 1980s.

Tax Shifting. The problem of lost jobs led to the next idea, known as tax shifting. Again, a tax would be placed on fossil fuels, but this time other taxes would be reduced by the same amount, so government could not be accused of getting rich at the expense of taxpayers, or even having the tax revenues to use for a while. Which taxes to reduce would then be the important question. The most logical ones would be taxes on employment, with Social Security and unemployment taxes being the most obvious. Revenues from the fuel tax would be transferred to these accounts to reimburse them for the taxes lost in encouraging firms to hire more workers.

How effective such tax reductions would be in encouraging new jobs is the next question, and it is not a pleasant one. Of the many ways the government has tried to create jobs, from being the employer of last resort to subsidizing the creation of jobs in the private sector, all left much to be desired; often they were among the first programs voters wanted to see cut back or eliminated. The only effective way the government has found over the years of encouraging jobs has been through fiscal policies that put more money into people's hands, either by cutting taxes or increasing spending. When the money is spent, workers are hired to produce the items being bought, with everyone benefiting from the increased economic activity—consumers, workers, and businesses. This was the breakthrough of Keynesian economics, but its very success discredited it; there were so many beneficiaries from fiscal stimulation that it got out of hand, contributing to budget deficits and the charge that we were trying to spend ourselves rich. And for the purposes of sustainability, job-creating policies cannot be the answer, since they lead to more consumption. This is the essence of the dilemma we face. The sustainable economy will be an asset to the mainstream economy only if it puts human resources to work in ways that do not add to the burden on the planet. Reining in consumption is just as important as shifting to renewable resources, but this compounds the job problem—as illustrated by the most straightforward way of reducing the least valuable forms of consumption.

A Luxury Tax. This tax was proposed by Robert Frank in *Luxury Fever* (and mentioned in Chapter 3) and is a steeply graduated tax on spending above the level at which consumption turns ostentatious. Such a tax would be paid primarily by the wealthiest individuals, those who have received the lion's share of increased national income in recent decades and compete as strenuously in spending it as in earning it. Frank's argument is that competitive consumption is a zero sum game—that the thrill of having the most expensive car is equal to the chagrin of being displaced from that position—so nothing would be lost if some of the money going into such consumption was taxed away with a luxury tax. Such a tax is backed by a well-established economic principle known as declining marginal utility, which states that each additional item consumed provides a smaller amount of satisfaction, with satiation the point at which an additional item purchased provides no added satisfaction. It is those purchases that can be taxes away with little loss of satesfactions.

Still, the luxury tax only highlights the basic dilemma, that reducing even the least useful consumption hurts the workers laid off, the companies they work for, and the communities they are a part of. For any consumption tax to be constructive, from fossil fuels to luxuries, the revenue would have to be used in ways that increase work in the sustainable economy, but this is the kind of work that is very hard to find. The virtual absence of such jobs is the major stumbling block in moving toward simpler ways of life in the sustainable economy. For the vast majority of Americans it is not an alternative.

Work in the Sustainable Economy

A good number of people may be attracted to ways of life away from the mainstream, but the fully evolved urban industrial society offers few niches for this. The trend is in just the opposite direction, toward two incomes being necessary to support a family, and usually in the urban regions where growth is strong but costs are high. Even the word "job" carries connotations that make it less appropriate for sustainable ways that involve working to meet household needs and earning supplemental income in various ways. This does not mean self-sufficiency, which is not a realistic goal since it requires an excessive amount of work to provide a low standard of living. Local self-sufficiency is the more realistic ideal, since it encourages specialization in the use of local resources, reduces transportation, and brings people together for the benefits of exchange. But a cash income will always be necessary, and that can be hard to find; rural areas have renewable resources but urban areas offer more income-earning opportunities. Both are parts of a sustainable economy, with both benefiting from exchanging the products they produce for those produced by the other. If towns and cities become smaller and more dispersed across the landscape, transportation would be reduced significantly, especially when urban densities are high enough to make cars unnecessary—which in itself would reduce the cost of living greatly. Food can be grown on the periphery of denser cities and towns, recycling organic wastes in the process. Towns and cities will be different in the future, but their basic logic will remain the same, with one way of imagining them being the way they functioned in the past. The big unknown, of course, is how the familiar scenes of pre-industrial settlements will be changed by the modern technologies that find roles in the sustainable economy.

Whether rural or urban, however, making ends meet is the immediate challenge, and it is a daunting one. It is hard to avoid the conclusion that, initially at least, some form of subsidy will be necessary to make experiments in the sustainable economy feasible. Subsidizing work in the sustainable economy is not a politically attractive thought, there is no question of that. But unless some ways can be found for creating jobs in the sustainable economy to make up for those lost in the mainstream economy, the process may have to wait until conditions get desperate. The breadlines and shanty towns of the Depression come to mind, but it could be worse in the future since now there are fewer farms in families and practical skills than in the thirties.

Using subsidies to create work in the sustainable economy would put it on thin ice politically, except if the benefits were clearly of value to the whole nation. How might this happen? The mainstream economy benefits from a stable workforce—an adequate supply of labor at steady wages. When the economy is strong, the concern is with inflation, that the need for workers will outstrip the supply, driving up wages and prices in ways that could turn boom to bust. With a weak economy, the concern is with unemployment, of more workers than jobs, leading to unemployment and downward pressure on wages. This is deflation, and it is apt to be the greater problem as the economy slows, for whatever reason. Deflation is dangerous because unemployment reduces spending, causing more layoffs, less consumption, and so on—the downward spiral that, if not halted, leads to depression. If it becomes apparent that the jobs lost are gone for good, there will be a critical need for other forms of work, and subsidizing it in the sustainable economy may be the only way of meeting this need. And if doing so turned out to be both the least expensive way of creating work and with greatest long term benefits for the mainstream economy, it could gain support—even from those with no interest in the sustainable economy.

The workers who decide to use the subsidy to give the sustainable economy a try will improve the prospects of those who remain in the mainstream by reducing the surplus of workers and the downward pressure on wages. But this will be helpful for the mainstream economy only if they still have money to spend, since spending it is what preserves jobs, and business profitability, too. If those who moved into the sustainable economy managed to achieve self-sufficiency (to simplify the issue), their contribution to the economy would be nil; with both their labor and consumption withdrawn, the result would be a wash, as if these individuals did not exist. The value of unemployment and welfare checks has been well established; they sustain spending by the unemployed, even if at a reduced rate. The absence of such checks during the Depression is what allowed unemployment to snowball to a quarter of the workforce. Now, when government checks are spent, workers are kept in their jobs and the mainstream economy benefits. In effect, the productivity of the mainstream economy would be used to help the sustainable economy get started—the economy that will take up the slack as the industrial economy slows.

This assumes, of course, that the subsidy can be offered in a way that constructively meets the needs of both mainstream and sustainable economies. There may be other ways of doing this, but the one that keeps coming back to me is one proposed by President Nixon during his second term. It was a welfare reform measure known as the Family Assistance Program (FAP), and it would have passed if Democrats had been willing to let a Republican president take credit for such a progressive measure. It included an incentive for recipients to find work by allowing them to keep a portion of their FAP payments as their incomes rose; by the time a modest income was reached, the FAP payment would have declined to zero. Because the FAP would be administered through the IRS, it was often referred to as a negative income tax. Part of it was passed in the form of the earned income credit which provides money to the working poor in an amount based on how much their incomes are below the level at which income taxes are first paid. It remains a popular program, popular enough that conservative challenges to it in recent years have been turned back.

The FAP has several practical advantages in addition to the incentive it offers to earn additional income. Being a part of the income tax system simplifies its administration and reduces the need for costly welfare agencies. Advocates for the poor like it since it reduces the stigma of welfare; the stigma would be reduced even further if FAP payments went to anyone, including those who gave up well-paying jobs to try the sustainable economy. Innovative and educated people could be among those most interested in experimenting with sustainable ways, but so could those who wanted to live in more traditional ways, such as religious groups. It would be helpful to the poor living in inner city neighborhoods, and African-Americans with memories of life in the South could give that a try again. It could even function as a universal educational support for college students.

FAP would be advantageous for the mainstream economy if it helped assure a stable workforce at stable wages. This could be accomplished by varying the payments under FAP according to the changing needs of the economy. If more workers were needed, FAP payments could be reduced enough to draw those marginally involved in the sustainable economy back into the mainstream workforce. If, on the other hand, there was a surplus of people looking for jobs in the mainstream, FAP payments could be increased to entice more workers into the sustainable economy to reduce the downward pressures on wages. Such incremental changes would be analogous to the way the Federal Reserve raises and lowers interest rates based on the needs of the economy. Also, FAP payments could be introduced incrementally, beginning, for example, in a region with especially high unemployment rates, to see how it works. If it was in place when problems in the mainstream economy arose— from falling exports to hemorrhaging dollars to pay for oil imports—a political decision could be made for a stronger move toward sustainability. Heavier taxes could be placed on oil or luxuries so FAP payments could be raised to accelerate the movement toward national self-sufficiency. To realize how important this tool could be, think of how vulnerable the economy would be to recessions, even depressions, if there were no longer enough resources to keep people fully employed in mainstream jobs. The existence of a second economy and a mechanism to draw people into it could be a godsend if the alternative was a deepening recession that would destroy other jobs and hit everyone hard.

The FAP should be thought of as a tool to be added to those the nation already has to regulate the economy, but with one major advantage; it would avoid the dependency on growth. It would permit the maintenance of a "healthy economy" without the qualifier that now goes with it: "growing." No longer would it be necessary to make a virtue of waste to keep the economy strong, nor would it be necessary to spend huge sums of money on unnecessary public works projects to put people to work, or provide export subsidies, investment credits, or the other costly forms of corporate welfare that are justified by the need for jobs. A FAP program could reduce federal spending significantly if it encouraged low-paid work in the sustainable economy rather than high-paid jobs in the mainstream economy. Which would be a better use of public funds, to support one worker on an unneeded freeway or, say, four families on FAP payments (especially if more people relying on FAP made new freeways unnecessary)? Rather than billions of dollars going to big aerospace corporations to build an anti-missile defense system that is unlikely to be needed or to work, would it be better for small amounts of money to go directly into the hands of far more ordinary people, including the small shopkeepers, craftsmen, and farmers who were squeezed out in recent decades? Most federal assistance now goes to large corporations because they have the capacity to create new jobs in the high-tech growth industries. If over-capacity became the problem, such corporations would still gain from FAP payments as they were spent, but they would no longer have the power they now have to obtain government benefits. The income inequalities in our society would be moderated, too, especially if luxury taxes were part of the effort to move work toward sustainable activities.

Other money-saving policy changes would be possible if the need for growth no longer trumped all other needs. Tax incentives to encourage debt could be removed if it was no longer necessary to direct so much money into new investment. Tax policies that penalize savings and ownership could be changed in ways to encourage holding assets for future generations. Similarly, tax laws favoring the speculative "cut and run" use of resources could be changed to encourage long-term management. Outright ownership of assets that support a way of life in the sustainable economy will be important, but so will the stability of the communities that ownership fosters. It is when land is productive, craftsmen are skilled, and shopkeepers provide what people need that community becomes a source of security and enjoyment.

Over the substantial stretches of time that hopefully will be available for industrial society to move toward sustainability, the need to subsidize the sustainable economy should decline and at some point end. This, of course, is speculative territory, but it does suggest how one program could respond to changing circumstances to smooth the transition from a single global economy to simpler, more diverse ones that are closer to sustainability.

Why would the majority of Americans who continue to work in regular jobs year after year support a program under which their taxes go to support economically unproductive individuals? The immediate reason is that they, too, could take advantage of the FAP if they decided to give the sustainable economy a try—or were forced to by layoffs or deteriorating economic circumstances. It could also be something their children could utilize if they wanted to. More importantly, however, FAP would preserve the way of life they preferred in the mainstream economy, and with less fear of being laid off. At the same time, the opportunity to live and work in the sustainable economy could be seen as the ultimate luxury of a highly productive economy with a problem of over-production.

Still, there would undoubtedly be ridicule of a program that could so easily be described as a bizarre new way for government to waste taxpayers' money. Even thinking about voting for such a program could send chills down the spines of legislators. And FAP could fail, as other seemingly good ideas have failed, especially those dealing with unemployment and welfare. Timing could be a problem, too, since it would be hard to pass a FAP at a time when the economy was strong and the "end of welfare as we know it" seemed possible, while later it could be felt to be something the nation could not afford. But timing could be an advantage if unemployment rose and better ways were needed to deal with it than the old, discredited welfare programs. It may not be until people begin losing jobs through no fault of their own that FAP would be seriously considered. Then the cost of the program would have to be funded by the reduction of costly programs to create jobs— something that may be harder than passing the FAP itself.

Does all this sound like too much to hope for? It is certainly optimistic, and I will not be offended by skepticism about it working out this way. It would be much preferable if something other than a subsidy could be found to encourage the sustainable economy. High-powered economists may be able to find better ways, but it is also possible that encouraging "uneconomic" activities may be too contradictory in a society built on growth. Or worse: such an economy could unravel in response to efforts to slow it down. It is in thinking about such things that it could be wished that the first energy crisis had been a real one, since the market-driven changes then were unfolding smoothly at a time when there was less dependency on a single, highly integrated global economy. It is ironic that the worst case scenario could be the one most hoped for now, of continued growth so that after several more decades overshoot would lead to the steep collapse from which it may not be possible to pull out of. Our society may not resist change any more than other societies, but the consequences of our resistance could be much rougher.

Preserving Biological Productivity and Diversity

To this point little has been said about the needs of the environment, which is perhaps to be expected in a society in which human needs generally take precedence over nature's. But this will change as we have less energy to overwhelm nature with our machines; then there will be little choice but to move toward relying more on the natural productivity of the environment. Even if the distance to move is great, the directions are at least right—toward smaller-scale, more decentralized economic activities, greater reliance on renewable resources, fewer wastes that poison the environment, and the many ways in which biological productivity is preserved—perhaps even enhanced. We will be learning to work with nature once again, rather than overcoming it as an enemy. The price mechanism of the marketplace will be helpful in this, since higher prices are a fine way of focusing attention on what is scarce and where the new opportunities are. Similarly, lower wages and profits will draw economic activity away from industries that are dependent on the heavy use of resources and toward those with better long-term prospects. It may be helpful to think of the process ahead as reversing the changes brought on by the Industrial Revolution, but this takes us toward the speculation that can be misleading, especially when it is so hard to know which modern technologies will have staying power—or which of our cultural ways will become new taboos. Speculation may be enjoyable, but it is actual experiences that will shape the evolutionary process. Think of how wrong the early visions of modern cities were, with futuristic towers tied together with elevated causeways and helicopters zipping around overhead.

There was a certain amount of ridicule of the back-to-the-land movement in the 1960s and 1970s, much of it because of the youthful naiveté of those involved and their soft muscles. But the legacy of that movement survives in the work of many groups associated with organic farming, alternative energy sources, and new building methods. Much has also been learned about what does not work, such as communities built on the premise that everyone could "do their own thing" and still function as a community. All such learning is helpful, but there is still a long way to go. And even though the learning curve may be long, the willingness curve may be longer yet, especially if such changes are seen as a failure of nerve in keeping to the heroic paths of the modern era. American history could be a problem, too, since there were always virgin lands to move to instead of facing the harder tasks of preserving the productivity of land already in use. Then new industries could also be developed, and new cities built so the old ones could be left to those who could not escape them. This same thrust is reflected in the visions of space as the next frontier, even as we learn how hostile the space environment is, the immense distances involved, and the energy required to reach even nearby bodies, let alone colonize them.

Other societies that failed to come to terms with their circumstances did not survive, and there is no law that says this cannot happen to us. But this should not happen if the evolutionary process functions as it has in the past. Rather than grand projects, there will be many small ones going on continuously, with the consequences of any one failure being small—unlike the one grand experiment with the global economy. As the experiments that work spread, the sustainable future will take shape. If done smoothly and constructively it could be one of the finest eras in human history. But even if the process is muddled, as is more likely, it will still be an interesting and creative time, as well as one with tremendous implications for the quality of life in the future.

To argue that the American political process is capable of facilitating this transition to sustainability does not mean this will happen. It could, but that depends on the signals politicians receive from voters. If Americans continue to press for their own interests—on the assumption that others are doing this too—it will reinforce the "win at any cost" partisanship that makes politicians so cautious and change so difficult. But there could just as easily be a spontaneous movement toward peaceful cooperation as the urban industrial way of life weakens. Our political system has the potential for taking us in either direction—depending on what the mass of Americans ask of it.

Still, if cultural evolution is to be placed on a surer footing, at some point it will probably be necessary to move toward ways that are more clearly cooperative and less competitive. How this will occur cannot be known, but we do know how other societies managed to put their economies on such a basis. The selflessness the great faiths ask for make such societies the best record of the efforts to encourage peaceful cooperation. Since these cultures are different from ours their ways are unlikely to be ours, but they still provide insights into how religions have functioned to order societies in stable and satisfying ways. These are the ways that worked before they were displaced by free-market ways. The following chapter provides a brief introduction to these achievements—of how other societies managed to meet their needs without letting economics shape everything. They will serve as a background for Chapter 9, and what can be learned from the more checkered experiences with religion in our own heritage.

CHAPTER EIGHT

Putting Economics in its Place

Every society, regardless of how spiritual, must have some method of meeting its material needs. It must have some form of economic organization. The selflessness asked for by the great faiths makes economics easier to manage, but it is just as important that there be enough economic incentives as to not let economics shape everything. Finding a balance in this has always been difficult. The more successful faiths did not restrict economic urges so much as incorporate them into the quest for ultimate goals. Since traditional societies have everywhere been weakened by modern forces, the focus here must be primarily historical, with recent experiences used to shed light on why some have been resilient while others have broken down.

The Eastern civilizations have the best record of ordering societies effectively, as reflected in the long eras of stability and continuity they achieved. For this reason, India and China will be discussed first, followed by two cultures that were shaped by less fortunate circumstances, Africa and Russia. The chapter concludes with a region that evolved in circumstances close to our own, the Middle East. The treatment is necessarily brief, focusing on the elements that best express the nature of each cultural solution, including what left them either resistant or vulnerable to modern pressures. The purpose is not so much to suggest ways that may be useful for us in the future as to provide a feeling for the process of cultural evolution, and how different cultures responded to the challenges they faced. (Additional sources are listed under the name of each culture in the References.)

The Paradise of the Gods

India can be thought of as the region that has been most deeply absorbed in religious matters, and the one that is most often accused of not providing enough economic incentives. It is as otherworldly as the West is worldly, and the source of what religious scholars consider the most sophisticated religious tradition, the Hindu-Buddhist, that spread over much of Asia. It is the source of the tolerance and nonviolence that made Asia's history so different from the West's, and helped put the East ahead of the West for most of recorded history. Its success is why Columbus wanted to get there, and while the people he encountered in the New World were called Indians. We learn little about India's heritage from the media today, with most coverage dealing with its poverty, its caste system, and the difficulties between Hindus and Muslims, including now the nuclear weapons India and Pakistan have. There is little mention of India's rich cultural heritage, or that most of the country remains peaceful, especially in the villages where three-fourths of the population lives. This peacefulness is a significant achievement in a country with four times the population of the U.S. living in an area one-third the size. Many of India's problems reflect its growing population, but India is one of the most ethnically diverse of nations, with thirteen major languages and many minor ones. Ethnic conflict would seem to be inevitable under such circumstances, especially when Muslims are a significant minority. There is a Hindu nationalist movement, but most of the nation remains largely at peace.

One reflection of India's otherworldliness is that it was not politically unified until the British took over in the eighteenth-century. Even then, the French were England's main competitors for this most valuable of colonial prizes. The Moguls who ruled northern India at the time were in decline, and the English effectively used the concept of divide and rule to control the many independent states that have characterized India for most of its history. India never offered effective resistance to invaders, which meant its culture was not militarized as Western culture was. The most destructive invaders came from Afghanistan, especially after the twelfth-century when fortified with Islam. The Mongols made the mistake of trying to invade India from China but were stopped by the deep river canyons and dense vegetation in a region that was not crossed until World War II when the Stillwell Road was built. The invaders from Afghanistan in the fourteenth-century who became the Moguls were Turks who had adopted Mongol ways, but in the process of ruling India they became more Indian than Mongol. India's response to invaders has long been to adopt what was of value from them while converting them to Indian ways. This occurred with Islam, to a degree at least, until the time of independence when Muslims demanded their own country, leading to the partition that involved so much bloodshed. With so many different ethnic groups, the continuity and vitality of Indian culture must be considered a major achievement. Even with the growing pressures now, visitors to India are struck by how little the temper of day-to-day life has changed.

India's religious tolerance appears in its earliest texts, the Vedas: "Truth is one, but sages call it by different names." All religions are considered valid, the different languages in which God has spoken to different peoples, or the different paths to the same end—oneness with God. Even with the centrality of religion in Indian civilization, there was never anything comparable to the bodies which govern Christian churches and define their beliefs. Anyone can hang out a shingle in India as a holy person if they feel they have a path to enlightenment, much as Buddha did 2500 years ago. Yet there was no anarchy; for thousands of years India was held together by the basic tenets of Hinduism.

The West has learned little about the timeless ways in which Hinduism functioned to order this huge, diverse society.

Even when India gained its independence, a saint was the moving force behind it. Gandhi achieved this first great victory over colonial authority, and it was through non-violent resistance to British rule, not the wars of liberation that would be fought elsewhere. This changed with Nehru, Gandhi's successor, who even while professing neutrality took over Kashmir and Goa and built up India's military power. India is the world's largest democracy, but it is still the part of the world where traditional society has survived most intact, even with the pressures building up within and around it.

The two great faiths of Indian origin, Hinduism and Buddhism, are more closely related than generally realized. Buddha's Four Noble Truths are the core of Hinduism, too:

1. Life is suffering.
2. Suffering is caused by desire.
3. The way to overcome suffering is by ceasing to desire.
4. Cessation of desire is accomplished by following the Eightfold Path.

Buddha's Eightfold Path can be thought of as one of the many paths that can be taken to reach the goal of ceasing to desire, but Buddha's way differs from Hinduism's by its austerity, which contrasts with Hinduism's multitude of reincarnated figures and forms of worship. Buddhism can be thought of as Hinduism reduced to its essence, as a reformation against the excesses of Hinduism that was almost successful in India. But Hinduism's counter-reformation succeeded, unlike Catholicism's in Europe, mainly because Hinduism adopted many of Buddha's reforms. Hinduism regained its dominance in India, leaving Buddhism to spread to most other countries in Asia but with less than one percent of India's population being Buddhist now.

One reason for Buddhism's failure in India was that Buddha rejected caste, which had been a part of Indian civilization since the time of the earliest Aryan invaders around

1600 B.C. The word for caste in the Sanskrit language of these invaders from the West means *color*; caste was part of the effort of these light-skinned conquerors to preserve their ruling position in India. It is interesting that caste in India and feudalism in Europe both had their origins in unsavory military activities, but in both cases the people adversely effected by them ended up holding to them firmly. This is almost certainly because of the secure economic niches both created. They enabled people to meet their daily needs, even if minimally, while leaving energy for other pursuits, especially the spiritual, which became so important in both India and medieval Europe. Caste may bring condemnation to India, just as serfdom did in Europe, but this is a reflection of our values, especially how deeply individualism and economic achievement shape our stance toward the world. Buddha's rejection of caste, which was done in order to rely more on self-control, is the higher vision, but the difficulties of reaching it could account for at least part of the violence that has racked most of the purely Buddhist countries of Southeast Asia—Sri Lanka, Burma, Cambodia, and Vietnam. Could it have been too high an ideal?

Unlike serfdom, which had no religious meaning, caste plays a central role in the integration provided by Hinduism, both horizontally—between people—and vertically—in answering ultimate questions. Many of Hinduism's characteristics stem from its different concept of the divine, as a spirit in all living things. This world spirit is *Brahma*, and even though it is in all people it is usually encrusted over with selfish desires that are the source of suffering. If these selfish desires can be thrown off, however, the result is not only enlightenment but an end to reincarnation and the endless cycle of death and rebirth. Anyone is theoretically capable of achieving enlightenment in this way, but it is felt to be difficult for ordinary people because of the lack of training and the time required to reach it. The path for most people is to move toward enlightenment by living good lives, fulfilling their duty (*dharma*) in order to increase their *karma*. Karma can be thought of as a moral accounting of one's thoughts and actions, with good ones increasing karma and bad ones decreasing it. At the end of one's life, one's karma determines the caste one is reborn into in the next life. As individuals rise up through the castes by living good lives in succeeding reincarnations, their karma increases, and with it their chances for gaining release from the endless cycle of rebirths. The classic route for a *brahmin*, a member of the highest caste, is to retreat to the forest after his duties to his family have been completed in order to pursue the religious exercises designed to help overcome all desires. A brahmin may have the best chance of reaching enlightenment, but anyone is theoretically capable of doing so.

Caste thus has two central functions in India: it encourages good behavior while also organizing the traditional economy, since all work is done by the appropriate castes. To try to rise above one's caste would be to violate the central beliefs of Hinduism that encourage acceptance of one's position in life, much as serfdom did in medieval Europe. Since it is not possible to rise up to a higher caste during one's lifetime, the pressure we experience in trying to advance in a competitive society is removed; it is not an alternative. In the same way, membership in a low caste, the ones most Indians are born into, does not carry the stigma of personal failure, since it was determined by previous lives. And while caste does not permit people to rise up, it protects them from falling down, too, so there is little of the fear of failure that hangs over individuals in our competitive society. Caste takes Indians off the proverbial treadmill that is driving us in such stressful directions, with the result being that emotional energy is left for other pursuits, including the spiritual, that are pushed to the margins of our busy society. Caste explains much of Hinduism's effectiveness in shaping Indian society for thousands of years, but it is under pressure now in several ways. Violence has occurred when Hindu nationalist parties capitalize on India's democracy to get jobs traditionally reserved for higher castes. Also, the free-market economy that is vigorous in India's cities cannot include caste in its functioning, although the upper castes generally have advantages, including better education.

Untouchability is another matter, and it correctly brings condemnation to India, especially as the number of untouchables has grown large. The untouchables do work defined as unclean, and stems from the ritual purity the Aryans used in their effort to preserve their elite status. Untouchability has thus existed in India for a long time, but the number of untouchables increased greatly as castes found it harder to care for the unfortunates among their members, as was their traditional obligation. It grew under British rule, for example, when India became an important market for English machine-made goods, such as cloth and metalware. Cheaper and often of a better quality than handmade items, they flooded into India and undermined entire castes, including their capacity to help needy members. When individuals were reduced to doing unclean work to get by, they found themselves among the untouchables. Gandhi spent much of his life trying to reduce the stigma of untouchability, even by renaming the untouchables *Harijan,* meaning children of god, but it survives simply because work is scarce and many people have no other way to survive than by doing work deemed unclean.

After Henry David Thoreau's death in 1862, a number of Hindu texts were found in his library, and also in Emerson's, whose philosophy of transcendentalism was heavily influenced by Hinduism. (The main difference in New England was that nature became the route to enlightenment, while in India nature is *maya*, or illusion, a word with the same roots as magic; nature, and physical reality in general, stand between the individual and the true reality behind it, the spiritual.) Thoreau's life was Hindu in many ways, certainly when he wrote that "A man is rich in proportion to the things he can do without." He expressed the logic of ceasing to desire in a characteristically American way— mathematically: Happiness is the result when achievements are divided by desires. In striving to fulfill desires, the highest number that can be reached is one, when all desires are achieved.

But this is unlikely since desires tend to rise with achievements. And usually, achievements fall short of desires, with the result being dissatisfaction, or suffering. The solution of both Hinduism and Buddhism is the opposite of this, to reduce desires to zero, since as they approach zero the figure for happiness approaches not just one but infinity. In Hinduism this is *Moksha*, but the Buddhist term is more familiar—*Nirvana*.

I went to India in 1959 after graduating from college in part to explore the possibility of working in foreign aid. I had seen news reports of India's poverty and expected to see a great deal of misery. It was disturbing, then, as I traveled around India on local trains, to see people who, even though often quite poor, seemed more at ease than people back home. It left me wondering if I was missing something by only being able to observe people going about their daily activities. Most spoke different languages, and the Indians who spoke English were disdainful of village ways and almost embarrassed by what was going on outside the train window. Women were out in the world and confidently at work in everything from market stalls to professions. Things were clearly not as straightforward as I had expected, and I returned home without looking for a job. For years I remained intrigued by the goal of ceasing to desire, but finally came to the conclusion that such a goal was out of my reach as a Westerner, that I could not remove my mind and replace it with one shaped by Indian ways, no matter how intriguing they were. I returned to India in 1987, when its population had doubled, and was surprised that it seemed to have changed so little, except that cities were larger, had fewer open sewers, and there were fewer people sleeping on sidewalks.

India's ways regularly gain my respect, especially when things the West looks down on turn out to be major achievements. One is the role of cows, which for decades was the target of much criticism—their excessive numbers, the food they ate that hungry people needed, and the absurdity of worshiping "holy cows." It turned out that cows have no special holiness in India other than the spirit that is in all living things; they are honored because they embody so well the Hindu ideal selfless service to others. A family with a cow and a bullock is blessed with milk and the power to pull a plow and cart, with both producing the dung that is an important cooking fuel when wood is so scarce. It also turned out that the foods cows ate were mainly crop residues that, while not particularly nourishing, were recycled through cows in a way that provided important family needs—food, labor, and dung. It would be better if the dung was put directly back into the soil if other cooking fuels were available, but burning it leaves most of the nutrients in the ash, which is returned to the soil. The main nutrient lost in burning is nitrogen, but it is replaced by the numerous legumes grown in India, especially lentils. Vegetarianism is a logical result of seeing divinity in all living things, with cows providing a continuous supply of animal protein in the form of milk, compared to the once-only supply of meat when a cow is slaughtered, and with far less impact on the environment per unit of protein obtained.

The crowning achievement of India's cows may be one that is sill only a hypothesis, that they are responsible for the uncharacteristic fertility of central India. This is a plateau area on a latitude that elsewhere in the world supports only thin populations. Known as savanna, biological productivity is usually low because heavy seasonal rains leach the soils of their nutrients. This should be the case in central India, too, given the geologically old rocks of this plateau landscape. The only way to explain the larger population it supports is that cows brought nutrients into the farming cycle, probably by grazing rough lands and collecting the nutrients in the form of manure that was incorporated into the fields and subsequent crop cycles. If this hypothesis is correct, India's cows have been constructive all across the spectrum—economically, ecologically, and religiously. What achievement can we point to with equal merit, especially in the long term? Such are the achievements that a long and peaceful evolutionary process make possible.

When scholars describe the religions of India as highly

evolved, it is because Hinduism and Buddhism both avoid the need for heaven and hell, a devil to blame evil on, and a fall from the Garden of Eden to explain sin. Neither found it necessary to disapprove of pleasure or worldly success, since it is only by trying them that they will be found unsatisfying, leading naturally to the next steps, of serving others and finally seeking release. Hinduism established four different paths to enlightenment—knowledge, love, work, and psychological exercise—to satisfy the needs of a diverse people. The achievements of this heritage suggest that India may be able to cope with the times ahead as well as any part of the world, regardless of the problems it faces now.

*   *   *

Buddha was criticized during his lifetime for offering not a religion but a rational method for overcoming self-concern. His Eightfold Path applies to virtually all aspects of daily life: right knowledge, aspirations, speech, behavior, livelihood, effort, mindfulness, and absorption. Notice that none are specifically theological. Buddha felt that to argue about theology was to argue about the unknowable. His way was devoid of ritual as well. In part this was to break the grip of the brahmin priestly caste over the common people, but he also felt the priests were keeping people from Hinduism's spiritual discoveries. When Buddha was asked if he was a saint, angel, or god, he answered simply that he was "awake," the meaning of the word *Buddha*. In his now classic *Religions of Man*, Huston Smith describes Buddha as throwing off the dream-like ways in which people go through life to find its essence. And unlike the West, which crucified its greatest religious teacher, Buddha lived for four decades after discovering the path to enlightenment, enough time to establish an order of monks and train them to help others reach this goal. The path was all he was concerned with: "Here is a path to the end of suffering. Tread it!" He retained karma and reincarnation, but when asked if there was a supreme being he did not answer but simply held up a lotus, the symbol of enlightenment ever since, the pure white flower growing out of the mud, a beautiful metaphor for the evolution of peaceful ways out of the violent.

E. F. Schumacher was a student of Gandhi and Eastern religions, and his essay "Buddhist Economics" was included in *Small is Beautiful*, the book that was so influential in the early days of the environmental movement. Based on the Right Livelihood of the Eightfold Path, he condensed the role of work into three essential functions: to give people the chance to utilize their faculties, to overcome ego-centeredness in a common task, and to provide what is needed for a "becoming existence." Schumacher contrasted Buddhist economics with Western economics in which production had become the ultimate end, one measured by quantity alone and aptly named the "Gross" National Product. Land, labor, and capital have been turned into simple costs of production with no spiritual meaning whatever. It brings to mind the old quip about economists knowing the price of everything but the value of nothing.

Buddhism gained ascendancy in India with one of its greatest empires, the Mauryan, reaching its peak with the reign of King Ashoka from 273-232 B.C. An encounter with Buddhism led Ashoka to feel remorse for the harshness of his conquest of northern India, and he spent the rest of his life spreading Buddhism. He had moral discourses inscribed on tall pillars throughout his empire, a number of which still stand. Buddhism led to a renaissance in India, as it did in all the countries in which it was adopted. In Southeast Asia and Sri Lanka it is known as Theravada Buddhism, and is close to the austere ways prescribed by a Buddha who is seen essentially a teacher. Elsewhere, however, Buddhism was shaped by the cultures that adopted it, China especially, where its character changed significantly. It became Mahayana Buddhism in which Buddha is the Compassionate One, a figure more like Christ, a savior who can be appealed to for help. The difference between the two forms of Buddhism turns on whether they are defined by

Buddha's words or by his actions after discovering the path, when he stayed in the world to help others find the path rather than following it directly to Nirvana. Buddhism took on different forms yet in Tibet and Japan, as might be expected in countries as distinctive as these. In the same way, Buddhism changed when it came to the West, with the goal of meditation changing from losing one's self in the eternal oneness to finding one's true self. The Four Noble Truths are as unfamiliar in American Buddhism as the Great Commandment is in Christianity, to love God first and then love your neighbor as yourself. This should not be surprising given the classical heritage of the West with its focus on individualism rather than the quest for oneness.

The Chinese Complex of Religions

The fact that Buddhism found acceptance in China, and later Islam and Christianity too, tells us something about Confucianism as the central organizing force in China: It did not answer the ultimate questions of life, at least not adequately. Confucius was primarily interested in ethics, in how people acted in the here and now, and his ways effectively provided the horizontal integration that held China together for thousands of years. Taoism contributed a subjective element that helped balance the objectivity of Confucianism, but Taoism was too esoteric to be of much value to common people, where it came to function more as magic than religion. The need remained for accessible answers to the ultimate questions, and Buddhism has been the main source of this throughout most of Chinese history. All three religions—Confucianism, Taoism, and Buddhism—coexisted harmoniously throughout Chinese history, making up what is commonly referred to as the Chinese complex of religions.

The Chinese speak of Confucius as the First Teacher, although he described himself simply as "a lover of the ancients." He lived during the period of the Warring States of the declining Chou dynasty and looked on the past as a golden age. He collected the old ideas, sifted them, and put them into a set of principles that worked so well that they became deeply embedded in Chinese life. Even now Confucian ways are being used by China's leaders to help strengthen their legitimacy as the faith in communism fails. Confucius put together canons of personal behavior that established the responsibilities of the emperor, the state, and the family, and with his backward-looking impulses created a society that was intrinsically conservative. To reject the ways of the ancestors would be to dishonor them, making ancestor worship the closest thing to the supernatural in Confucianism. Family names come first, followed by given names—Smith John rather than John Smith—and the Chinese countryside was dotted with grave mounds housing the remains of the ancestors until the communists leveled them to provide more farmland.

Many factors contributed to the extraordinary continuity of Chinese civilization, but an important one was the heavy obligation Confucius placed on leadership at all levels of society. According to *The Great Learning*, which is often said to be the core of Confucian teachings, all leaders, beginning with the emperor, had to "rectify their hearts" and "regulate their families" to provide an example for others if China was to be harmonious and tranquil. If the emperor acted this way, it influenced the officials, often referred to as mandarins, who handled day-to-day matters, and then parents, too, who had authority in the household. Correct relations were established between husband and wife, father and son, elder and younger brothers, friend and friend, as well as between ruler and subject. Everyone had to set a good example; misbehavior of children reflected poorly on their parents, bringing dishonor on the family, the community, and the nation as a whole.

Some form of the Golden Rule is found in all societies, to "Do unto others as you would have them do unto you." It is, in effect, a way of operationalizing selflessness, since it asks people to think of how they would like to be treated by others as a basis for their own actions. In China it is stated in the negative: "Do not do unto others what you would not want them to do to you." This may reflect the important role of the officials in China, which is often described as a bureaucratic society. But it is a unique one in that its officials were selected by examinations, half of which were on the teachings of Confucius and half on the writing of poetry on topics assigned during the examination. This led to a different kind of bureaucracy than we are familiar with. The Chinese were looking for officials who were cultivated and had the personal qualities necessary to maintain harmony. Education was essential for this, and was highly regarded and available to any youngster with the necessary intelligence, no matter how poor. Confucius was in this category, since he was raised by his impoverished mother after his father died when he was three.

Another reason for the extraordinary stability of Chinese civilization was the economic hierarchy it established. Great honor was conferred on the peasants as the foundation of the empire, and they were given a status just below that of the officials, with businessmen on the bottom. China's stability has been described as due to an alliance between the officials and the peasants against the businessmen, who were seen as a threat to the timeless ways of China, a hierarchy that Mao would reaffirm later. Cities were the seats of Confucian authority in China, in contrast to the West, where they were the centers of trade and political ferment that encouraged the princes to challenge Church authority. Yet the Chinese are good at business, and they were free to pursue profits as long as they did not disturb the Confucian order. If they did, however, the officials had the power to tax or regulate them into submission, even to confiscate their business. This not only served to make businessmen properly respectful of the officials but also provided protection for the peasants. When dynasties broke down, it was usually because corrupt officials and the wealthy colluded for their own benefit, leading to the landlordism, poverty, and even banditry that drove peasants to revolt. If an emperor failed to hold to the Confucian way, he was deemed to have lost the Mandate of

Heaven, and the people were authorized to overthrow him. The leader who emerged out of the chaos that followed and was able to reestablish the Confucian order could claim that he had received the Mandate of Heaven and become the new emperor. Such revolutions were the rare events in China that punctuated its dynastic history.

China was thus solidly organized by Confucianism, but in ways that were quite unlike those of India. The two cultures are often spoken of together, as if the "East" is intrinsically different from the "West." But China's emphasis on strong, centralized government, education, disciplined work, and the peripheral role of religion leaves it closer to the West than to India. It is because of these qualities that the Chinese economy was able to grow so rapidly in the last decades of the twentieth-century, and other Confucian countries, too.

An important part of China's stability was the balance provided by Taoism. Founded by Lao-tzu, who may have been a contemporary of Confucius in the sixth century B.C., the word "Tao" means "the way"—the way of nature. In contrast to Confucianism's heavy emphasis on individual responsibilities, Taoism counseled withdrawal from such responsibilities and living simply and close to nature. The ideal is the sage, the person of quiet wisdom who finds peace and serenity in accepting the natural rhythms of life. The Taoists were opposed to education, seeing it as producing scoundrels, and preferred the anarchy of natural ways to those of government, with its rulers, armies, officials, and tax collectors. The Tao is reflected in Chinese painting, with a small human figure almost lost in a mystical natural landscape of mountains, trees, and waterfalls. Taoism was also the inspiration for most Chinese poetry, adding a subjective element to the practical Chinese society. And the Confucian order had the wisdom to accept it, even though it was subversive to Confucian ideals in many ways.

A well-known expression of this balance is the concept of Yang and Yin, which represents the duality of all life—male and female, dark and light, winter and summer, active and passive, happiness and sadness, perhaps even Confucianism and Taoism. China deemed both to be necessary, since without both balance is lost, the balance we in the West have a hard time finding. We try to be happy all the time, but are often bored or jaded. We are so active that we find it hard to be passive or contemplative, or to enjoy simple pleasures—the beauty in a single flower, for example, rather than a huge arrangement. We have for so long honored masculine ways that we now miss the feminine qualities of compassion, forgiveness, and understanding. We ridicule good manners and the Chinese urge to "save face," and then wonder why our "in your face" ways lead to the anger that has cut into so many of life's pleasures.

The achievements of Chinese civilization reflect maturity and sophistication, but its highly centralized political order led China to claim it was superior to other societies. The Chinese word for foreigner also means barbarian, reinforcing China's characteristic isolation. Its proud leaders assumed China had no need for the things other societies had, including the brash Westerners who kept demanding that China open its ports to trade. In the mid nineteenth-century the West finally broke in by force, mainly over the violation of the private property rights it claimed for the opium it was smuggling into China. The Opium War of 1839-1842 led to the collapse of China's proud but rigid social order into a century-long humiliation, including the conquest by what was seen as a primitive Japan. The void left after World War II was filled first with communism, and then with a crass form of capitalism which, while growing rapidly, has few of the qualities that caused Chinese civilization to endure for so long and to be so admired, especially by Voltaire and the French Enlightenment. Confucianism is alive and contending with communism, but conditions in China are so different now that it is hard to imagine how it could regain the position it once held, except if the economy broke down, when all bets would be off.

Limitations of Landscape and History:
Africa and Russia

If it is assumed that human nature is much the same everywhere, it may have simply been that India and China were more fortunate in their circumstances than people in other areas. The same could be said for the evolution of industrial society in Europe, which had the necessary resources and access to the oceans, as well as a heritage that left its people vigorous, creative, and aggressive enough for the task. In other parts of the world, however, circumstances were different, and cultural evolution moved in other directions, ones that, even if less impressive, still made life good in less than ideal circumstances. These, too, are important to be aware of, perhaps more so, since the circumstances ahead could well be difficult, with large populations, damaged environments, and a significant potential for violence. We will look at Africa first, especially the effects of its difficult landscapes and colonial experiences, and then the Slavs, who endured one of the most tragic histories imaginable but turned it into a village culture that most Russians still yearn for.

The frequent mention of Africa's vast, untapped potential may be one of the most common forms of racism that still exists, because the reality is that the African environment is a tough one. Astride the equator, the continent's three major biomes—rain forest, savanna (or bush), and desert—all present difficulties to those who live in them. The rain forests may look fertile with their verdant vegetation, but heavy rainfall has leached their soils of nutrients, so that the few remaining nutrients are primarily bound up in the vegetation. This is why slash and burn agriculture works, since burning the vegetation leaves the nutrients in the ash that supports a brief period of cropping. When this fertility is depleted, the forest is left to return and recover the nutrients. That it works at all is surprising, but also that it seems to be sustainable, at least if the fallow period is long enough. This is usually around twenty years, meaning that only a low population density can be sustained. Continuous cropping using chemical fertilizers does not work, since continuous exposure to air and sunlight causes most tropical soils to turn to brick. And infertile soils cannot be expected to produce nutritious foods; the root crops that are most productive in tropical areas are low in protein, generally around one percent. Animals are scarce, too, because of the lack of nutritious feed, making protein deficiency a major problem, while insects and diseases are favored by the year-round warmth and humidity.

The savannas surrounding the tropical forests are better, but they receive heavy rainfall for part of the year, so soils are still leached even if not so heavily, while the long dry season presents other challenges to farmers. Herding works better in the savannas, but cattle do not utilize the savanna vegetation as effectively as wild animals, and in many places are plagued by diseases that wild animals are resistant to. Game ranching seemed like a good idea, but it proved difficult, mainly because the larger animals depend on migration for their food supplies and harvesting was difficult. For these reasons, the deserts are rather useful, mainly because the scarcity of rainfall at least leaves the nutrients in the soil and discourages disease. Still, a scarcity of water makes herding the mainstay, and the number of animals that can be sustained without overusing the vegetation is small. Droughts reduce the number even more, with tragic consequences for animals, the environment, and the people. The difficulties of the African environments were the main reason why it was the last continent to be colonized, and also why most colonial powers were willing to leave after World War II. The exceptions were in the better environments of southern Africa, the part that finally dips into the benevolent temperate zone—the one we enjoy—and where the richest mineral deposits just happened to be as well.

South America is astride the equator like Africa, but it is blessed with the Andes and the environmental diversity they provide. They are a source of water to irrigate the deserts along the Pacific coast and of the sediments that form pockets of alluvial soil in the Amazon basin. But the best soils are in the highlands of the Andes, especially where volcanic activity adds fresh nutrients from deep in the Earth. Africa, in contrast, is largely plateau country composed of ancient rocks and with little volcanic activity to provide fresh nutrients. One result is the myriad of tribal societies that still characterize Africa.

Because of the absence of writing, the historical record prior to the era of European contact is limited, but the pattern that emerged was so widespread that it must be considered a productive adaptation to the environmental circumstances. The best insights about this way of life may well be from the novels written by Africans that are based on stories told to them by old people. One of the best known is Chinua Achebe's *Things Fall Apart*, and it describes a way of life that, while perhaps not ideal from a Western perspective, still had vitality. A striking thing about the village life Achebe writes about is the small amount of time devoted to work. All a young man needed when getting married was a supply of seed yams, since the tribal lands around the village were available for his use. Dwellings could be put up using local materials, and the year-round warm weather meant clothing needs were modest. The uniformity of Africa's landscape meant there were few benefits to be gained from trade, and with virtually no other economic opportunities village life was focused on other activities. In the Nigerian village of Achebe's novel, status was based on securing honorific titles and winning wrestling matches. The animistic origins of the tribal religion were clear, as was the functional role of religious beliefs in holding the village together. Decisions were made by tribal elders, but the village oracle was important too. Things began to fall apart when the missionaries proved their god was more powerful than the tribal gods. Most anthropologists agree that it was the collapse of tribal religions that took the life out of African villages.

The ease of meeting basic needs and the limited economic opportunities offered by the environment led to the relaxed, modest way of life Achebe describes, but it also left Africans unprepared for the hard work demanded by colonial authorities and the disciplined ways of the modern economy. Yet it was also clear to the Africans that their colonial rulers did not work with their hands, and this was the method of leadership Africans learned—to give orders and have them obeyed. Leadership was backed up with arms under colonial rule, as is so often the case today, and it is still symbolized by the big house and retinue of servants. The West's continued criticism of Africa for its failure in democracy and free enterprise brings to mind Gandhi's response to the question of what he thought about Western Civilization: He said it was a good idea.

Whatever the reasons—environment, culture, history, or all of them—there is little question that Africa is not making progress in the modern sense. Per capita incomes are falling, birth rates are the highest of any major region (as are its death rates from AIDS), and its role in the global economy is declining, with exports increasingly limited to oil, minerals, and plantation crops, much of it produced by foreign-owned corporations. Paradoxically, this could be an advantage if the global economy stumbled or oil production headed downward. With little dependence on trade or fossil fuels, Africa could return to its village ways without fundamental changes. It would be harder for those living in the cities, where wealth and Western influences have long been concentrated, but the villages would come back to life as the cities declined. Tribal ties remain strong—one of the few things that continues to work in Africa— and even though it would take time to recover the richness of the life Achebe describes in his novels, chances are it would happen, perhaps when the tribal gods prove they have power after all.

*   *   *

It would be harder to have such optimism about the Russians, especially after the 1930s when Stalin drove the peasants into huge collective farms and factories. The peasantry, which made up 80 percent of the population at that time, hated Stalin for this. But they loved him later when his forced industrialization enabled the Soviet Union to drive back the invading Germans, something few Russians thought their country would ever be strong enough to do. And when the Soviet Union set off its own atomic bomb and then put the first man into space, the Russians enjoyed a degree of protection they had never felt before. Stalin was acting like a new tsar when he provided what was most important to Russians—security. Not only was the Red Army strong enough to repel foreign invaders but the security forces protected Russians from the internal weaknesses that had cost huge numbers of lives, as when a tsar failed to produce a strong heir or famines occurred. Now Russians are thinking again about the upheavals of the twentieth century that took some 60 million lives, and there are fears of famine again. An abrupt rise in death rates is attributed to a failing medical system compounded by the heavy consumption of vodka by a disillusioned people. Many observers agree that if Stalin were running for president today he would win easily, and that the majority of Russians would be thankful if he put to death the crooks and politicians who are seen as destroying Russia.

The Russian landscape is vast, with much of it unproductive and its weather harsh. Its border is the longest in the world, and most of it is without natural defenses against dangerous neighbors in all directions. But Russia's tragic history is due mainly to its leaders, especially those who learned their ways from the mounted nomads who dominated the steppes for thousands of years. The Mongols (who are known as Tatars in Russia and were among the last mounted warriors to attack Russia), regularly killed everyone in their path, and at times used conquered peoples to lead attacks so Mongol horsemen could finish off the defenders easily.

The steppes of southern Russia were a paradise for mounted horsemen, but their ways were poles apart from the Slavs, who arrived on the historical scene relatively late, in the fifth-century A.D. They came northward out of the Carpathian

Mountains to settle in the large marshy areas of southern Poland and western Ukraine, areas that were relatively safe since horsemen could not pursue them through areas interspersed with water. The Slavs were left free to continue their peaceful ways as fisher-farming folk, with early accounts describing them as patient and hard working, and preferring to flee from attackers rather than fight. They lived in small groups, governed themselves democratically, were hospitable to travelers, and had close family ties, especially between brothers and sisters.

As their numbers grew, however, they spread out from the marshes in several directions, including onto the fertile steppes dominated by the nomads, where the attraction was the black, fertile prairie soils. The first affliction they suffered there was to be taken as slaves; so many Slavs were taken to the slave markets of the Mediterranean that they gave their name to the institution. The next and more long-lasting torment was serfdom, first under the mounted nomads and then under Slavic chieftains who, in fighting the nomads, had adopted their harsh ways. Still, most Slavs held to their peaceful ways, and in 1480 Ivan the Great finally overcame enough of the Russian chieftains to unify Russia and throw off the Tatar yoke. But it is his grandson, Ivan the Terrible, who the Russian people most love. He was the first to name himself Tsar (the Russian word for Caesar) in 1547, and after carrying out important reforms turned to the suppression of the nobles who were a threat to him but were also tormenting the peasants. Forever after, the mass of Russians looked to the tsars—and then Stalin—for a strong leader who would protect them from the lords who had such power over them, a trust that continued no matter how much it was betrayed. Under Catherine the Great, the lords were allowed to do virtually anything they wanted to their serfs except kill them—because the peasants were producing Russia's wealth and manning its armies.

The peasants had little choice but to hunker down in their villages and cope with the lords as best they could, but in the process they created a collective way of life that is still the ideal of most Russians. Their solidarity was bolstered by the deep distrust of almost everyone outside the village, which was the domain of their feudal tormentors. Their endurance became legendary, as Europeans learned during the Napoleonic invasion and World War II. Russian patriotism, too, was impressive, but always it was in defense of the Russian land rather than whatever government was in power. The people coped with the party bureaucrats during the Soviet era much as they had their feudal lords, and see those who are doing well in Moscow and St. Petersburg now as the equivalent of the old nobility, and just as treacherous and self-seeking, and just as detrimental to their own prospects and those of the Russia they still deeply love. The mass of people deal with such circumstances as they always have, by enduring, some by planting gardens but most with a passivity born of getting by in the Soviet police state. The Soviet way met their needs, even if minimally, but since its demise things have degenerated as the former Soviet bureaucrats grew wealthy by selling off state assets to cronies. Russia's GDP dropped 50 percent in the ten years after the end of communism, and it exports little other than oil and natural gas. The Soviet system may not have worked well, but the optimism in the West about a liberated Russia moving smoothly toward democracy and free enterprise was clearly unrealistic given its cultural heritage.

Even with the late appearance of the Slavs, the difficult environment they lived in, and the torments they endured, the Slavs grew to be Europe's largest ethnic group by far, fanning out in all directions from their core area; their peaceful ways enabled them to survive better than the more violent peoples all around them. Religion helped with this, from the original Slavic beliefs to the Christianity that was introduced a thousand years ago; together they enabled faith to survive the seven decades of Soviet repression. The Russian Orthodox Church is the institution that best reflects Slavic ideals of peacefulness, close family ties, and love of the Russian land; following the collapse of the Soviet Union churches, monasteries, and seminaries were restored and reopened all over Russia. Georgi Fedotov, in the definitive work on the Russian religious mind, (1953) describes the Russian attachment to the land this way:

> Beneath the beautiful veil of grass and flowers, the people venerate with awe the black moist depths, the source of all fertilizing powers, the nourishing breast of nature, and their own last resting place. . . Earth is the Russian 'Eternal Womanhood,' not the celestial image of it; mother, not virgin; fertile, not pure; and black, for the best Russian soil is black. (p. 13)

The Orthodox faith introduced from Greece in 988 was warmly embraced by the Slavs because its ideals were so compatible with their Slavic beliefs. The people undoubtedly hoped Christian ethics would restrain the nobles, but this did not happen; even a church nobility was formed, the black priesthood—because of the color of their garb—of the monasteries, which accumulated large amounts of land and wealth. The white priests who served each village and were chosen by its members, were looked down on by the nobility almost as much as they looked down on the peasantry, and were almost as uneducated. Later, even the village priests were separated from their communities when Peter the Great took over their appointment and required that any incriminating words heard during confessions be reported to the government.

The Russians still like themselves best when in village-like circumstances, when they can be passionate, generous, and expansive, all the ways that reflect the great soul of Holy Russia. They want human relations to be based on intimacy, affection, and loyalty, on the qualities that make Russian friendship such a powerful thing. They dislike prescribed forms, pretense, the detached legalism of Western law, the manipulativeness of its politics, and the miserliness of the market mentality with its cold, calculating ways. Slavophile intellectuals accepted the tsarist rule, no matter how enfeebled it became, as better than letting politics tear the community apart.

The quality of life in the old Russian villages is reflected in the different ways the peasants were seen by the nobility compared to the foreigners who began passing through the Russian countryside on their way to Moscow in the eighteenth-century. The nobility's view of the peasantry is the one found in most books and sees them as ignorant, brutal, dishonest, greedy, and superstitious. The accounts of foreigners, on the other hand, pictured them as naturally polite, gay, cooperative, generous, hospitable, and deeply religious. The surprising thing is that both are correct; they simply describe the peasants' behavior under different circumstances. In the village, the peasants were bound by a traditional ethic that was known, trusted, and accepted, one in which solidarity was essential for everyone's survival. Outside the village, however, the peasants were at the mercy of the nobility and were free to use any devices they could to fend off the lords' predations. Cunning and guile were essential, which the nobles saw as greed and dishonesty. The peasants claimed they could do no more than what the lord was already demanding of them, while the lord assumed the peasants were feigning poverty and had rubles buried in the ground.

The different behavior of the peasants is described by Richard Pipes in *Russia Under the Old Regime* (1974):

> When he did not want to do something, he played stupid; when found out, he feigned contrition. 'The peasants show the landlord almost in all circumstances of life the darkest side of their nature', complained Iurii Samarin, a Slavophile expert on rural conditions. 'In the presence of his master, the intelligent peasant assumes the pose of a clown, the truthful one lies right to his face, untroubled by conscience, the honest one robs him, and all three call him 'father.' This behavior toward his betters contrasted vividly with the peasant's honesty and decency when dealing with equals. Dissimulation was not so much part of peasant

character as a weapon against those from whom he had no other defense.'   (p. 156)

His manner toward equals was surprisingly ceremonious. Travelers to Russia were struck by the elaborate manner in which peasants greeted one another, bowing politely and tipping their hats. . . . Foreigners also commented on the peasant's gay disposition, readiness to mimic or break into song and his peaceful disposition: even drunk he rarely came to blows.

(p. 159)

The gaiety is especially impressive given the nature of Russian feudalism, which scholars considered to be more like slavery in the American South than feudalism in Europe. Peasants endured whippings with the infamous *knout*, which had pieces of rawhide woven into it that literally peeled skin and flesh from backs. Peasants made a virtue of suffering, since it was necessary to hold off the demands of the nobility. An American doctor in Russia before the Revolution reported that "boys and girls, men and women would have two or even three teeth pulled out in a single session without any anesthetic, and without showing a quiver of fear." Such endurance is what enabled Russian soldiers to survive the winter warfare that, in the end, defeated Napoleon and Hitler. The Russians claim, with much justification, that Western freedom was bought with Russian blood.

The peasants' experiences with their lord led them to assume that anything he suggested was for his benefit, rather than theirs, and automatically to be resisted. This frustrated even enlightened nobles who tried to introduce agricultural improvements; Tolstoy eventually freed his serfs but could not get them to use the long-handled scythes instead of the sickles that required them to bend over to harvest the grain. This fear of people outside their immediate group remains a problem in Russia today, causing it to be termed a "cellular society," one in which people do not trust anyone outside the small group they know and trust. This unwillingness to cooperate with larger groups makes the prospects for democracy and large-scale enterprise poor. An old Russian expressed the common view of free enterprise when he said: "I know what capitalism is. The rich get richer and the poor die"—which is pretty much what is going on in Russia today. The cellular society is also hostile to members who try to better themselves, as reflected in the old peasant saying, "The tallest corn is the first to be cut." And the Russian soldiers who were part of the occupying force in Europe after World War II gained a bad reputation for their treatment of people they had no ties with. Visitors to Russia often feel a stand-offishness, but if they gain a Russian's trust they will be embraced in a friendship that has no equal in the West.

The fear of famine today has its roots in the past when it was common for bread to have sawdust added to it to stretch grain supplies through the winter. Cabbage was the other staple, and even at the time of the Revolution tea was a luxury reserved for holidays, while sweets were only a dream. In the spring, farm animals often had to be helped back to their feet, having come close to starvation before the spring grass returned. For centuries the knout was the penalty for peasants who tried their hand at private enterprise, since the tsar and the nobility held monopolies on all trade goods, even for the coffins peasants were buried in. In 1800, when the peasantry made up 96 percent of the Russian population (the nobility was two percent, as was the newly forming professional class), serfs worked three days a week for their lords, twelve hours a day in summer and nine hours in fall and spring, while in winter the frozen roads were the time to haul goods, often to the lord's house as far away as Moscow or St. Petersburg. Peasants paid most of the taxes, maintained the roads, delivered the mail, billeted soldiers, and if drafted into the army, served for life, leaving their wives to mourn them as dead. The nobility, for their part, paid no taxes, and after Catherine the Great managed to shed even the obligation to serve the tsar. In Europe, Catherine was seen as an important figure in the Enlightenment, but in Russia feudal exploitation reached its zenith under her rule. Peter the Great before her was seen as the Antichrist by most peasants, since he started conscription, established the secret police, and sold whole villages to European industrialists to man the factories he contracted with them to build and operate. Still, all Europe saw in Russia at this time were the glittering courts in Moscow and St. Petersburg, and the U.S. is seeing Russia in the same way now. Imitation is the surest flattery and helps us see what we want to see in Russia.

The peasants' first experience with democracy, the Duma set up early in 1917 following the abdication of the tsar, only confirmed their distrust of the privileged classes it was composed of. Even the parties claiming to represent the peasantry did not go along with the two things the peasants asked for, withdrawal from World War I and redistribution of the land. If there had been real democracy, both would have happened quickly, since the peasantry made up 86 percent of the population at the time. But the West wanted the Russians to stay in the war and the elites wanted to prove that they were good Europeans, as well as regain the honor lost when Japan sent the Russian fleet to the bottom in 1905. There was little thought given to the gray mass of Russian society, the ignorant, backward peasants whose only function had always been to do what the elites told them to do. So many peasants were conscripted for World War I, their horses too, that women and old people were left to till their fields, often harnessed to plows themselves and driven by the fear of famine. Casualties rose to seven million, another of those astronomical figures so common in Russian history but so hard for us to comprehend. Many soldiers slept in the snow rolled up in their overcoats, and some had to wait for comrades to be killed before they had a gun to use. The government used the one asset it had in abundance— men. It was said that the officers' horses were better fed than the soldiers, and this at a time when starvation stalked the countryside.

All of this was a huge gift to Lenin, who in November of

1917 took over the government easily by promising the peasants what they wanted, to withdraw from the war and redistribute the land. Yet their tribulation continued as twenty million died in the civil war that followed, much of it a war for bread. The West was again on the wrong side, supporting the elites for their own purposes, eyes closed to how self-serving this was. How different subsequent events in Russia might have been if American actions had reflected its own democratic ideals. Should it be surprising, then, that the still gray mass of Russians continue to recoil from the West? Or that they see us as still more interested in the high life in Moscow and St. Petersburg than in the poverty and hopelessness elsewhere? Or that most Russians still see democracy as fraudulent when there are so few leaders working for ordinary Russians, as opposed to the sources of money today, including foreign investors, after soviet assets ended up with the new rich?

The mass of Russians are, after all, still Slavs; nothing has happened to change the circumstances they must cope with. The tragedy now is that, unlike the Africans, it is so hard to imagine them returning to their beloved villages. Each was governed by a *mir,* which was simply a meeting of all villagers to discuss issues and make decisions. There was no leader, only a steward appointed to conduct the meeting and balloting, an obligation that was passed from person to person. Once a vote was taken, a second, unanimous one followed. No peasant would dream of going against the will of the mir, so important was unity in the village. *Mir* is an interesting word because of its two other meanings—peace and world. The first meaning—the village government—was the source of the second—peace — since the mir created the peace in the village that was essential for everyone's' well-being, even survival. And the village was their world, the third meaning of mir, because outside of it was the hostile world of the nobility, who were of a mind to use the peasants in any way they could. Even in the factories that poverty forced peasants into, they spontaneously formed councils—the Russian word for which is *soviet*—to protect their interests and function like mirs. After the tsar's abdication in 1917, which caught Lenin off guard, the soviets were providing what order there was in Russia—until Lenin and the Bolsheviks took them over and imposed their own oppressive order. In other words, Russia does have a democratic heritage, but on the small scale where trust is possible. Whether the country can reform itself is problematic, since even the trust among the peasants was crushed in the large collective farms where unguarded words to an informer could mean being send of to the gulag.

Alexandr Solzhenitsyn came to the U.S. in 1974 as a hero after being deported for his writings, which so powerfully challenged the Soviet system. But then he turned his attention on the United States, and his Harvard Commencement Address in 1978 may be one of the most trenchant critiques of American society ever written. He spoke of our insipid faith and cult of earthly well-being, of having substituted self-indulgence for moral behavior, of seeking liberation without responsibility, of reducing the free press to the pedaling of fashionable ideas rather than hard truths, and of turning democracy into the triumph of mediocrity. After this speech he disappeared from the American media; it was more satisfying to hear him criticize the Soviet Union than the U.S. He became almost a recluse in his home in rural Vermont before returning to Russia in 1994.

Cultures are all of a piece. It is not possible to mix and match them, to enjoy the best of cultures around the world without their downsides. This is the mistake we make when we think we can have democracy without divisiveness, free enterprise without self-centered drive, affluence without depleted resources and damaged environments, and individual freedom along with trust, loyalty, and warm personal relationships. Choices must be made, choices that are influenced—but not determined—by a cultural heritage. If self-knowledge is important for personal growth, then cultural knowledge is equally important for national growth—for knowing what is possible and what is not. Flattering assumptions about Russia embracing Western ways after the collapse of communism led to futile efforts to help them, but with unfortunate consequences for the majority of Russians, ones that in the end only confirmed their distrust of the West.

Having a clear, even hard-headed, understanding of who we are and what our choices are is of great importance in coping with the future. But it is important for the present, too, so before venturing into our own territory we will visit a region we are related to by a common heritage—plus the conflicts that make it the most dangerous part of the world today.

Closer to Home: The Trials of Middle Easterners

Americans are appalled by the hostilities in the Middle East and the Balkans, and see them as reflecting the almost barbaric ways of the Islamic ethnic groups in the region. We tend to forget that until recent times such ways were characteristic of Europe, too, ways that escalated into two world wars in the twentieth-century. The ancient hostilities there could still be alive if it were not for the incentives for unification created by the global economy. The U.S, too, went through its "ethnic cleansing" of Native Americans and its slavery and Civil War, both of which left hostilities that are still with us. Even now, after Middle Eastern violence has reached our own shores, we tend to forget that we are deeply involved in the Middle East and the two most important sources of conflict there, our need for their oil and the creation of Israel out of Arab lands.

The age-old source of such conflicts remains the same, the quest for national self-interest regardless of its consequences for others. The U.S. has been strong enough to get much of what it wanted in the Middle East, but not without generating a good deal of antagonism. It is the fundamentalists—the militant believers—who are most apt to respond, and in the violent ways that justify our dehumanizing of them as terrorists. This justified the war against terrorism, a war that is seen by the people of the region as against Islam in general. The potential consequences of this have grown huge, especially as the global economy becomes more dependent on the oil resources of the region. The result could well be the downward spiral of violence that leads to the war of all wars, especially since Israel has nuclear weapons. In pushing for our interests so single-mindedly, we are acting very much as any other ethnic group in a region plagued by conflict, a region that was shaped by nomadic herders in the first place.

The Arabic word for desert dwellers is *bedouin*, and they were the traditional aristocrats of the region and famous for their proud and independent ways. Fighting skills were honored, but so was the hospitality, generosity, and loyalty that were necessary for survival in the desert. These qualities made the region attractive to Arabists, such as T. E. Lawrence—Lawrence of Arabia—who lived with the Arabs, adopted their ways, and wrote about them for a fascinated Western audience. Located at the world's most important crossroads, between Europe, Asia, and Africa, trade was inevitable, and it functioned to keep the nomads profitably employed in trade, transporting goods and defending the trade routes. A crossroads is a place where residents are most apt to come into contact with new ideas, but it also attracts attackers hoping to profit from trade. These factors left the Middle East more advanced than Europe for centuries and strong enough to control the trade with the East. This forced the European to turn their attentions to improving the maritime skills that would enable them to sail around Africa to avoid the Arabs, and when they were able to do this they found the entire world was within their reach. Exploiting this fabulous prize demanded new skills and disciplined behavior, contributing to the Renaissance that ultimately enabled Europeans to dominate the world. The Middle East was effectively by-passed.

The conflicts between the Christian West and Islamic Middle East have a long history that obscures the many ties between the two faiths, and Judaism, too, since all three faiths worship the same god. Allah, or al-Lah, is Arabic for "the God" that is the same one Jews and Christians worship. All three faiths accept the Old Testament and its prophets, and Islam believes Christ is a prophet, too, but not the son of God. Likewise,

Mohammed is not God but the last and the greatest of the prophets. Even the origin of Islam is biblical. In Genesis, God promises Abraham that he will be the father of a great nation, and his first son, Ishmael, was born of the servant girl Hagar when his wife, Sarah, was unable to conceive. In her old age, however, Sarah gave birth to Isaac, and she demanded that Ishmael and Hagar be sent away. But God had promised Ishmael that he would be the father of a great nation, and it formed around the simple stone temple in Mecca that Abraham is believed to have built and is known as the *Ka'aba*, or cube, and covered with black silk. There are other similarities between Christianity and Islam—heaven and hell, judgment day, the Ten Commandments, and the Golden Rule. Because of their common roots, Jews and Christians are accorded a special position within Islamic society, as People of the Book, although the Koran asks for tolerance of all religions. Because of their common origins and similarities, Islam and Christianity are considered the major Western faiths, in contrast to the Eastern faiths of India and China.

But the differences between the Islamic and Christian realms are there, too, and they can best be understood as reflecting the different circumstances Mohammed faced in the vast, desolate Arabian Peninsula in the seventh-century, with its warring tribes and clans. The Roman Empire was gone, and with it the *Pax Romanum* that maintained order in the Middle East when Christ was alive. This meant Islam had to function as a government as well as a religion in an area where scattered tribes tended to fight continuously. To "turn the other cheek" was not possible as it was at Christ's time, so Islam became the most masculine of the great faiths. Still, Mohammed advanced the ethics of the region significantly. He improved the status of women and gave them important protections, but women were still left in a position quite different from that of men. The requirement that women dress modestly stems from the same reason that the Koran bans gambling and alcohol: all could inflame the male passions dangerously, the passions of a proud desert people. The fundamentalist who translate "dress modestly" into "completely covered" provide an example of how taking religious principles to extreme positions is a way of creating conflict, and thus betraying their founder. The more important way in which Islam protected women is by establishing a women's world that is separate from men's, something many Muslim women defend but is used by the U.S. as a justification for aggressive actions against Islamic governments.

For a new religion to survive in the unstable circumstances of Arabia, constant effort was necessary. This is *jihad,* which in the West is usually translated as "holy war," as it is by Islamic fundamentalists. But scholars point out that among the many Arabic words for war, jihad is not one of them. It is correctly translated as "struggle," the struggle to create the *umma,* the community of Islam, and in all senses—moral, spiritual, and political. It may include war, but the most common use in the Koran is the struggle for justice under the laws of Allah within the community of Islam. This unity was Mohammed's main goal, and to a significant degree he was successful. Within twenty years of his death, the two superpowers of the time, the Byzantine and Persian empires, had been defeated, and in less than a century the Islamic realm extended from Spain to Afghanistan. The West likes to use the phrase "conversion by the sword" to explain this explosive growth, but it was more an authentic conversion of a large part of the Christian realm at a time when Christianity was badly torn by theological divisions. The unity offered by Islam made it attractive then, and this is still the case. The words of Mohammed were committed to memory by his followers, recited regularly to maintain their purity, and written down in the Koran after his death much as Mohammed had spoken them. (The word *Koran* means recitation.) It is thus highly consistent, certainly compared to the Bible, which was written by many people over long periods of time and is full of the contradictions that have led to endless theological disputes. Islam is the fastest growing faith in the world today, in part because of this straight-arrow quality, but also because it has been genuinely colorblind, in contrast to the color consciousness of the West. Its strength is also reflected in how traditional the Middle East remains today, with low rates of divorce, drug use, and crime, strong family ties—and high birth rates, the second highest in the world, after Africa. This traditionalism is also why it is so offended by many Western ways, especially those reflected in films, television, music, and the internet.

As might be expected with two such closely related religions, the treatment of economics is much the same in the Koran as in the Bible. Trade would have been impossible to restrain in such a prime trading location, so the Koran focuses on the rules that guide it. Justice is the highest value, as it is in the Old Testament, in contrast to love in the New Testament. One of the Five Pillars of Islam is charity, and it is as central a theme in the Koran as in the Bible:

True piety is this:
to believe in God, and the Last Day,
the angels, the Book, and the Prophets,
to give of one's substance, however cherished,
  to kinsmen and orphans, the needy, the
  traveler, beggars,
and to ransom the slave,
to perform the prayer, to pay the alms. (Sura 2:172)

The great age of Islamic civilization was during the time when Europe was struggling to overcome the Dark Ages. By the time of the Crusades some of its creative vitality had ebbed, but when the Crusaders reached the Holy Land late in the eleventh-century they still encountered a civilization far ahead of their own. Arab libraries contained Greek texts that had been lost in Europe, math and science were flourishing, and the Arab leaders the Crusaders encountered were cultured and humane compared to the half-barbarian Crusaders. When the Crusaders first took Jerusalem, they slaughtered all of its inhabitants, but when

Saladin retook it, none of the defenders were put to death. The Crusades failed, but they weakened the confidence of Islamic civilization, and it was shattered by the Mongol conquest of the thirteenth-century that left large areas devoid of life. At a time when Europeans were preparing for the breakout of the Renaissance, Muslims were being driven back to a fatalism that contrasted sharply with Islam's great age. The political void was filled by the Ottoman Turks, a small but vigorous clan from among the last invaders from Central Asia. Their military advances took them almost to Vienna, but by the nineteenth-century their vitality had ebbed, and it collapsed during World War I. By this time Europeans had already established protected enclaves in the Middle East that were used for trading purposes, and later oil production, and were ruled by Emirs who were dependent on Europeans for their existence.

As the Ottomans weakened, European power expanded, and during World War I the French and English promised the Arabs their freedom if they helped drive the Turks from Arab lands. Lawrence of Arabia helped with this, but he did not trust the promise; indeed, when it was made the British and French had already secretly signed the Sykes-Pecot Agreement to divide the region after the Turks were driven out. Emir Faisal of the illustrious Hashemite line of rulers entered Syria in 1918 as a conquering hero, was proclaimed king, and then exiled by the French. In Iraq, the British installed the first of several puppet rulers that so offended Arab sensitivities, the last of which was overthrown after World War II. Out of the political chaos came two of the worst leaders in the Middle East, Hafiz al-Assad in Syria and Saddam Hussein in Iraq, both by gaining control of the military and security forces. The unfortunate consequences of this have fallen most heavily on the people of the two countries, but there have been major international repercussions as well. Saddam Hussein offered to obey the UN resolution ordering Iraq to withdraw from Kuwait if Israel obeyed the many UN resolutions ordering it to withdraw from occupied Palestinian territory. But the U.S. simply declared this "non-negotiable" and in 1991 unleashed $60 billion worth of military force against Iraq—to preserve the "international rule of law." Most Middle Eastern countries supported the war, since Saddam was a threat to them, too, but there was sympathy for someone who would point out the blatant injustice in U.S. actions, especially after it bombed water treatment facilities, power plants, and bridges. The Iraqis then endured a trade embargo for many years, the consequences of which included the rise in infant mortality that so disturbed Middle Easterners. We blamed it on Sadam.

Israel is the sharpest thorn in the relationship between the West and the Arabs. The West felt the need to atone for the Holocaust in some way, but not by creating a homeland for the Jews in Germany, for example, the scene of the worst horrors, or elsewhere in Europe. It was convenient that the Zionists wanted the Holy Land, since there the price could be paid by those who had little power to resist it. Jews had lived as a minority in Palestine for over a thousand years and there had been no pogroms against them or any need to make them a "final solution" for Arab problems. Many of the Jews who were expelled from Spain (for refusing to convert to Christianity after the Muslims were driven out) settled in Turkey, where they remain a respected group to this day. The objections of the Arabs to the injustice of carving out a homeland for the Jews from their territory were ignored, and the wars to resist this only led to the expansion of Israel with its overwhelming military superiority. With the support of the U.S. the Israelis could ignore the UN resolutions against them, leaving Palestinians with no alternative but primitive forms of violence, starting with rock throwing youths and escalating to suicide bombers. This was convenient since it meant they could be called "terrorists" and "fanatics"— for acting in ways Americans would in similar circumstances.

Imagine if the tables were turned and a militarily dominant China demanded half of California as atonement for injustices done to the Chinese in the past. Would we shrug our shoulders and say, "Oh well, that's just the way things are?" Of course not; think of the field day our "freedom fighters" would have, regardless of the military power employed by an occupying force and how effectively they had collected every weapon they could find. Or imagine if Islamists gained influence in Europe, through the selective allocation of oil for instance, and then established military bases there to work against unfriendly governments while providing assistance to those that moved away from secular ways—including how women dressed. Think of the outrage this would create, and how strong the urges would be to harass Muslims to get them to leave. Should we be surprised, then, that Middle Easterners should feel this way toward us? They are a proud people, too.

It was not until World War II that the U.S. became the major power in the region. Our initial goal was to resist the spread of Soviet communism, and this justified the CIA coup in Iran that brought the Shah to power. But it was nice, too, that he opened up investment opportunities, including the development of oil resources. For several decades Iran was a shining example of effective American foreign policy; we were encouraging the "enlightened progress" that is so often a euphemism for self-interest. We helped train the Shah's army so it could resist the Soviet Union, but also the security forces that often brutally drove modernization ahead. The westernized Iranians in Tehran were happy as high-rise buildings transformed city's skyline and foreign entertainments came in, but the mass of Iranians were not, and it took a religious fanatic backed by a genuine popular revolution to overthrow the Shah and his police state. The pendulum, having been pushed too far toward the West, swung back too far in the Islamic direction, and to the fundamentalist who violate the words of Mohammad as much as the religious right violates those of Christ. The Ayatollah became the man Americans loved to hate, but not to accept that we played an important role in bringing him to power.

In Afghanistan it was the Soviets who staged the takeover, which was unfortunate for the Afghan people since it gave the U.S. a chance to weaken its arch foe by sending huge amounts of military hardware to its enemies. Much of it went to the fundamentalists who were the most ardent fighters against communism, but after the Soviets left U.S. interest faded, especially as the new commanders turned their weapons on each other to see who would fill the political void. A group of seminary students, the Taliban, finally managed to stop the fighting, but they evidently needed the assistance of outsiders to do this, especially ones smarting for a jihad. Many were from Saudi Arabia, including Osama bin Laden, who not only had the money to buy influence with the Taliban but also to fund strikes against the U.S. The horrendous loss of life that resulted from the bombings of the World Trade towers not only discredited Islam but generated strong support in the U.S. for a war against the Taliban. It remains to be seen whether the result will be a turning point in the war against terrorism or greater animosity toward the U.S. The danger is that it will lead to the downward spiral of anger and violence that is the opposite of the peace everyone hopes for.

The only sure way of halting such a process is by working as hard for peace as for war, but this goes against the strong predispositions of both sides, and for deep seated reasons. With the Arab-Israeli conflict, it is hard to imagine either side compromising, but Saudi Arabia could be a more significant problem. With the world's largest reserves of oil, the Saudis receive extensive military assistance from the U.S. in return for assuring a steady supply of oil at reasonable prices. The U.S. supports the Saudis even though its Islam is as conservative as Iran's, but without the parliamentary elections that in Iran provides a degree of balance. This has allowed corruption within the 30,000 member royal family to grow bad enough to alienate the Wahhabi religious leaders who have long legitimized the monarchy. The Wahhabite leader was jailed for criticizing the royal family for its corruption in 1995, and in 2001, the clerics issued a *fatwa,* or edict, authorizing a Jlhad against the kingdom's rulers. King Faud had a major stroke in 1995 and is no longer able to rule, but he remains on the throne because of divisions over his successor. The Saudis give money to the most dangerous fundamentalists to keep their attentions focused on other countries rather than Saudi Arabia with its vulnerable oil handling facilities. The government refused to provide the U.S. with information about the Saudis who were the majority of the terrorists involved in the aerial bombings in the U.S., assuming we had no choice but to continue backing them. The government is also losing the support of the common people, especially the many educated but unemployed men who have been most attracted to the excitement of a jihad. It is not pleasant to think of what the results might be if radicals took over the country, since oil exports could be cut heavily with no adverse effects except on the royal family and their huge incomes.

One wonders what the Middle East would be like today if it did not have its huge deposits of oil. The region now has the largest food deficit of any region in the world, and there are limited opportunities for reducing it when so much of the land is deserts and mountains. The most hate-filled terrorists come from places where there is plenty of anger and no future, such as the Algerians living in dismal public housing projects in Paris, Chechens driven to the hills by Russians, and rich Saudis with nothing to do. They were the ones that committed atrocities in Bosnia in response to the equally hate filled actions of Christian Serbians. All are prescriptions for the darkest kind of future, and it is not clear how best to go about defusing it. The U.S. tends to attack such issues directly without accepting that the fund-amentalists are a small minority among the Muslims, and in so doing alienates moderate Muslims, including those who had hoped the U.S. would encourage democratic reforms.

As it is, the U.S. supports many anti-Islamic govern-ments regardless of how undemocratic or repressive they are. Most are the remains of the leftist, one-party, socialist governments that took over as the colonial era ended, often through wars of liberation. Socialism was the fashionable altern-ative to capitalism at the time when these leaders were studying in Europe, but they know that the rising Islamic tide is now the main threat to their rule. When Islamic leaders are jailed as "extremists," it justifies the radical Islamists who see violence as the only answer. One of the saddest parts in all of this is that the most effective rulers in the Middle East are among the few traditional leaders to survive, Jordan's King Hussein, a Hashemite, and King Hassan in Morocco, who traced his ancestry back to Mohammed. King Hussein allowed Islamic parties to participate in elections, and they have done so without violence.

If we could put ourselves in the shoes of the people in the Middle East, it would be clear why Islam is enjoying such a renaissance; it is the way of separating themselves from a West that has worked mainly for its own interests. Israel receives more U.S. military and economic aid than any other country in the world, with Egypt second, provided as an inducement to sign a peace treaty with Israel. We claim the "moral high ground" when we work against the proliferation of "weapons of mass destruction," but not when we blithely accept Israel's denial that it has them, and a policy for using them ominously termed the Samson Policy. We may sleep better because of this, but imagine how Middle Easterners feel with such a Sword of Damocles hanging over their heads and with no capacity to defend themselves against it. The military supremacy of the Israelis enabled them to annex land beyond the boundaries established by the United Nations in 1948, to turn Jerusalem from an international city to the capital of Israel, to confiscate land without payment in occupied territories to build Jewish settlements that function as armed camps of an occupying power, to take most of the water from Palestinian regions to support agriculture in Israel, and bar most Palestinian economic activity so they are dependent on jobs in Israel, and then can be barred from entering Israel as punishment when their suppressed anger explodes. If any other country in the world acted in such ways it would be deemed an international pariah, rather than the U.S.'s best friend in the region.

The evolutionary process—and practical common sense —would suggest that Israel's best hope for the future would be in making peace with its neighbors rather than taking steps that inflame their sense of injustice. The U.S. worked to encourage a negotiated settlement, but Israeli intransigence about the status of Jerusalem and the settlements made such an agreement too bitter a pill for the Palestinians to swallow. They wanted other European and Islamic countries to be involved in the peace process, not just the U.S. with its close ties with Israel, but the U.S. and Israel would have none of that. At times it seems that Israel almost wishes to encourage violence to justify a heavier military presence and the control of more land.

The terrible truth the Israelis should keep in mind is that, in a world where national self-interest is the rule, if it became a choice between oil supplies and Israel's survival, the U.S. could well come to the point of seeing oil as more important. History could be in the process of repeating itself, since it was the incessant rebelliousness of the Jews that led the Roman authorities to expel them from Palestine in the first place. The atrocities done to the Jews since then leave them feeling justified in doing whatever is necessary to secure their homeland, but if this causes the pendulum to swing back too far in the direction of injustices to others, history could repeat itself. Injustice to one's neighbors is not the way of improving security; it is the way violence is sustained.

The U.S. acts in balanced ways when it can, as when it supported Muslims in Bosnia, Kosovo, and Somalia. But it jeopardizes its national interests whenever it sees what it wants to see in the Middle East to justify policies that have powerful support in the U.S. but unfortunate effects in the Middle East. Egypt provides a good example, since all we hear about it is when the government arrests those accused of being extremists. This is usually the leaders of the large Islamic parties that have been banned from politics but gained support by acting in ways the Koran asks for. They established Islamic banks, for instance, which do not pay interest on deposits, as the Bible and the Koran both ask, and charge only administrative fees for loans, many of which go to poor people who have no other source of credit.

They operate medical clinics staffed by volunteers and free to those who cannot pay the modest fees charged while providing better service than the government medical facilities, where bribes determine the service received. They operate Islamic schools that demand high standards for both teachers and students. It is in such ways that mainstream Islam is gaining momentum, but Muslims are distressed when such activities rarely make it into a Western media interested only in terrorists and reactionary governments.

In other words, the Western heritage of aggressive self-interest is alive and strong in the Middle East, and it is still generating the hostilities that are the age-old source of violence. Islamic, Christian, and Jewish fundamentalists have much in common, but their actions, rather than reflecting the teachings of their founders, suggest the anger and violence that could well shape the times ahead. Still, the core of this religious heritage is a peaceful one, so it remains to be seen which paths will be followed.

CHAPTER NINE

The Great Instability

The near-vertical growth lines this book began with—of population, economic activity, technology, resource use, and environmental impact—all have their origins in the West. Why this revolutionary change occurred here is a question that has absorbed historians for centuries and been approached in many ways. Here it is approached through the process of cultural evolution, especially the changing fortunes of peacefulness and aggressiveness. This means to focus on religion, since it is the cultural device that has been most effective in encouraging peacefulness through the ages. Christianity's difficulties with this reflect its origins in the Middle East, yet it managed to build a traditional agricultural society in Europe out of the breakdown of the Roman Empire and the chaos of the Dark Ages. The medieval Age of Faith was the longest period of relative stability in Western history, but it weakened as the classical heritage recovered, and with the Industrial Revolution Christianity turned from being the main source of resistance to a market-based society to a powerful force driving it forward.

With such a contradictory heritage it is not possible to know whether Christianity will be an asset in moving toward peaceful cooperation in the future or another source of conflict to add to the many that already exist. Plausible scenarios can be written for both, but there is no way of knowing the probabilities of either. What can be known, however, is important—how Christianity functioned in Western history to encourage both peacefulness and aggressiveness. This is important because of the tendency for setbacks to cause a return to roots—as is happening in the Middle East, with Islam the source of both constructive and destructive activities.

The recovery of traditional values may have a good deal of support today, but it is important to keep in mind what this actually involves—a return to the obligations and responsibilities of traditional societies shaped by the selflessness of the great faiths. This is the opposite end of the spectrum from the market faith that so powerfully encourages self-interest and requires individual freedom. Even to think of the selflessness of the great faiths would be a form of romantic escapism if it were not for the unsustainability of industrial society. The future may be unknowable, but we can gain a better understanding of our heritage, especially how it worked to order medieval society and then contributed to the great instability known as urban industrial society. The focus of this chapter is on the forces that shaped Christianity initially, how it built a new order following the fall of Rome, and then contributed to the market faith and the rise of urban industrial society. The complex role of Christianity provides an illuminating example of the changing fortunes of self-lessness and aggressiveness in the Western historical experience.

Greek and Jew in Western History

Traditional agricultural societies are usually tough nuts to crack. Having reached a stable equilibrium, they stay with it, enduring famines, natural disasters, and periods of chaos to get back to the place that is most comfortable—where they started. They were conservative in the pre-modern sense, of valuing old ways enough to look backward for answers rather than forward. But the unstable circumstances of the Middle East and Europe rarely permitted this degree of stability; the Church may never even have had an opportunity to organize Europe if it had not been for the breakdown of secular authority that led to the Dark Age. And even though the medieval Age of Faith that followed was the longest period of relative stability in Western history, it was still regularly disturbed by nobles with their urge to fight, merchants and bankers with their economic ambitions, religious enthusiasts with heretical beliefs, and a Church that was often more concerned with preserving its power than its faithfulness. (Russell, 1968) And the order that the Church had slowly and laboriously put together started to unravel well before the Renaissance, especially among the upper classes who felt most constrained by it. The common people held to the old ways resolutely, especially in the rural areas where most lived, in many cases until the Industrial Revolution left them no choice.

Clearly, there are competing forces at work in the Western historical experience, and the two most important ones can be understood as stemming from the differences between the Greeks and the Jews. These differences are so significant that reconciling them was rarely possible; one or the other has usually been dominant at different times in Western history. The differences found their way into the Bible, too, leading to the contradictions that enabled Westerners to disregard the parts of the Bible they did not care for, including much of the Law that Christ said he came to fulfill. The result is the unsavory reputation Christianity has gained today, both in the West and around the world, and the questions about its role in the future.

The Jews were like other groups of nomadic herding peoples caught up in the violent circumstances of the early civilizations in the Middle East. Their roots were in Mesopotamia, out of which Abraham led his followers sometime around 1800 B.C. The fought as much as other herding groups, but their tribal loyalties enabled them to hold together, and this was aided by their genius for religion. Their faith helped them conquer the promised land, but the instincts of nomadic herders also led to problems, ones that resulted in periodic setbacks, such as the exile in Babylon. But even though the Jews were small in number and left none of the grand monuments of the great empires, their worldwide impact has been far greater in the three religions that originated among them.

The Greeks, in contrast, were the source of great

intellectual and artistic brilliance and were among the most successful of conquerors. Worldly and sophisticated, their love of disputation let to the philosophical differences that caused the great age of Greece, the Periclean in the fifth-century B.C. to be short, lasting for less than a century before being brought down by wars the Athenians started. The achievements of Alexander the Great that followed were spectacular, but even though he was educated by Aristotle he became increasingly murderous as his conquests spread beyond Persia toward India. Even the epics that sustained Greek civilization, the *Iliad* and the *Odyssey*, were full of violence, while their gods were almost larger-than-life humans, and full of jealousy, pride, anger, and vengeance; they meddled in human affairs so much that the Greeks could blame them for their own violent behavior. Hellenism remained important after the decline of Greece, but the long *Pax Romanum* was based more on Rome's administrative, engineering, and military skills. The Roman gods were essentially Greek ones with new names, and their behavior reflected the individualism of the Greeks more than the ethical restraints characteristic of the tribal Jews.

The early experiences of the Jews required that their Law be strong if they were to survive in a dangerous part of the world. This made Old Testament ethics harsh in many ways, but also functional; an eye for an eye assured enemies that hostile acts would be met with retribution. As in many herding societies, guilt was collective; if one member of a clan committed a sin, the entire group was punished, sometimes for generations. Still, no Jew would think of opting out of the Law if he disagreed with it, since a lone individual was unlikely to survive in such times, except as a slave. The survival of the individual and the group was one and the same, and this gave the Jewish Law its strength. The common way of referring to faith in the Old Testament is "the fear of God," which, although not sitting well with modern ears, reflects the nature of the world the Jews lived in.

By the time of Christ, however, the Jews had moved toward a settled way of life in a location with excellent trading opportunities on the Mediterranean. There may have been more Jews living in the Diaspora at this time than in Palestine, and some scholars argue that Judaism had a cultural influence comparable to that of Hellenism. The Jews bitterly resented Roman rule, but for Jesus it provided the stability that enabled him to turn to fulfilling the Law the Jews had strayed from in their worldly success. But the Jews were looking for a leader to drive out the Romans, so when Jesus turned out to be a religious reformer rather than a political one, they turned against him, had him put to death, and returned to their struggle for independence. The Romans grew tired of the Jews' rebelliousness and in 70 A.D. tore down the temple in Jerusalem. Another revolt in 135 led the Romans to expel them from the Holy Land altogether.

Hellenism had been important in Palestine ever since Alexander the Great conquered it in 332 B.C., and Greek was so widely spoken at the time of Christ that Palestine was almost bilingual. But the worldly ways of the Greeks were the opposite of the tribal solidarity of the Jews that Jesus sought to recover. The critical juncture in the new faith came after Judaism had closed ranks against the Christians in Jerusalem and the apostles were taking the faith to Jews and gentiles around the Mediterranean. Peter and Paul were most important in this. Peter was the one Jesus had designated as the rock on which his church was to be built and ultimately became the leader of the church in Rome. Paul never knew Jesus and declared himself to be an apostle after his conversion on the road to Damascus, but he is known as the great evangelist for his work in converting the Greeks. The first major question the new church faced was which Jewish ways should be retained and which would have to be given up if Christianity was to become a world faith rather than an ethnic Jewish one. Paul was the spokesman for those who wanted to liberalize the Law, and in several of his letters, he speaks against the "Judaizers" who resisted this. Whether this included Peter is not known, but Peter is credited with putting together the compromise that preserved the Jewishness of the new faith—including the importance of the Law—while still permitting its adoption by gentiles.

Peter was an unlettered fisherman before he became an apostle, in contrast to Paul, who was born in Tarsus, a Greek city in what is now Turkey and known as the Athens of Asia Minor. Paul knew Greek, Hebrew, and Aramaic, the vernacular language Jesus spoke, and in the course of his evangelical work wrote letters to the new churches, mostly in Greece, many in response to difficulties they were experiencing. The thirteen epistles of Paul make up half of the books in the New Testament, and they introduced the metaphysical elements that so absorbed the Greeks. Peter, in contrast, has only two books in the Bible, and they are brief and stylistically different, suggesting they may have been taken down by others, the second possibly written by someone else. One result is that little is known about Peter, or how it was that the Christian community in Rome managed to live in such exemplary ways, with people sharing everything they had and suffering periodic persecutions with courage and fortitude. It was their good behavior that in 313 A.D. led Emperor Constantine to adopt Christianity as the faith of the Empire, even though Christians at that time represented only some ten percent of its population.

Constantine had hoped that the Christian example of good behavior would serve to reverse the decay of the Empire, but it had descended too far in that direction to have its course altered so easily. Worse yet, once Christianity became the religion of the Empire, it became enmeshed in royal politics in Constantinople, where Constantine had moved the capital for the better protection it offered against the barbarians than Rome. Even earlier, the new faith had become an outlet for the Greek love of disputation, so that within a century of Christ's crucifixion many church fathers were writing in a form that was clearly classical, and more influenced by Plato and Aristotle than the Judaism of Jesus' world. The Greeks took what they saw as a primitive Jewish faith and made it into a triumph of Greek thought—of theological thought, however, rather than the ethics that were less congenial to the classical mind. With Constantine, these theological issues became political as well, and disputes began to tear the new faith apart. The most divisive one was over the nature of Christ, whether he was god, man, or something in between. It was to resolve these disputes that Constantine called the Council of Nicea in 325, which adopted the Trinity as official Church doctrine, as expressed in the Nicene Creed. But this did not stop the arguments; they continued for centuries and often turned violent, leading to the fragmentation that contributed to the victorious spread of Islam over much of the Christian world in the seventh-century. Differences in the interpretation of Christ's nature simply could not be tolerated, an ominous turn for a religion supposedly based on love.

The controversies over the nature of Christ are in stark contrast to the struggles Jesus himself went through to learn what role God intended for him, as reported with such humanity in the Gospels. He consistently refers to himself as "the son of man," which in Old Testament Hebrew was a synonym for "man" or "humankind," while in the Aramaic Jesus spoke it simply meant "the man," or even "someone." Later, the "son of man" was taken to mean God manifested on Earth, but that was not its meaning when Jesus used it. To him, the disputes over his nature would have seemed like the arguments of the Pharisees, which he described as "blind guides, which strain at a gnat but swallow a camel." Elsewhere Jesus praises God because he has "hidden these things from the wise and learned, and revealed them to little children."

Jesus' words in the New Testament are heavily Jewish in character. The Mosaic Law was the tradition he was born into and absorbed him all of his life. He said that he had come to fulfill the Law, and did so by balancing the often harsh, masculine ways of the Old Testament with the softer, more feminine ways of forgiveness, tolerance, and "turning the other cheek." By "Giving unto Caesar what is Caesar's," Christianity avoided the catastrophe that would befall the Jews with their incessant rebellion. Indeed, the revolutionary statements Jesus made during his lifetime were so out of character with the times he lived in that it has long been speculated that he had come into contact with Eastern religions, which could have reached Palestine along with trade goods from the East. But Jesus' life was spent primarily in the rural area around the Sea of Galilee, and religious scholars who have studied the matter point to the Zoroastrian influences in both Christianity and Hinduism, suggesting that common elements in them could have spread east and west from Persia. That Christ's roots were in the villages of Palestine, rather than its cities, is suggested by Richard Critchfield when, in *Villages*, he describes the revelation he experienced in reading Mark, the earliest of the four Gospels:

> Jesus spoke just as many of my villagers did, making the same observations from village life and sometimes using the same phrasing. . . Even the cry from the cross, "My God, My God, why hast thou forsaken me?" finds contemporary echoes in the despair of villagers badly treated by fate despite the utmost faith and piety. (p. 280)

As striking as Jesus' words themselves is the fact that they survived to form the basis of a great faith, a message of love and forgiveness in a part of the world characterized by violence and long-standing feuds. But this is where Paul's role is both historically important and controversial. It has been argued that Christianity may not have survived without Paul's evangelical work, but to be successful among the Greeks required that he downplay the ethics that so absorbed Jesus. Even Paul, with his Greek upbringing, may have been uncomfortable with the Jewish Law, leading him to focus on the theological issues the Greeks were more comfortable with. The fateful step in this was expressed in several of Paul's letters in which he argued that Christ's sacrifice on the cross freed Christians from the Law, that faith in Christ is what led to salvation, by God's grace, and not the works that could be contrived for public display. "Christ," he wrote, "is the end of the law"—the Law Jesus came to fulfill.

Even though most of what Paul wrote is consistent with Christ's message and his words about love in I Corinthians 13 are among the most beautiful every written, with the Reformation it was Paul's words about salvation by faith rather than works that came to dominate Christianity. Perhaps it was the ambiguities in Paul's teachings outside of the Jewish context that opened them up to the negative interpretations of the Law, or the complex of forces at work from the Renaissance to the Industrial Revolution, but somehow Christianity came to reflect the loophole in the law that enabled them to do what they wanted and still claim salvation—even when acting in ways clearly opposed to what Christ asks of them. Christianity survived as a world faith, but tarred with the contradictions that displaced love with aggressiveness and a "holier than thou" attitude to others— including now blaming government when things turn sour. Many Christians today should be called Paulists, since they reflect the classical heritage of Paul more than the Jewish heritage of Christ. That Paul's theology is better suited to life today is suggested by the frequent reference to it as the gospel of freedom, and also that books about Paul significantly outnumber those on the four gospels in the libraries of theological seminaries.

The Dark Ages and the Opening for the Church

If Christianity was able to function as a great world faith, it was primarily because the fall of Rome broke the proud classical spirit. The barbarians had the vitality Rome had lost, and in many ways their morals were no worse than those of the Romans, who had grown increasingly cruel in trying to hold their disintegrating empire together. The barbarians continued to move into Europe for centuries after the first sacking of Rome in 425, with the Vandals, Goths, and Visigoths followed by the Franks, Germanic tribes, Lombards, Jutes, and finally the Norsemen five centuries later. Rome was the first target, but other cities quickly followed, and finally the towns were sacked.

Trade dropped to almost nothing as bandits preyed on merchants moving goods from place to place, causing cities to waste away since trade was their lifeblood. City dwellers were left with little choice but to retreat to rural areas where at least food could be grown. But even rural areas were dangerous as warrior chieftains fought for control of large areas.

The anarchy of the times forced the Church to fall back on the Law to create a workable order out of the chaos. The way of life that evolved was a traditional agricultural society in most respects, except that the elites were the old barbarian chieftains. They retained their violent tendencies even as the Church worked to incorporate them into the medieval order, mainly by honoring them as "nobles." The circumstances the common people found themselves in were difficult enough to create the intense religious feelings of the age, as well as the steady stream of heresies that would disturb the medieval era.

The Dark Ages were a harsh time for the common people. Population declined, and people desperately needed protection from the marauders ranging across the countryside, taking their food if nothing better could be found. Ordinary people had little capacity to defend themselves. Not only were horses, armor, and weapons far beyond their economic means, but their rural ways were no match for the hardened fighting ways of their predatory tormentors. Their best hope was to put themselves under the protection of a chieftain strong enough to protect them, cultivating the land he controlled in return for giving him roughly half of the food they produced on his land. This is feudalism, and in most cases people voluntarily accepted it, in effect negotiating a contract with a lord to trade their labor for his protection and the use of his land. The lord did not have unlimited power over his serfs, but because of the nature of the times the terms were hard. The serfs were considered his property, and were not allowed to move away unless a substantial fee was paid.

The Church in Rome survived the collapse of Rome because it did not pose a threat to the invaders. Its wealth was taken, but learning was preserved in the monasteries, and the Church slowly came to provide the organization that the feudal lords could not. Missionaries were sent out from monasteries in Italy and then the windswept western coasts of Ireland and Scotland that had escaped being sacked because of their remoteness, until the Norsemen got them later. The process of conversion was irregular, but slowly the nascent order provided by the Church came to be seen as a defense against the chaos of the times. But the Church had to come to terms with the lords, too, and it accepted their feudal position over the peasants in return for the lords' acceptance of the Church's authority in religious matters. And since religion was deemed to cover much of life, the Church's position was strong. Slowly, the structure of medieval society took shape and, to the extent permitted by the times, it was patterned on the Bible, the closest thing to a constitution that Europe had for centuries.

The medieval Age of Faith was the period when the West was most like India, partly because of the deep faith but also because the Bible has much to say about economics. The quest for wealth was a sin, since it led to oppression of the poor, while charity is the most pervasive obligation in both the Old and the New Testaments. Periodically the common lands around a village were redistributed so everyone had an equal share to work; the goal was to encourage collective solidarity by distributing resources equitably. The urban counterparts of this were the guilds of the towns and cities, which fixed the prices, materials, and workmanship of the items each guild produced. Everyone was born into a station in life, with those born into positions of wealth and influence obligated to use them for the glory of God and the good of others. People could expect to have what was deemed appropriate for their station in life, but not more, since beyond this one's energies were to be directed toward the more important things of the spirit. The ideal of biblical economics was the Great Commandment, to love others as oneself, and even if it was rarely reached, it still guided behavior in ways that were quite different from those of the market faith that has shaped our society.

The cities offered more freedom than rural areas, mainly because trade was more difficult to control than agriculture and the crafts. Still, every possible method was used to suppress the economic urges that found their outlet in trade. Usury, the lending of money at interest, was banned on the principle that only the work of one's own hands was to be rewarded, not the unearned income from lending money. The same principle applied to windfall profits from trade; the Church had no problem with merchants recovering the costs of purchasing and transporting goods plus a reasonable profit, but not speculative profits beyond that. But controlling trade was difficult, and as it spread to distant markets and found protected niches in certain cities, controlling it grew more difficult. Still, the rate of change was slow, as was population growth, contributing to the sense of timelessness of the medieval era. This is most clearly reflected in the way buildings were built to last for centuries, as many have.

A pattern emerged of a predominantly agricultural society, with villages sorting themselves out around market towns, which were distributed around the cathedral towns where Church authority resided. Nobles had the obligation to defend the people—their key role in the feudal contract—and also to assure that churches were built and mills to grind grain. Monasteries and convents absorbed what could otherwise have been surplus population while performing roles as varied as copying manuscripts, praying for the people around them, caring for the sick, or experimenting with new agricultural methods. Most regions were close to self-sufficient, with long-distance trade mostly in luxury items for nobles and high church officials. There were alternatives for those who did not fit into the niches they were born into, such as monastic life, becoming a mercenary for a lord, or, for peasants vigorous enough to purchase their freedom, moving to the towns where there were more economic opportunities. For the most part, however, medieval life strived to reflect the Beatitudes which open the Sermon on the Mount and are often said to be the core of

Christ's message, that it is the meek, the merciful, the pure in heart, the peacemakers, and those who hunger and thirst after righteousness who are close to God, not the wealthy and the powerful.

The history books often make serfdom into something akin to slavery, but the great majority of villagers saw it differently. They undoubtedly would have preferred to own the lord's land and keep all the fruits of their labor for themselves, but since this was not an alternative they worked instead to preserve their rights to cultivate the lord's land. In England, this effort was pursued in the village courts, and over the centuries this evolved into the common law that is the basis of our legal system today. Land was the basis of the livelihood for most people and they wanted to preserve their rights to it, especially when the lord sought to turn it to the production of cash crops instead. Feudal rights were not extinguished until late in the eighteenth-century in a legal process known as enclosure, but it was begun earlier, especially as wool became England's most valuable export. The enclosure movement was slowed when there were few other ways of making a living, but still, the English country-side is full of what are euphemistically called "lost villages," but are in fact the remains of villages pulled down so the land could be turned to grass. It was said that the land was producing sheep rather than people, even as the weaving of cloth became a cottage industry. The chancellor in Parliament still sits on a wool sack to keep members of parliament from forgetting how important wool was to England's wealth and power for several centuries before the Industrial Revolution.

Initially the people thrown off the land who could find no other way of making a living survived on a primitive welfare system known as the Spenhamland Law, which provided them with bread. It was not until this law was repealed that people had no choice but to enter the alien world of factories, mines, and cities. It is interesting that, at a time when Europe was creating so much turmoil around the world with its conquests and colonial empires, many people at home were going through experiences that may have been equally as wrenching. Most of the common people held to their ancient ways as best they could, and some emigrated in the hope of reestablishing them elsewhere, the hope that was behind the Jeffersonian ideal. It was only in recent decades that these hopes were thoroughly obliterated by the triumph of the urban industrial way of life.

The classicists who wrote the history books picture the medieval era as a time of feudal exploitation, stagnation, and superstition, of peasants slogging through the mud and oppressed by powerful lords and churchmen. This is history written by the winners; there is some truth in this, but it is a highly selective truth, much as the Soviets described capitalistic societies. The paucity of accounts of daily life makes it hard to say much about what everyday life was actually like. Chaucer's *Canterbury Tales* provides one of the clearest pictures—earthy, bawdy, but steadfast and devoted, too. The paintings of Brueghel give a similar impression, of peasants working together to harvest a grain field or cavorting at feasts in ways suggestive of the pilgrims on their way to Canterbury. The European landscape is perhaps the best evidence of what the medieval era was like, since landscapes are a clear reflection of the cultures that produced them and much of rural Europe was left untouched as the cities became the center of activity. Europe's medieval landscapes remain one of its main tourist attractions, along with the fewer parts of medieval cities that have survived. The gothic cathedrals are symbolic of the era, soaring heavenward to the glory of God. Built mainly during the eleventh and twelfth centuries, they dwarf the houses and shops that huddle below them, perfect symbols of the centrality of faith at the time—as much as skyscrapers symbolize market-based society now. Even nobles contributed to the collective effort to build the cathedrals, quarrying stone and carting it to building sites. There is no record of who designed the cathedrals, only the names of the chief masons who directed the work over the long years it took to build them. They were built for the glory of God rather than the glory of the designers and artists who decorated them.

The cathedrals also tell us something about the technical advances of the times, since they are essentially tall piles of stone held together by gravity, weak mortar, and iron pins. But the stones were cut and fitted together so well and the forces on them were so balanced that they have stood for centuries. Other technical advances were occurring, but slowly too. Wind and water power were applied to tasks such as grinding grain and pumping water, and the efficiency of sailing vessels improved. Iron was used, but in limited quantities because of its cost. Woodwrights made up for this with their skill in using wood for such complex mechanisms as windmills, employing different woods for different purposes so effectively that they lasted for centuries if maintained. Agricultural changes were the slowest, limited by the conservative nature of peasants and the common management of the land, but also reinforcing the sense of timelessness of the era.

A much humbled Western Civilization had regrouped around the order provided by the Church, and for ordinary people it was a comforting change, especially as the warlords came under the Church's influence. Obligations were placed on them, too, ones that reflected their noble status and reinforced the effort to overcome their warrior ancestry. Fighting among them continued, but it relied on knights primarily, and included rules establishing when and where fighting could occur.

The first indication of things to come was the Crusades. On the surface they reflected the religious faith of the times and the urge to regain control of the Holy Land from the infidels. But they also provided an outlet for the fighting urges in places other than Europe, while merchants and bankers saw the Crusades as an opportunity to clear the Mediterranean of Muslim control to open it to European trade. The religious objectives of the Crusades were achieved only briefly and many powerful nobles were either killed or impoverished, but the advancements of the merchants and bankers were important and long-lasting.

The first Crusades went by land and, in addition to being

slow, they reflected badly on the Crusaders, especially those attracted by the opportunities for adventure—and plunder. Later Crusades went by sea, but for this large sums of money were needed, much of which the Church borrowed from Venetian bankers. Throughout the medieval era, Venice was the largest city in Europe, with a population of some 100,000. Located on low-lying islands that made it safe from bandits, it grew wealthy on the trade on the Adriatic Sea, which was a "Christian Sea" protected by its narrow outlet to the Mediterranean. It also permitted trade with Greece and from there to Constantinople and the Silk Road to China, all of which made Venice wealthy and led to the oriental quality of its architecture. The loans to finance the Crusades enabled the Venetian bankers to influence them in ways favorable to their objectives, with the low point of the Crusades—and the crowning achievement of the bankers— being the sacking of Constantinople in 1204. It was the seat of the Eastern Church, but the Venetians wanted its rich booty as well as access to the Black Sea. This act of treachery was especially unfortunate in its impact on the Russians, who were turned into implacable foes of the West, seeing it as hopelessly tainted with humanism even in the early thirteenth-century.

The Crusades opened the Mediterranean to trade, and the Church had been a part of it. The medieval order began to decay as the Italian bankers and merchants grew wealthy, and then the Church, too. The election of a pope became enmeshed in the politics that were to inspire Machiavelli, and the wealth trade generated was used to support artists and architects. Perhaps most important of all, it led to the translation of Greek texts obtained from Arab libraries that had been lost in Europe. All of this contributed to the opening up of the world of classical thought that gave confidence to the new worldview, a confidence that was spectacularly confirmed by the Age of Discovery. Soon wealth began pouring into Europe from around the world, and it gave the new order a momentum that challenged the medieval order everywhere. Proud Church officials began to build them- selves palaces so as to not be outdone by bankers, merchants, and nobles. Fine Renaissance churches were built, too, ones honoring architects and artists more than God but requiring ever more money from the faithful.

Barbara Tuchman argues in *The Distant Mirror* that the real turning point in all of this was the century before the Renaissance, the fourteenth-century, a time she saw as much like our own, when the confidence in a way of life first began to falter. (1987) The common people held to their faith as their main hope, but the unsettling events of the time led William Langland in 1377 to decry the new pride in *Piers Plowman*:

> Loud laughed life
> And armed him in haste, with words of harlotry
> And held Holiness for a jest, and Courtesy
>   for a waster,
> And Loyalty a churl, and Liar a gentleman.
> Conscience and Counsel, he counted it a folly.

A widely read book during the medieval era was a devotional titled *The Imitation of Christ*, which responded to Christ's dictum to "Be ye therefore perfect." It was this clear, untroubled faith that was unraveling at the time. To the elites it at least offered opportunities, but for the common people it only threatened everything that was important to them, not only their faith and their economic well-being but the whole medieval way of life. Everything seemed to be under siege by princes, wealthy merchants, and arrogant Church officials, all of whom seemed to have little loyalty to anything beyond themselves. The paintings of Hieronymus Bosch in the late 1400s reflect the dread of this time perfectly, with scenes of rapaciousness, lust, and gluttony that included clerics and greedy peasants as well as rich merchants and princes, all of it leading to a monstrous hell.

Slowly but relentlessly the spread of trade, wealth, pride, and ambition undermined the Age of Faith. Kings and princes challenged the power of the pope, mainly over the right to appoint bishops, making it necessary for the pope to raise his own army and act in other ways much like a Renaissance prince. As the Church in Rome grew worldly, so did the discontent of the faithful, especially in the still pious north, making the Reformation inevitable.

The Reformation and the Unintended Revolution

Luther was medieval in most ways, especially in his attitude toward feudalism and economic restraint; his goal was to bring the Church back to the true path. But in two ways he was instrumental in bringing on the modern, even if this was far from his intent, by encouraging individualism and nationalism. He encouraged individualism by giving people a personal relationship with God. Rather than allowing priests and the Church to act as intermediaries between people and their God, people were encouraged to read the Bible themselves. But this led to different interpretations of the Bible, with the result being not only the end of a unified Christendom and a Protestantism that fragmented into many different sects but the theological disputes that have divided Christians ever since. Nationalism was encouraged because Luther needed the support of the German princes in resisting the efforts of the Roman Church to suppress Protestantism, but this led to other problems. Since Luther had rejected Rome's authority, the peasants felt they could reject the authority of their lords, leading to the German Peasant Revolt that began in 1524. Luther's dependence on the princes meant he had no choice but to support their bloody suppression of the peasants, with an estimated 150,000 deaths. This was the beginning of the most tragic consequence of the Reformation, the almost unending religious wars that followed. Their names describe their lengths—Thirty Years, Sixty Years—but not the vast numbers of deaths, mostly of the common people who were pulled into the conflicts; the population of Germany was reduced by more than half before the religious wars were over. Not only was the unity of Christendom broken, but with it came the violence that has so disgraced Christianity along with the West.

The real revolutionary of the times, however, was not Luther so much as Calvin, because he was instrumental in eliminating religion as the main source of opposition to the quest for wealth. A contemporary of Luther, Calvin was the pastor of a church in Geneva, an important trading city strategically located near the headwaters of the Rhone, Rhine, and Danube rivers. His congregation was composed of prosperous merchants who embodied the values of thrift, hard work, careful calculation of profit, and the discipline of low wages for hired workers. But as pious Christians, they festered under the pervasive biblical proscriptions against the quest for wealth. God may have promised wealth to the Jews as a whole, as a sign of his favor, but there is only one example in the Bible of wealth going to an individual as a reward. The book of Job is one of the oldest books in the Bible (with earlier versions in Mesopotamian literature), and it concludes with God rewarding Job for his faithfulness with great wealth. This was the part of the Bible the Calvinists chose to follow, bringing to mind the old saw that the devil can quote the Bible to his ends.

The times in which Luther and Calvin lived caused both of them to see human nature as sinful, and that people were unable to achieve salvation by their own efforts. They looked to God's grace instead as the only way of coping with a sinful era that seemed to be moving away from Christ's way. This led Luther and Calvin to fall back on predestination as a way of determining who was saved, the belief that God determines at birth who will go to heaven. Predestination is a minor theme in the Bible, one associated with God's plan for humankind, but Paul tied it to grace in the letter to the Romans when he quotes God saying to Moses in Exodus: "I will show mercy to whomever I choose; I will have pity on whomever I wish." Christ, it is important to note, never uses the term grace. He speaks instead of gifts, like the sun and rain that are available to all, with individuals responsible for accepting the gift of faith and living by it. But because of the deep insecurities during the time of the Reformation, when it seemed that the sinful were prospering at the expense of the faithful, the belief in predestination gained credence. Still, it left people with the problem of not knowing if they were among the elect, and destined for heaven, or were headed for the fires of hell. It was Calvin's followers who later resolved this question by seeing economic success as a sign of God's favor, that as with Job, prosperity meant they were among the elect destined for heaven. Similarly, poverty was a sign that they were likely to be among the damned.

It is hard to imagine a more unchristian concept given Christ's special concern for the poor in the gospels, that they were close to God and would be lifted up, while the rich will be sent away empty and the powerful brought low. The effect, however, was to create an incredibly powerful theological incentive for making money, one that reinforced the already strong economic incentives. Together they gave Calvinists the drive to pioneer the Industrial Revolution. Known as Puritans in England and North America, they felt no hesitation in working employees twelve and fourteen hours a day, women and children, too, since this was felt to be good for them, a stimulus to improve themselves and possibly to find that they were among the elect. With Calvinism, it was the wealthy that were close to God, not the poor and the merciful of the Sermon on the Mount. This theological justification for wealth may have fallen away, but it survives in its secular form, the market faith, in which individual worth is determined by economic achievement.

This is close to the modern economy, but not quite there. The Calvinists opposed spending their wealth on palaces and beautifying cities, since this is what the Italian bankers had done and had corrupted the Roman Church. But they also opposed providing charity for the poor, since it allowed them to be lazy. The only thing left to do with their profits was to reinvest them, the breakthrough of capitalism. Investing profits rather than spending them caused production to soar, and factories began producing the goods that became today's abundance. This required discipline, which was certainly what the Puritans had, and the growing size and complexity of factories led them to appreciate the importance of education. In Massachusetts the Puritans established Harvard College in 1636, only seventeen years after landing at Plymouth Rock. Sensitive to criticism for their harsh treatment of workers, the Calvinists moved toward educating them, and then toward improving their working conditions, even if slowly and without allowing laborers to organize themselves. Perhaps most importantly, their hostility toward the aristocrats—their main political opponents in England—led the Puritans to support democracy as a way of breaking the power of the nobility; it was also the way of breaking the power of the southern plantation owners in the U.S. The Protestant north in Europe, and then the U.S., became the progressive part of the West, the part that made industrial society work.

It worked so well, in fact, that it is now creating the deep forebodings that mirror those of the fourteenth-century. Unlike that time, however, when the fears were focused on the changes that were actually causing the problems, today there is an unwillingness to even consider that economic forces may be the cause of the problems that so disturb us. And in what may be the supreme irony of this age, the religious right is one of the strongest opponents of any restraint on economic activity.

Not the Selfless Way

There are good Christians in our society, as reflected in the work of some of the best charitable organizations and many personal acts of kindness. But in this media-driven, highly politicized era, those who try to live by Christ's words are part of the anonymous background. They do not thrive on its competitiveness or seek media attention, and thus do not have much influence on the directions of change. Their faith is undoubtedly a comfort to them, but it is increasingly a personal faith, since public life is moving in such unchristian directions. Dislike of these directions undoubtedly motivates the religious right, but targeting government as the problem requires that they ignore the multitude of ways in which the modern economy works against the ways that Christ asks of his followers. All across the board, in fact, the policies pushed by the religious right are contrary to the tenets of Christianity as expressed so clearly in Christ's words in the Bible. Let us look at a few of them.

Prayer in the schools? Christ's words about public prayer are so explicit that they deserve quoting in full:

> And when you pray, do not be like the hypocrites, for they love to pray standing in the synagogues and on the street corners, to be seen by men. I tell you the truth, they have received their reward in full. But when you pray, go into your room, close the door and pray to you Father, who is unseen.

Welfare? Rather than being angry at the poor and blaming the government for their existence, the pervasive biblical obligation is to be charitable to the poor. In the first printing of the King James Bible in 1611, the Greek word for love, *agape*, was mistakenly translated as charity. This was an easy mistake to make since the word love is used consistently to suggest charitable behavior toward others; love means to be concerned for the well-being of others. This is the Great Commandment, but whether love or charity, it is hard to find it in the political agenda of the religious right, with its efforts to leave economic forces in charge of everything and the poor standing by roads with signs asking for work. It was the failure of private forms of charity during the Depression that led to the first federal social welfare programs.

Political activity? Stay away from it. Christ's words are straightforward: "Give unto Caesar what is Caesar's, and to God what is God's." Christians are to take care of their households and their communities, and to show the rightness of their way by their example rather than political activity: "By their fruits you shall know them." One of the Ten Commandments is "Thou shalt not kill," but the religious right strongly supports the death penalty and creating ever more powerful military weapons at a time when U.S. military dominance is unchallenged. Forgiveness? When Peter asks Christ how many times he should forgive his brother, Christ answers, "I tell you, not seven times, but seventy times seven times." Judging others? "Do not judge, or you too will be judged." Christ is especially critical of judging others without first looking into one's own heart. "Why do you look at the speck of sawdust in your brother's eye and pay no attention to the plank in your own eye? . . You hypocrite, first take the plank out of your own eye, and then you will see clearly to remove the speck from your brother's eye." When Christ came upon a woman about to be stoned to death for adultery, he says to her accusers: "He that is without sin among you, let him cast the first stone at her." When none did and all had departed, Jesus said to the woman, "Neither do I condemn you. . . Go now, and sin no more."

The only issue that is biblically safe for the religious right is abortion, but only because it is not mentioned in the Bible. The Bible is undoubtedly pro-life, but this is expressed most consistently in the requirement that children be loved and cared for at all stages of their growth. This was straightforward when Christ lived, since with population low and growth negligible, each new life was a gift, a treasure. We can only speculate about what his thoughts might be today with overpopulation a real threat and so many children receiving inadequate love and care. Even if the religious right were active in helping the "throwaway children" our society is producing in such numbers—by opening their homes to foster children, for example—its politics would not seem quite so unchristian. But taking injured children into one's own homes is not as satisfying as righteous indignation expressed in high-profile political activity.

If Christ's words grow intemperate, it is when they are directed against the spiritual pride of the Pharisees, who were the defenders of traditional morality of his time. But at least the Pharisees held to the letter of the Law, even if they ignored its spirit. The religious right, thanks to salvation by faith rather than works, can reject both the letter and the spirit of the Law, and then be rewarded with huge sums of money from powerful economic interests for saying what they want said, about reducing government regulation, taxes, and spending. The result is to reinforce the shameful reputation that Christianity has been gaining for centuries, of small, mean-spirited people following ways that suggest that selfishness is righteousness, and ready to fight anyone who threatens what they have.

Biblical Economics

The religious right says little about the economics of the Bible, which is understandable since a market-based economy must be close to the polar opposite of what the Bible asks for. The economics of the Bible is not liberal or conservative, socialist or capitalist. It includes private property but restricts it heavily, and goes to great lengths to avoid the concentration of wealth. At its core is a community that is responsible for assuring that everyone has a role to play in it, a role that is honored for its contribution to the community while discouraging the quest for more. There is no welfare in the conventional sense, but charity is a pervasive community obligation as well as a source of security. At its core is the belief that "Man does not live by bread alone." The unending quest for more is replaced by the urge to make life a reflection of God's love and the love of others.

Americans are usually surprised to learn that the Bible is so hostile to the quest for wealth, since it is the force that gives the free-market economy its momentum. What is heard at times is that the Bible is not opposed to wealth, which, while technically correct, is highly misleading. It is not hostile to wealth *per se,* since in a static, hierarchical society wealth is determined at birth by the position one is born into. Those born into favored positions have the obligations that go with their greater wealth: "From those who have been given much, much will be demanded." There is no call for the equal distribution of wealth, but to be satisfied with what is appropriate for one's station in life.

How are the specifics of this worked out in daily life? In the Old Testament, Proverbs is the book in which are collected the sayings by which traditional societies facilitate day-to-day life. Collected over several hundred years after the time of Solomon, it is full of the pithy sayings that establish the tone of a community's life:

> Better a little with the fear of the Lord
> than great wealth with turmoil.
> Better a meal of herbs where there is love,
> than a fattened calf with hatred. (15:16-7)

> A good name is more desirable than great riches;
> to be esteemed is better than silver and gold.
> (22:1)

> He who oppresses the poor shows contempt for
> their maker, but whoever is kind to the
> needy honors God. (14:31)

> A kind-hearted woman gains respect,
> but ruthless men gain only wealth. (11:16)

In the end, it is both wealth and poverty that are wrong:

> Give me neither poverty nor riches,
> but give me only my daily bread.
> Otherwise, I may have too much and disown you
> and say, Who is the Lord?
> Or I may become poor and steal,
> and so dishonor the name of my God. (30:8-9)

Christ only continues a long tradition:

> No one can serve two masters. Either he will love the one and hate the other, or he will be devoted to the one and despise the other. You cannot serve both God and Mammon (money). (Matthew 6:24)

> Be on your guard against all kinds of greed; a man's life does not consist in the abundance of his possessions. (Luke 12:15)

> For what will it profit a man if he gains the whole world but loses his soul. (Matthew 16:26)

A rich young man who obeyed the commandments asked Jesus what he still lacked:

> Jesus looked at him and loved him. "One thing you lack, "he said. "Go, sell everything you have and give to the poor, and you will have treasure in heaven. Then come, follow me. At this the man's face fell. He went away sad, because he had great wealth.
> Jesus looked around and said to his disciples, "How hard it is for the rich to enter the kingdom of God. . . It is easier for a camel to go through the eye of a needle than for a rich man to enter the kingdom of God." (Mark 10: 21-2)

John's message of love also touches on wealth:

> If anyone has material possessions and sees his brother in need but has no pity on him, how can the love of God be in him? Dear children, let us not love with words or tongue but with actions and in truth.
> (I John 3:17-18)

And Paul too:

> Those who desire to be rich fall into temptation, into
> a snare, into many senseless and hurtful desires that
> plunge men into ruin and destruction. For the love of
> money is the root of all kinds of evils.
>
> (1Timothy 6:9-10)

In all of this, it is more than just opposition to the quest for wealth; in the deepest sense it is an openness to life itself, as expressed in some of the most beautiful language in the Bible:

> Therefore I tell you, do not worry about your life,
> what you will eat or drink; or about your body, what
> you will wear. Is not life more important than food,
> and the body more important than clothes? Look at
> the birds of the air; they do not sow or reap or store
> away in barns, and yet your heavenly Father feeds
> them. Are you not much more valuable than they?
> Who of you by worrying can add a single hour to
> your life?
> And why do you worry about clothes? See how
> the lilies of the field grow. They do not labor or spin.
> Yet I tell you that not even Solomon in all his
> splendor was dressed like one of these.
>
> (Matthew 6:25-28)

Poverty was at the core of the religious genius of Saint Francis. His conversion occurred when he gave up the wealth of his prosperous merchant's family so he could "walk in the footsteps of Christ" with no possessions other than what he wore. His humility led him to establish his "minor" orders of "lesser" brothers early in the thirteenth-century, a time when most monks and priests were from the upper classes, were well dressed, and did not walk from place to place as did the Franciscans. The Poor Clares, too, were granted the "privilege of poverty," the need for which reflected on the wealth of the Church and the antagonism it caused. The result was that the common people trusted the Franciscans, and the movement grew rapidly to be an important part of the religious renaissance of the Age of Faith that was largely the work of lay people.

The Bible places heavy responsibilities on those with wealth, and it was not to be a source of pride. It is the wicked man who in Proverbs says, "My power and the might of my hand have gotten me this wealth," rather than thanking God for it, as the righteous would do. All roles were to be honored for their contributions to the ongoing life of the community. The important things were not material: "Having food and raiment, let us therewith be content." Or more simply yet in the Lord's Prayer: "Give us this day our daily bread."

As in all traditional societies, work is a positive value in the Bible. Everyone is expected to provide for their needs with their own labor and to help the less fortunate.

> Let the thief no longer steal, but rather let him labor, doing honest work with his hands, so that he may be able to give to those in need. (Ephesians 4:28)

The obligation to contribute to the common good is sustained by family honor. Each family wishes to be known not only as taking care of its own members but as providing for the needy as well. And to do so with a good heart. This is a common theme all through the Bible, including the Mosaic Law in the first five books of the Old Testament:

> Give generously to him and do so without a grudging heart; then because of this the Lord your God will bless you in all your work and in everything you put your hand to. (Deuteronomy 15:7)

But as with the sharing in hunting and gathering societies, being able to help others could create problems if it becomes a source of pride for the giver and humiliation of the recipient. Assistance was to be provided in the most constructive way possible, and in the medieval era this was accomplished by making the community responsible for ensuring that everyone had a productive role in it and the resources necessary to fulfill it. This was not only practical, since it made the poor productive, but it also contributed to their emotional well-being, by being able to meet their own needs and help others. And the resources to do this were to be provided as a matter of right, as a member of a community, and not as alms to a beggar. This is what led villagers in the medieval era to periodically redistribute the land so every family had an equal share, even to the point of providing it in small parcels scattered throughout the common fields so each had an equal share of the better and poorer soils. Efficiency was less important than equality and solidarity

The obligation to contribute to the community left it with assets that could be put to other uses that were important parts of medieval life, the feast days and holy days that crowded the medieval calendar and the mendicant orders of monks and nuns who obeyed Christ's call to rely on the generosity of others to support their work. Direct assistance was provided to widows, orphans, and the infirm, and the cottages built for them are still some of the most desirable properties in villages across Europe. Kahlil Gibran described work as love made visible, and this is very much in the spirit of biblical economics.

Taken together, these provisions did much to reduce the disparities in the economic circumstances within a community, but the Mosaic Law added other requirements:

When you reap the harvest of your land, you shall not reap your field to its very border; neither shall you gather the gleanings after the harvest. As you shall not strip your vineyard bare, neither shall you gather the fallen grapes of your vineyards; you shall leave them for the poor and the sojourner.   (Leviticus 19:9-10)

To borrow money is discouraged, but if adversity strikes, loans are to be provided without interest or collateral, and every seventh year—the sabbatical year—all loans are to be forgiven. It could be considered a form of charity except that family honor led people to strive to repay loans. If a family became so poor that it had to sell its land, it could not be sold in perpetuity, but was returned in the year of the jubilee, every fiftieth year—seven sabbaticals plus a year. When Isaiah charges, "Woe to you who add house to house, and join field to field, until no space is left, and you live alone in the land," he is condemning those who had so much land that others could not support themselves. As the Israelites grew wealthy they had strayed from the Law, and the great reformer was exhorting them to return to it.

It is said that justice is to the Old Testament what love is to the New. A feeling for justice requires that everyone have an honorable role in the community, one that enables them to contribute to it and help those in need. Individuals are protected by this, but they also have obligations, with the result being the security and emotional comfort that made villagers all over the world so resistant to "development" by outsiders. Biblical economics avoids the deep frustration we generate by demanding that everyone work while tolerating unemployment in the millions to keep inflation under control. The biblical way would be to share the available work rather than let the hardship fall on a few, who are then looked down on as failures. Perhaps the most important difference for the future is the modern quest for efficiency and higher productivity compared to keeping needs to a minimum to leave time and energy for the more important things, including the spirit.

*   *   *

The biblical economics reflected in medieval life can be thought of as the "totally other" of our religious heritage—the ways of a traditional society that are radically different from our own. They are far more different than Marxism, for example, which handled the ownership of productive assets differently but was otherwise just as production oriented. That there are still cultural memories from the Age of Faith probably accounts for the sense of loss felt as we move further from its ways, but also telling us how different we have become.

This brings us to an important question: Would such religiously defined ways be useful again in the future? One factor suggests the answer is yes, the depletion of the fossil fuels, that could drive us toward the small-scale, decentralized, and less mobile ways that renewable resources can sustain. This suggests that a smooth evolutionary process may be possible, but is there any way of assessing the prospects for this?

Again, all we can really do is look to the past to see what can be learned that might apply to the future. Fortunately, some impressive work has been done in this field.

CHAPTER TEN

Evolutionary Openings

The principle is straightforward: evolutionary progress depends on effective adaptation to changing circumstances. The problem is reality, and knowing which adaptations are life-giving ones and which are movements further into a dead end. Ambiguity plagues us now, making decisions difficult and turning resolve into inaction. In one decade, the 1980s, the stock market seemed stuck below 2,000, inflation and unemployment were both high, and the era of cheap energy was widely declared to be over. In the next decade, the 1990s, oil was cheaper than it had ever been, the stock market passed 10,000, and inflation and unemployment were both low. No one predicted such wide swings; indeed, there would have been no basis for doing so. But people changed accordingly and the stock market went from being a risky place for one's money to one promising retirement as a millionaire. The steady stream of changes in both decades were at times wrenching, but the effects on long-standing trends were virtually nil. They were simply "blips" in the dominant pattern of economic advance, not unlike the Vietnam War and the energy crisis.

In the longer period since World War II, however, one thing has clearly changed—the confidence in where the dominant trend is taking us. Still, there seems to be no choice but to continue on the path we are on. The memories of simpler times are there, but so pervasive are the ambiguities that it is even hard to say whether we prefer the old or the new. Is it better to have the freedom to rise as high as we can but with failure an ever-present possibility, or to have one's livelihood determined by a family's farm, shop, or craft? To live in a close but demanding family, or in circumstances of our own choosing but possibly alone and without help when needed? To live in a community with set ways, lifelong ties, and clear responsibilities, or in free, wide-open ways but little that can be trusted or counted on? Is it better to listen to quite average music played by friends and neighbors, or the world's best music reproduced electronically? Is it just romanticism that makes growing one's food and cutting firewood anything but hard labor, or is it just paychecks from jobs in an impersonal, highly competitive economy that makes work anything more than a way of making ends meet? Is our way of life breaking down barriers to a fuller, richer life, or are superficial, short-lived gimmicks replacing wise, time-tested ways?

It is fortunate that everyone responds to such questions differently, since this is the source of what stability there still is. Yet it also means that steps are not being taken to avoid the barriers our way of life is coming up against. Industrial society has reached the point where a cold, hard, scientific view of things leads pretty much toward what *The Limits to Growth* study came up with several decades ago, of a long grinding-down process ahead. From such a theoretical point of view the obvious thing to do would be to begin as quickly as possible to divert the growth lines in sustainable directions, but this seems unlikely given the freedom and affluence we still have. Theory is one thing; it tends to be straightforward, neat and clean. Reality is different; it is usually messy, and rife with contradictions and dilemmas. Where might we find help in at least understanding the ambiguities we face and how they could work themselves out?

Dynamics of Rise, Fall, and Transformation

The process by which civilizations in the past rose and fell was the lifelong focus of perhaps the most eminent historian of the twentieth-century, Arnold Toynbee. His work was done at a time before academic specialization became the rule—a specialization that now seems almost a way to avoid thinking about where we are heading. For several decades before World War II Toynbee put his prodigious energy into a ten-volume *Study of History*, and its organizing principle was challenge and response—how societies responded to the forces that threatened their futures or failed to, just what we face today. He collected a vast amount of information about the rise and fall of civilizations, and it helps us to place our circumstances in a larger historical context.

Toynbee summarized his conclusions in the opening essay of *Civilization on Trial*, (1948) which was published a year after he finished his *Study*:

> A majority of the score of civilizations known to us appear to have broken down already, and a majority of this majority have trodden to the end the downward path that terminates in dissolution.
>
> Our *post mortem* examination of dead civilizations does not enable us to caste the horoscope of our own civilization or any other that is still alive. . . [But] when we make an empirical comparative study of the paths which the dead civilizations have respectively traveled from breakdown to dissolution, we do here seem to find a certain measure of Spenglerian uniformity, and this, after all, is not surprising. Since breakdown means loss of control, this in turn means the lapse of freedom into automatism, and whereas free acts are infinitely variable and utterly unpredictable, automatic processes are apt to be uniform and regular. (p. 12)

This was written before the free-market economy had become the dominant organizing force of modern life. The "Spenglerian uniformity" Toynbee warns of would now be the spreading order created by the global economy, since it has displaced the political faiths, fascism and communism especially, of the pre-war decades when Toynbee was working on his *Study*. The "loss of control" would now be reflected in the fear that any change could jeopardize the stability of the economy on which everything depends, causing our ways to be ever more "uniform and regular." It now takes an expert to look at a photo of an urban center and identify the continent it is on, since everywhere they look the same. Manufacturing facilities are similar, too, and if transportation networks remain different it is only because poorer countries cannot afford to build the complex networks the wealthier can. Students trying to plan their lives feel clearly the "lapse of freedom into automatism" when only a handful of fields offer solid prospects for a job that makes marriage and family reasonably secure, and even grade-school children are told in no uncertain terms that they must be proficient with computers if they want to get a job. And even though the growth of e-commerce was vigorous and diverse for a while, it is settling down, as other innovations have, to that which is "uniform and regular"—and profitable enough to survive. This is in contrast to the "infinitely variable" ways that made travel so much more interesting in the past than it is now.

Toynbee describes the cultural traps that "dead civilizations have respectively traveled from breakdown to dissolution," but he also points to the openings we should look for, the "free acts [that] are infinitely variable and utterly unpredictable." It may be the autumn of the industrial age, but it is the springtime of the sustainable age, the niche that is open and ready to be explored and occupied. But how the new is created will be related to how the old ends, and Toynbee continues with a fuller description of the process of decline, and to the matter ultimately of most importance, that of transformation. The terminology is different, reflecting the changes that have occurred since Toynbee's time, but the conclusion reached could well be the one we are headed toward:

The process of disintegration does not proceed evenly;

it jolts along in alternating spasms of rout, rally, and rout. In the last rally but one, the dominant minority succeeds in temporarily arresting the society's lethal self-laceration by imposing on it the peace of a universal state. Within the framework of the dominant minority's universal state the proletariat creates a universal church, and after the next rout, in which the disintegrating civilization finally dissolves, the universal church may live on to become the chrysalis from which a new civilization eventually emerges. To modern Western students of history, these phenomena are most familiar in the Greco-Roman examples of the *Pax Romana* and the Christian Church. . . The same relation between a declining civilization and a rising religion can be observed in a dozen other cases. In the Far East, for instance, the Ts'in and Han Empire plays the Roman Empire's part, while the role of the Christian Church is assumed by the Mahayana school of Buddhism.   (pp. 13-14)

The "rout, rally, and rout" would be the booms and busts of the economy, while the "peace of a universal state" would not be something imposed by a dominant minority but by the majority of voters in a democratic society. If there is a state church, it would have to be the market faith that integrates our society so effectively and gives it such power. Christianity has been so heavily associated with the market faith that it could be pulled down with it, but if this were the case it would leave the question of what would function as "the chrysalis from which a new civilization eventually emerges." The Eastern faiths have the best record of effectively ordering societies, but they ask for ways that are so alien to the West, especially the cessation of desire, that they are unlikely to function as an integrating force here. There are westernized versions of the Eastern faiths and a plethora of modern faiths, but they reflect the quest for a personal spirituality, a quest that, while making sense in the context of the market faith, says little about the selflessness that enabled the great faiths to organize societies. The quest now is for a good "religious investments," ones that pay off well and with low costs, in personal freedom especially. While understandable in a market-driven society, such faiths would have little capacity to establish a new order to replace a failing market one.

The tendency for societies in crises to turn to a new faith could, in our case, be facilitated by the unchristian ways of our times. After experiencing the consequences of moving so far from our religious heritage, a revitalized Christianity could provide a new opening by making a conscious decision to return to Christ's ways. Americans regularly describe this country as a Christian nation, but the overall tenor of our times is close to the opposite of what Christ asks for, of love, forgiveness, charity, and finding satisfaction in doing for others. The one advantage of Christianity for the future is that the biblical heritage is still there, and still fresh. Could it "become the chrysalis from which a new civilization eventually emerges"?

This is what Toynbee seems to expect. He compares the cyclical view of history of the Greeks and Indians with the progressive view of the Jews and Zoroastrians. He speaks of the greatest Greek and Indian, Aristotle and Buddha, as accepting without question that history is a "dreary round of vain repetitions," and contrasts this with the Jewish and Zoroastrian idea of a "divine plan which is revealed to us in this fragmentary glimpse, but which transcends our human powers of vision and understanding in every dimension." The latter would seem to be a description of the mysterious process of cultural evolution, but Toynbee concludes by arguing that the two are not necessarily contradictory:

> While civilizations rise and fall and, in falling, give rise to others, some purposeful enterprise, higher than theirs, may all the time be making headway, and, in a divine plan, the learning that comes through the

suffering caused by the failure of civilization may be the sovereign means of progress.

He concludes the essay with a profound question:

> Will some comparable spiritual enlightenment be kindled by the 'displaced persons' who are the counterparts, in our world, of those Jewish exiles to whom so much was revealed in their painful exile by the waters of Babylon? The answer to this question, whatever it may be, is of greater moment than the still inscrutable destiny of our world-encompassing Western civilization." (p. 15)

The Parable of the Boats

Many years ago I came across a parable that stayed with me even though its author's name did not. It spoke of the quest for God as people rowing boats upstream against the current of human selfishness. Progress was slow and required continuous effort; periodically individuals would falter and be swept downstream toward degradation and violence. But on the whole, progress was made; the boats moved slowly upstream. Then, in recent times, some rowers turned their boats around and, rowing easily downstream, convinced others that their rapid progress was proof of the logic of their actions. Soon most boats had turned around, and so strong is the current of human selfishness that we have moved a good ways downstream, so far that we are beginning to feel the pain of being far from God. We also hear what sounds like a cataract ahead, and instinctively fear it.

Enough has been said about where the currents may be taking us; it is easier to find fault with the currents of our times than ways of turning around and returning to the task of moving upstream. Concerns about the difficulties involved are, unfortunately, reasonable; they are a measure of our predicament. It may be hard to imagine how we can turn away from the path we are on, but it is even harder to imagine how our ancestors overcame primate instincts for sex and dominance or the warlord kings of the early civilizations. But they did, and in the end we have no choice but to strive for this, too, if our species is to survive on this small, beautiful planet. The longer we wait, the harder it will be. The only questions now are how smooth—or rough—the process will be and whether the final results will enhance our humanness or drive us back toward the ways of our primate ancestors.

The faith we can have today is in the process of cultural evolution, that it will work its mysterious ways again as it has in the past, and by favoring the same peaceful genes. The selflessness asked for by the great faiths, perhaps even the universality of the religious impulse, may well be the expression of the peaceful genes that has been the critical element in cultural evolution. Regardless of whether religion is considered to be the ultimate truth or a man-made crutch, it has proven itself capable of binding people together in stable and satisfying ways. The struggle between reason and faith will end when it becomes clear that faith simply makes life better—easier and more comfortable as well as more secure and in balance with the environment. If religion is a crutch, it is one that a frail humanity needs because of the aggressive genes it still carries along with the peaceful ones. Any progress made in moving back upstream against the current of human selfishness, no matter how slow and halting, will still bring with it the confidence that we are moving in the right direction once again, that we are in the mainstream of human evolution rather than trying to stand above it like technological gods. We will be moving in a direction with proven evolutionary potential.

Because of the explosive growth of recent centuries we have constraints our ancestors did not have, but we also have advantages they did not have. Knowledge is the most important one, not only the extraordinary amount of information that has been accumulated but also the opportunity to test it with the equally extraordinary cultural contacts of our times. It is when information is placed in the light of experience that it becomes knowledge, perhaps even wisdom. This is the way of seeing through the ethnocentrisms all societies collect, the way of giving the lie to statements such as life in the past being "nasty, brutish and short," that selfish genes are the source of evolutionary success, and that there is no end to how wealthy and free we can become. It is also essential to keep in mind that many of the most important technologies are sustainable, and that we bring unprecedented amounts of flexibility and willingness to change to the task of moving toward ways that work in the times ahead. New Legends of the Fall are almost certain to come out of the process—new taboos about elements of the modern that endanger sustainability in the future. The territory ahead will be new, but exploring it will be done in the old evolutionary ways, by pioneers finding out what works and what does not. And rather than seeing only a long grinding-down process ahead, it is more fitting to see the future as a time of incredible challenge and excitement, and with huge potentials for both gains and losses.

The evolutionary process provides us with information that can facilitate such a future, but there is no point in denying that it also presents us with hazards, especially those associated with high levels of population, resource use, and environmental damage, all compounded by the ubiquitous weapons and the willingness to use them. But there are hopeful trends, too, and we will look at the most important one before taking on the question of violence.

Convergence in the Midst of Divergence

As the global economy loses steam there will be a steady increase in diversity, in economics, culture, and uses of the environment. It will be initiated by the movement toward local and regional self-sufficiency as transportation becomes more expensive and renewable resources more important. This means a more dispersed population, smaller-scale economic activities, and a greater dependency on both the community and the biological productivity of surrounding environments. All of this is to the good, the movement toward the inevitable future. But there will be hazards, too. An important one is that, with the declining importance of the global economy, there will be fewer incentives to preserve peaceful relations between nations. This would apply primarily to countries in more desperate circumstances than the U.S., with larger populations and fewer resources, but disputes could increase here, too, between regions, communities, and even neighbors as circumstances grew tighter.

If this is not to be the case, it could well be due to the spread of an ethical pattern that enables people to live and work together without fear of being taken advantage of by others. There is a precedent for this—the ways of hunters and gatherers; its critical advantage was that groups could hold to their peaceful ways without fear of being left vulnerable to the aggressive. The most common justification for aggressiveness is that it is necessary as protection against those who would otherwise take advantage of us, even that offense is the best defense. If this is not to be the case in the future, it could be because people living over a wide area gravitated to a set of values that enabled them to live together peacefully—toward an ethic that made peacefulness safe.

There are indications that such a movement could be evolving now out of the convergence of the ethics of the great world faiths. The ecumenical search for unity, mutual under-standing, and respect among all faiths has led to the recognition of elements common to all of them, and this is especially striking in the similarities of the high points of the Eastern and Western traditions, Buddhism and Christianity. Neither Buddha nor Christ wrote anything themselves, but because Buddha lived until he was eighty years old and trained many monks, there is an extensive record of the kind of person he was and what he asks of his followers. Descriptions of him sound much like those of Christ, that he was strong-willed and authoritative but gentle in manner and speech, and with infinite benevolence—"the compassionate one." Buddha and Christ both accepted the theological answers they grew up with, and neither was interested in metaphysics; Buddha called it "the jungle, the desert, the puppet-show, the writhing, the entanglement of speculation" that leads only to disputes and resentments, never wisdom and peace. Christ said "anyone who will not receive the kingdom of God like a little child will never enter it." But while Buddha and Christ did not challenge the theological premises of the traditions they were born into, both advanced their ethical content significantly, and it is here that the similarities are so striking as to seem almost miraculous.

For both, saintliness was not in knowledge but in self-less and benevolent living. Like Christ, Buddha scandalized the brahmins by accepting into his order members of all castes, and then asking his disciples to "Go into all lands and preach this gospel. Tell them that the poor and the lowly, the rich and the high, are all one." As with Christ, the power of Buddha's words reflect the power of his inspiration: "Thus does he live as a binder-together of those who are divided, an encourager of those who are friends, a peacemaker, a lover of peace, impassioned for peace, a speaker of words that make for peace." He too asked that good actions be returned for evil, love for hate, and to not retaliate when slandered or abused. He took no thought for the morrow, was provided for by those he visited, and shocked others by eating with a courtesan, all as Christ had done. The importance of love is perhaps most surprising: "Let a man over-come anger by kindness, evil by good. . . Victory breeds hatred, for the conquered is unhappy. . . Never in the world does hatred cease by hatred; hatred ceases by love." The detachment that is such an important part of what Buddha asks for is reflected in Christ's words, that "Whoever wants to save his life will lose it, but whoever loses his life for my sake will find it." The greeting Buddha used, "Peace to all beings," is close to the Jewish "Peace be with you." Even the subsequent accretions of Buddhism and Christianity are similar, including the miraculous birth, saints (the Buddhist form being Bodhisattvas, or future Buddhas, who also refrained from extinguishing themselves in Nirvana in order to help others), and the drama and color of ritual, which must be accepted as part of the lifeblood of human-kind.

It is an attractive vision, of behavior coalescing around an ethical pattern that offers the best hope for a long and peaceful human existence on Earth. Many people would undoubtedly be attracted to such ways, but the scarcity of opportunities to do so only confirms the barriers to them now. One of the most important barriers is the "value free" ways claimed for the market economy, but as conditions grow more difficult this could easily lead to the free-for-all that degenerates into the violence of "take or be taken." How a universal ethic could emerge and spread is far from knowable, but it could be one of the paths that emerged as the mainstream lost momentum. The ways that led to peaceful cooperation would begin to stand out from those that led toward discontent, anger, or violence.

The most hopeful evolutionary process is one shaped by a solid, proven ideal that can be held to firmly—as by faith—while dealing with the inevitable "messiness" of the real world. The history of cultural evolution provides insights into this messiness, including what pulls societies down. The premise of this book is that humans yearn for peacefulness, and in the end this will win out, but also that the currents of our time could lead to the violence in which the violent genes, in the process of killing themselves off, could take many of the innocent with them. The question of how best to cope with violence is thus one that cannot be avoided, but also—and more hopefully—can be learned about from the past, especially how people and cultures managed to cope with violence and finally overcome it.

Dealing With Violence

The aggressive urges are held in check now by major expenditures in everything from security guards and local police to huge defense budgets and international peacekeeping efforts. There is little question that such expenditures are necessary, that there are individuals, groups, and nations ready to take advantage of their absence. How existing weapons might be put to use cannot be known, but to point guns out windows at neighbors, as the survivalists do, or bomb buildings full of ordinary people, as the terrorist do, could be the first indications of how the killer instincts might be expressed—but also how they may be killed off, or at least discredited. The weapons in military arsenals all over the world are a different matter; control of them could turn critical quickly, just as people on horses forced herding peoples to become mounted warriors. The great majority of people will yearn for the safe, peaceful circumstances that encourage the age-old comforts of family, community, work, faith, and the beauty of the world. As has always been the case, the tensions between the violent and the peaceful will be the stuff of history, and point to the role of culture in providing incentives for peacefulness and barriers to aggressiveness.

There could well be a new splitting of the ways between the peaceful and the aggressive, one similar to that which occurred when herders went their separate ways from farmers following the invention of agriculture. The individuals who would "rather fight than switch" now would be the counterpart of the hunters who resisted settling down to take up the digging stick and do what was condescendingly seen as women's work. These herders were almost certainly the more spirited and masculine among the hunters, but their peaceful heritage would not have led them to be so destructive if had not been for the unstable equilibrium created by the domestication of the horse. This forced all groups to become violent—whether they wanted to or not—if they were to survive. We, unfortunately, have the weapons as well as the heritage to use them. It is a chilling thought, since it means significant probabilities of violence in the future.

A case can be made that this is what we are programmed for, yet I persist in the belief that the peaceful genes are there, and that they are the dominant ones in the majority of people. This means they should have strategies for dealing with the violent individuals, and to do so without being militarized themselves. The potential for the dark age scenarios is there, but there is also the history of how violence has been held in check. We will take them in that order, from the darkest outcomes to the most hopeful ways of making things difficult for the aggressive genes.

The process could be started innocently enough by those who are unwilling to let go of the heady achievements of the fully evolved industrial economy, just as herders resisted giving up the excitement of the hunt. They will see moving toward sustainability as defeatism, weakness, or lack of courage, as turning away from the proud Western spirit that conquers barriers rather than adapts to them. There will be calls for more profits to motivate industry to undertake riskier investments, more government spending for defense, and more promises that the last of the resources can be exploited while keeping the productive and the beautiful from turning into the dying and the ugly. It is not an attractive vision, especially since it won't work, not for long anyway. And the setbacks, when they come, will require a scapegoat to blame them on, with the likely target being those who opposed the effort in the first place. Such "traitors" would have to be punished in who knows what unpleasant ways. It is a dangerous business, for everyone, since it could take events in the directions that made apocalyptic thinking so important in Western history.

The many ways in which violence could spread are reflected in the fertile imaginations of the science fiction writers, from space-based nuclear wars to neighbors reduced to fighting over the last scraps of food. There are many ways in which the killer genes could be killed off, but let us assume that the peaceful will try to go their own ways as much as they can while the aggressive try to control them for their own purposes. The consequences could range from the most murderous—the decimation of the world's population—to the peaceful finding ways of frustrating the violent. Nuclear war would at least destroy people quickly, and if the physical plant of industrial society was destroyed, too, it would at least reduce the chances of continuing the war until the Earth was barren of life. (That would be hard to do anyway, since nature is so resilient; it survived the natural debacle that killed off the dinosaurs and a majority of other species to return with more beauty and diversity than ever—even if it took the huge lengths of time that nature has but humans are unlikely to have.) And there is logic in MAD—mutually assured destruction—that keeps nuclear weapons sheathed. Chemical and biological weapons could be more pernicious, and more difficult to resist other than by trying to get as far away from them as possible.

The prospects for small-scale dark ages could well be more worrisome than large-scale ones since they are more likely —some argue they are already underway—and have the potential of leading to dreadful forms of stability, such as rule by drug lords or bandit chiefs. The Mongols were unusual in killing everyone they encountered; more common was for warlords to keep their prey alive so they could be forced to work as hard as physically possible and with a minimum of food and shelter. The interplay of the violent and the peaceful has at times been close to the predator-prey relationships in nature. Human predators may learn how to benefit from their prey on an ongoing basis, but this would require fighting off other predators eying the same prey, and then fighting over it like murderous animals—one of the ways in which the killer genes were killed off. Perhaps the prey could find ways of encouraging this, which would be safer than trying to kill the predators themselves, since violence tends to beget violence. Even the winners in the struggles with other predators could end up looking enviously on the ways of their peaceful prey, as preferable to constantly looking over their shoulders for those bent on killing them. Examples of peaceful-ness are undoubtedly more effective in controlling violent people than challenging them violently, since that only confirms the necessity of violence, even for those who have grown to dislike it.

The range of predator-prey relationships in human

history tells us about the depths human nature is capable of. In his book *Evolutionary Economics,* Kenneth Boulding places human activities in a biological context:

> The complexity of habitats means that competition in ecosystems is extremely imperfect and that a species threatened with decline in its niche often retreats to some protected habitat where the decline is arrested, sometimes for a very long time, from which it sometimes emerges again when conditions are favorable. We find the same thing happening in society, where persecution, for instance, or conquest may drive a particular people or culture underground or to the hills, where they survive until in some sense they emerge as the system changes. This husbanding of genetic material is an important principle in the evolutionary process.

Remaining poor has often been the best way of discouraging predators; it was the only strategy available to the Russian peasants, for instance. It works best in unproductive or isolated areas with little wealth to attract would-be warlords, but such areas also mean low material standards of living and the low population densities that limit cultural richness. Slavery is not feasible in most circumstances, since the supervision required cannot be justified by the returns. It was slavery on the large, impersonal scale of irrigated river valleys or commercial plantations that paid off well but also tested human endurance. Even under such circumstances, however, slaves still had incentives to work as little as possible. And slavery on the small household scale often softened to the point where slaves became members of the household.

As the skills of the warlords evolved they learned how to exploit their prey more efficiently. Feudalism can be thought of in this way, as a way of managing large numbers of subjects by providing the incentive of working the lord's land in return for a share of the food produced. The key advantage for peasants was that they gained the right to use the lord's land on their own, although at the cost of swearing loyalty to him. (The original definition of the word *peasant* was one who owed allegiance to a lord.) The work done for a lord can be thought of as the equivalent of rent in a monetized system, except that peasants were less vulnerable to fluctuating crop prices or increasing rents. The disadvantage was that feudalism offered few incentives to increase agricultural productivity, but this also meant less competitiveness. In Europe, where the Church and the village courts watched over the feudal relationship, it led to stability, attractive landscapes, and the Age of Faith. Feudalism has a hostile sound to us, but the decline of urban industrial society could make it useful again. For example, if falling values for urban assets left individuals without funds to purchase land and landowners without buyers for land they wanted to sell, both could benefit from an agreement of a feudal nature they freely entered into.

In some cases, predatory activities brought advanced ways with them. Whatever can be said against the Spanish conquest of Mexico, and there is much, it displaced a harsh warlord society, one that preyed on people in many ways but most notably for sacrificial victims. Cortez could never have conquered the Aztecs with 300 men and 16 horses if it had not been for the help of the peoples the Aztecs exploited. One thing cannot be disputed: no equilibrium will be stable unless it is supported by all parties involved, including the mass of people. It is when all parties feel secure that they will be willing to move in ways that are mutually beneficial. The village courts in Europe reflect the effort to create a symbiosis between ruler and ruled, something that is important for the higher faiths, since stability is necessary if they are to function effectively.

Cultures organized by the great faiths grew strong by using their ideals to integrate societies effectively. They developed ways that were advantageous to everyone so all could support them, rather than be torn apart by dissention and violence. Several of the cultures which achieved this were described in Chapter 8; here, three will be looked at again from the perspective of how they overcame aggressiveness to create the stability that characterized traditional agricultural societies. The ones that achieved this for long periods of time are the ones that offer proven instruction in this matter.

China's stability was aided by its isolation from most of the mounted horsemen, as reflected in the absence of feudalism. Private ownership of land encouraged farmers to work hard, and this enabled China to support a large population in a country with a high percentage of rough, unproductive terrain. It also meant the absence of a hereditary class of landed nobles, making it easier for the Confucian authorities to defend the peasants and honor them as the foundation of Chinese society. This alliance proved quite stable, especially since cities were the seat of Confucian authority. The strength of the Confucian system was its horizontal integration, its ethical/political order, but its vertical integration was weaker since its answers to the ultimate questions were less satisfactory. Other religions came into China to meet this need, but still, the lack of strong vertical integration weakened the internal controls that are so important if a religion is to effectively order a society. This left a heavy responsibility on the emperor and Confucian officials; China was very much a bureaucratic society, which is always a dangerous thing. It was when China's leadership deteriorated that landlordism and poverty led to the rebellions that marked the passing of one dynasty to the next. Its weaker vertical integration also meant pride was necessary to hold China together, even though in most of the higher faiths pride is a sin, the first of the Seven Deadly Sins of Christianity. China's experience's suggests one reason for the Old Testament warning against pride, that it goes before a fall. Pride caused China to look down on all foreigners as barbarians, so when the Westerners forced their way in, China's pride was dealt a severe blow, contributing to the abrupt collapse of its ancient order. The downfall of this powerful, well-organized society is something we should keep in mind, especially given the pride we have in our achievements and our dependency on government to keep things working.

The alliance that sustained medieval Europe was similar to China's in that it was between the common people and the Roman Church. But it formed relatively late and faced much more opposition, initially from nobles and princes, then merchants and bankers, and finally enlightenment thinkers and powerful kings, all bent on freeing themselves from Church authority. The "free air of the cities" is often seen as critical in the displacement of medieval economics by market economics. Yet Christianity must have provided an effective vertical integration since medieval ways persisted for centuries after the fragmentation of religious authority, especially in rural areas. Still, modern ways chipped away steadily at the old order, and as power gravitated from the landowning classes in rural areas to the commercial classes in towns and cities, the religious world-view of a traditional agricultural society was inexorably displaced by the rational, scientific worldview of the modern era. How adaptable this new way of life will be in the future could well determine whether sustainable ways evolve smoothly or rise from the ashes of a new dark age.

India, as the Paradise of the Gods, provides the clearest expression of the integration that religion can provide. With no centralized governmental (until the British took over) or religious authority, Hinduism ordered India for several thousand years, and it remains the traditional culture that survives most intact today. This cannot be explained using Western theories of political organization; India should be in chaos today, as it periodically is in places, but most of the country continues to function in its timeless ways. How can this be explained?

One key almost certainly is the Hindu/Buddhist concept of the divine as a spirit in all living things. This led to the non-violence that caused India to be relatively relaxed in resisting invaders and in dealing with them as rulers. This was helpful because India's conquerors, feeling little danger, felt less need to treat the Indians harshly. Rather than having to demonize Indians to justify severe controls, they could enjoy India's cultural achievements and, over time, absorb Indian ways. This was facilitated by the way Hinduism saw all religions as valid, as different paths to the same end, since that made religion less apt to be a source of contention. This was true even when invaders came in with very different religious beliefs, such as Islam after the twelfth-century.

The second key to the survival of India's traditional ways is the horizontal integration Hinduism provides, especially the caste system that orders its economy. Caste effectively ties every-day life to the quest for liberation through karma and reincarnation. No other religion provides such an integrated whole, with one result being India's capacity to cope with all manner of pressures, internal as well as external. India has been confident enough to allow foreign influences in without fear of falling apart, while China felt the need to force everyone into the Han way, including the minorities on its periphery. This has been continued by the communists, but still leaving a residue of hostility, as reflected in Tibet today. India's tolerance is at the core of a culture that over the centuries encouraged a rich, flexible, yet stable culture.

Even the classical heritage now dominant in the West has a non-violent side to it, even if in an unexpected form. It was presented in one of the most intriguing books to come out of the environmental era, *The Comedy of Survival,* by Joseph Meeker. (1974) A classicist, he distinguishes between two types of heroes, the tragic and the comic, as depicted in classical literature. The tragic hero is the one that is most honored, the individual who is willing to risk everything for a goal he knows to be right, is unswerving in defense of moral principle, and does not hesitate to take on powers greater than himself. Yet each individual sees right and wrong differently, and such single-minded zeal has led to conflict throughout Western history. Its extreme form today would be the terrorist who sees himself as giving his life for a noble cause—the same mentality that is apt to challenge resource limits. On top of this, the tragic hero is usually an unpleasant fellow to be around, taking himself seriously, unwilling to compromise, and condescending to those who disagree with him.

The comic hero, in contrast, is usually relegated to the status of a buffoon, as base and silly, although innocuous. His goal is simply to survive and enjoy himself as best he can. Unwilling to fight, he tries to outwit his enemies and the authorities. His victories are small; survival and life are what are important to him; no cause is worth dying for. The comic hero is friendly toward life and takes things as they are; he would rather win the girl than strive for abstract ideals. Life is an end in itself, rather than a struggle between right and wrong. Meeker suggests that it may be time for us to honor such virtues. He argues that it is the comic hero who will better insure our survival, the human animal adapting to the world as it is and enjoying what it has to offer, rather than trying to make it into something it is not—and probably cannot be. It brings to mind the book by Johann Huizinga, *Homo Ludens: A Study of The Play Element in Culture,* which sees much of the richness of the medieval era as organized play, as a way of continuing the enjoyable activities of childhood into adult life.

Above all, it is important to remember that history is not necessarily destiny. The dark ways of the Mongols turned toward the light of Tibetan Buddhism, and the bloodthirsty Vikings became the peaceful Scandinavians of today. Hitler and Stalin both failed, and the French and Germans are putting aside their animosities after centuries of warfare. There is much evidence that, in the end at least, the meek do inherit the Earth.

The Opportunity—If It Can Be Realized

All such considerations lead us back to the evolutionary movement toward sustainability, and to the importance of beginning it while the world is still relatively well ordered, resources are available, and before everyone is even more dependent on the global economy. Alexis de Tocqueville was insightful in so much of what he wrote in *Democracy in*

America; will he be equally insightful in what he wrote about religion?

> Religion, then, is simply another form of hope, and it is as natural to the human heart as hope itself. Men cannot abandon their religious faith without a kind of aberration of intellect and a violent distortion of their true nature; an invincible inclination draws them back. Unbelief is an accident; faith is the only permanent state of mankind. (1988, p. 297)

Evolutionary history supports this conclusion, in the past anyway, and, we may reasonably expect, in the future, too. Much depends on whether there are good outlets for peacefulness, and in this, too, there are reasons for hopefulness. When opportunities abounded it may have made sense to forego long-standing ties with family, friends, and community for ways that seemed to offer wealth and excitement. But as the age of expansion draws to a close, the values it encouraged will lose their usefulness. The new economic circumstances will be more like those of the past—those that religions have a proven capacity to order. Their logic of relying on peaceful cooperation to make life good will improve as resources grow scarce, mobility declines, and decentralization occurs. Under such circumstances, ties with others will become more important, and loyalty, trustworthiness, and generosity will once again be virtues by which an individual is known in a community. There will be fewer opportunities for the exploitive, self-centered behavior honored today, since they thrive in big cities, big firms, and big governments. Instead, there will be more honor for the individual who contributes to the quality of life in neighborhoods and communities. As these smaller institutions become more important, there will be less need to rely on government for so many things. A good name will permit full participation in a community, and labor will once again be more an act of participation in a collective life than the source of a paycheck.

Children will become more important, for both parents and the community as a whole, so everyone will have an incentive to see that they grow up in healthy ways.

Traditions are simply devices that evolve over time to make life better. All societies utilize them, and it is only our obsessive individualism that has turned them into something that interferes with the full development of the self. Traditions offer a different path to fulfillment, since if the family and community are good, life is good; humans are, after all, a social species. The era of technological advance and resource abundance will, in time, be seen as an aberration, an extraordinary one, no doubt, but one that was hard on people in its own ways. Sustainable technologies will help in the times ahead, but it is unlikely that they will support a totally new way of life, if for no other reason that it would have to be built from scratch, a huge evolutionary task. The most important changes ahead are more apt to be ones that build on a cultural heritage which, even if far from perfect, still has a logic to it that was lost in the age of affluence. The exotic philosophies and "feel good" religions that fascinate us now are apt to end up among the excesses of the modern era, as no longer useful in the circumstances that make the movement toward sustainability necessary.

It has been said that true heroism is to see the world as it is and to love it. This not only means to deal with the liabilities we have with understanding and good heart but to capitalize on our assets in the same way, especially the peaceful genes that are the great gift of our ancestors. They will provide the feeling of rightness that comes with the ways that enabled our ancestors to separate themselves from the other primates. There is much to relearn in this process, especially how to pull families and communities together, to raise healthy and happy children, to allow elders a useful and agreeable life, and to recreate the worldview that sustained such ways, including its rituals and festivities. Everywhere there will be opportunities for healthy work, much of it with one's own hands, and much of it in cooperation with other people and with nature. We will be exchanging the grand achievement of large-scale technological society for the modest accomplishments of life on a human scale. We will once again be a part of humankind's great journey, and with this will come the stability, continuity, and satisfactions that have sustained societies throughout history. They will permit the deepening of culture, the enrichment of lives lived simply, and the comfort of knowing that our relationship with the environment is sustainable. We will again act in ways that justify the name of our species, *sapiens*—intelligent and wise.

Warren Johnson

REFERENCES

Africa.
Chinua Achebe's novels, along with *Things Fall Apart,* include *Arrow of God, No Longer at East, Anthills of the Savannah,* and *A Man of the People,* all from Anchor Books. Barbara Kingsolver's *Poisonwood Bible* (New York: Haperperennial, 1999) provides a good feeling for the problems in the Congo, and West Africa in general. Anthropologist Colin Turnbull writes of his long experiences in Africa in *The Lonely African* (Garden City, NJ: Doubleday, 1963) In *The Africans* (New York: Vintage Books, 1987), journalist Richard Lamb describes the corruption and inefficiency in both government and business that has derailed modernization.

Billington, James H., *The Icon and the Axe* (New York: Knopf, 1966), an outstanding cultural history of Russia.

Boulding, Kenneth, *Evolutionary Economics* (Berkeley: Sage Publications, 1981), p. 19.

Campbell, Colin J., and Jean H. Laherrere, "The End of Cheap Oil," *Scientific American,* March 1998, pp. 78-83.

Carneiro, Robert L., "A Theory of the Origin of the State," *Science,* 28 August 1970, vol. 169, pp. 733-738.

Chagnon, Napoleon, *Yanomamo: The Fierce People* (New York: Holt, Rinehardt, and Winston, 1968).

China.
Etienne Balazs, *Chinese Civilization and Bureaucracy* (New Haven: Yale University Press, 1964.). Houston Smith's chapter on Confucianism in *Religions of Man.* Will Durant, *Our Oriental Heritage* (New York: Simon and Schuster, 1954) is a good introduction to all of Asia. Japan: Ruth Benedict, *The Sword and Chrysanthemum* (New York: Houghton Mifflin, 1969); and Edwin O. Reischauer's *The Japanese: Change and Continuity* (Cambridge: Harvard University Press, 1995

Clements, Marcelle, *The Improvised Woman: Single Women Reinventing Single Life* (New York: W.W. Norton, 1998).

Cobb, Clifford, Ted Halstead, and Jonathan Rowe, "If The GDP IsUp, Why Is America Down?" *The Atlantic Monthly*, October 1995, pp. 59-78.

Columbus, Christopher, *The Letter of Columbus on the Discovery of America* (New York: Trustees of the Lenox Library, 1892), p. 5.

Cox, Harvey, "The Market as God" in *Atlantic Monthly*, March 1999, pp 18-23.

Coward, Howard, and Daniel Maguire, eds, *Visions of a New Earth,* (Albany: State University of New York Press, 2000). The idea that the economy is functioning as a religion is being heard with increasing frequency.
Critchfield, Richard, *Villages,* (New York: Doubleday, 1993)

Dawkins, Richard, *The Selfish Gene* (New York: Oxford University Press, 1990).

Daly, Herman, *Beyond Growth: The Economics of Sustainable Development* (Boston: Beacon Press, 1996), p. 93.

Diamond, Jared, *Guns, Germs, and Steel: Fates of Human Societies* (New York: W. W. Norton & Company, 1998).

Economist, The, "Debt in Japan and America," 22 January 2000, pp. 23-25.
_____, "Shares without the other bit: In corporate America, paying dividends has gone out of fashion," Nov. 20, 1999. p. 93.

Friedman, Meyer, and Diane Ulmer, *Treating Type A Behavior and Your Heart* (New York: Fawcett Crest, 1984).

Easterlin, Richard, "Will Raising the Incomes of all Increase the Happiness of All?" *Journal of   Economic Behavior and Organization*, vol. 27, 1995, pp. 35-47.
_____, "Does Money Buy Happiness? *Public Interest*, No. 30, Winter 1973, pp. 3-12.

Fedotov, Georgi, *The Russian Religious Mind* (New York, Macmillan, 1953), p. 13.

Columbus, Christopher, *The Letter of Columbus on the Discovery of America* (New York: Trustees of the Lenox Library, 1892), p. 5.

Cox, Harvey, "The Market as God" in *Atlantic Monthly*, March 1999, pp 18-23.

Coward, Howard, and Daniel Maguire, eds, *Visions of a New Earth,* (Albany: State University of New York Press, 2000). The idea that the economy is functioning as a religion is being heard with increasing frequency.
Critchfield, Richard, *Villages,* (New York: Doubleday, 1993)

Dawkins, Richard, *The Selfish Gene* (New York: Oxford University Press, 1990).

Daly, Herman, *Beyond Growth: The Economics of Sustainable Development* (Boston: Beacon Press, 1996), p. 93.

Diamond, Jared, *Guns, Germs, and Steel: Fates of Human Societies* (New York: W. W. Norton & Company, 1998).

Economist, The, "Debt in Japan and America," 22 January 2000, pp. 23-25.
_____, "Shares without the other bit: In corporate America, paying dividends has gone out of fashion," Nov. 20, 1999. p. 93.

Friedman, Meyer, and Diane Ulmer, *Treating Type A Behavior and Your Heart* (New York: Fawcett Crest, 1984).

Easterlin, Richard, "Will Raising the Incomes of all Increase the Happiness of All?" *Journal of   Economic Behavior and Organization*, vol. 27, 1995, pp. 35-47.
_____, "Does Money Buy Happiness? *Public Interest*, No. 30, Winter 1973, pp. 3-12.

Fedotov, Georgi, *The Russian Religious Mind* (New York, Macmillan, 1953), p. 13.

Frank, Robert, *Luxury Fever: Why Money Fails to Satisfy in an Era of Excess* (New York: The Free Press, 1999).

Freuchen, Peter, *The Book of the Eskimos* (New York: Fawcett, 1967).

Freud, Sigmund, *Civilization and its Discontents* (London: Hogarth Press, Third Edition, 1946), pp. 60-64, 72-77, 131-144 deal with the issue of culture being the source of emotional problems.

Fukuyama, Francis. The original "end of history" case was made in a 1989 article in *National Interest.* It was followed by a book titled *The End of History and the Last Man* (New York: Avon Books, 1993), and then *The Great Disruption* (New York: The Free Press, 1999), dealing with recent difficulties but still expressing confidence that the spontaneous tendencies toward self organization can be expected to deal with them.

Gibbons, Anne, "Which of Our Genes make Us Human?"*Science,* 4 September 1998, vol. 281, pp. 1432-1434.

Grant, James, *The Trouble With Prosperity* (New York: Times Books, 1998). Huizinga, Johan, *Homo Ludens: A Study of the Play Element in Culture* (Boston: Beacon Press, 1986)

Hunters and Gatherers.
            Because a number of hunting and gathering groups survived into the modern era, the accounts of them are a true asset in understanding human nature. Peter Freuchen's *The Book of the Eskimos* is especially valuable since he married an Eskimo woman and lived with the Eskimos for a number of years. One of the earliest documentary films was made of the Eskimos early in the twentieth century, *Nanook of the North,* by Robert Flaherty. It provides a view much like Freuchen's, of people living in one of the harshest of environments but still quite happy. Farley Mowat's *People of the Deer* (Boston: Atlantic Monthly Books, 1998), deals with the people who live inland from the coasts of Alaska and Canada and survived on the caribou until they were overhunted by Canadians. The Bushmen of the Kalahari are the source of most scientific information about hunters and gatherers because of Richard B. Lee's ecological research; see his *The !Kung San: Men, Women, and Work in a Foraging Society* (New York: Cambridge University Press, 1979). An hour long film, *The Hunters*, made by John Marshall (Waterbury, Maine: Documentary Educational Services, 1979), provides a good feeling for the Bushmen's way of life. Colin Turnbull's *The Forest People*, (Garden City: Doubleday, 1961), describes how the BaMbutu Pygmies cherish the tropical forest that sustain them in the Congo. In The *Mountain People,* (New York: Simon and Schuster, 1968), he describes the collapse of a group of hunters and gatherers who were forced into farming when their territory was made into a national park. The Aborigines of Australia would have provided a fine opportunity to learn about hunters and gatherers except that, as in North America, the European newcomers wanted to see the worst in indigenous peoples to justify treating them badly. The hunters and gatherers among the American Indians were heavily concentrated in California because the oak trees provided a large, assured source of food. Some anthropologists argue that half of all Native Americans lived in California, and their peaceful ways led the early settlers to have a low regard for them, compared to the warlike Plains Indians. *The Ohlone Way*, by Malcolm Margolin (Berkeley: Heyday Books, 1981) is perhaps the most accurate account of this way of life because of the number of early accounts of their life around San Francisco Bay. The Indians who lived in the mountains above the Sacramento Valley were sometimes more violent, but this included the Yahi, the tribe from which Ishi came, the last wild

Indian in the U.S. Lewis Hyde, *The Gift: Imagination and the Erotic Life of Property* (New York: Vintage Books, 1979), is not limited to hunters and gatherers, but suggests how the original role of gifts continued into the era of traditional agricultural societies.

India.

L. Bashom, *The Wonder That Was India* (London: Sidgwick and Jackson, 1997). Louis Fisher, *Gandhi: His Life and Message for the World* (New York: Penguin, 1954). Kussum Nair, *Blossoms in the Dust: The Human Factor in Indian Development* (New York: Praeger, 1961). Helena Norberg-Hodge, *Ancient Futures: Learning From Ladakh* (San Francisco: Sierra Club Books, 1991). See also Huston Smith's chapters on Hinduism and Buddhism in *Religions of Man.*

Jeffers, Robinson, *Selected Poems* (New York: Vintage Books, 1962).

Kaplan, Robert *The Ends of the Earth: A Journey at the Dawn of the 21st Century* (Random House, 1996).
_____ "The Coming Anarchy," *The Atlantic Monthly,* Feb. 1996.

Kates, Robert W., "Sustaining Life on the Earth,"*Scientific American,* October 1994, pp. 114-122.

Khazanov, A. M., *Nomads and the Outside World* (New York: Cambridge University Press, 1984).

Kroeber, Theodora, *Ishi in Two Worlds* (Berkeley: University of California Press, 1961) a portrait of a man with the classic qualities of hunters and gatherers

Kropotkin, Petr, *Mutual Aid: A Factor in Evolution* (Boston: Beacon Press).

Krutch, Joseph Wood, *The Modern Temper* (San Diego: Harcourt Brace, 1929), Chapter 2.

Lefebuse, Leo. D, *The Buddha and the Christ* (Maryknoll, New York: Orbis Books, 1993). One of several sources which point to the similarities in the ethics of Buddha and Christ.

Loy, David R., "The Religion of the Market" in *Visions of a New Earth*. Edited by Harold Coward, above.

Loye, David, *Darwin's Lost Theory of Love* (Lincoln, Nebraska: iUniverse, 2000)

Marx, Leo, *Machine in the Garden: Technology and the Pastoral Ideal in America* (London: Oxford University Press, 1964)

McNeill, William H., *The Rise of the West: A History of the Human Community* (New York: New American Library, 1963), p. 35.

Meadows, Donella, et al. *The Limits to Growth: A Report for the Club of Rome's Project on the Predicament of Mankind*, (New York: Universe Books, 1972).

Meeker, Joseph, *The Comedy of Survival* (New York: Scribners, 1974).

Middle East.
        Karen Armstrong, *Mohammed: A Biography of the Prophet* (San Francisco: Harper San Francisco, 1993); Houston Smith's chapter on Islam in *Religions of Man*; David Shipler, *Arab and Jew: Wounded Spirits in a Promised Land* (New York: Penguin USA, 1987).   Edward Said, a Palestinian Christian, has written extensively on the Arab Israeli conflict.

New York Times, "In Principle, a Case For More 'Sweatshops,'" June 22, 1997, p. 5.

Oswald, Andrew J., "Happiness and Economic Performance," *The Economic Journal of the Royal Economic Society*, 1997, pp. 1815-1830.

Pipes, Richard, *Russia Under the Old Regime* (London: Weidenfield and Nicholson, 1974)

Pipher, Mary, *Reviving Ophelia: Saving the Selves of Adolescent Girls* (New York: Ballantine Books, 1995); *The Shelter of Each Other: Rebuilding Our Families* (New York: Ballantine Books, 1997); *Another Country: Navigating the Emotional Terrain of Our Elders* (New York: Riverhead Books, 1997).

Polanyi, Karl, *The Great Transformation* (Boston: Beacon Press, 1944)

Powers, Ron, "The Apocalypse of Adolescence," in *The Atlantic Monthly,* March, 2002,38- pp. 58-74. This article presents a disturbing way of understanding the mindless violence of young people, one related to the lack of healthy roles available to them.

Putnam, Robert, *Bowling Alone: The Collapse and Revival of American Community* (New York: Simon and Schuster, 2000).

Rappaport, Roy A, *Pigs for the Ancestors* (New Haven: Yale Univ. Press, 1984)

Reich, Robert, *Locked in the Cabinet* (New York: Vintage Books, 1998)

Rimland, Bernard, 'The Altruism Paradox, *Psychological Reports,* Vol. 51, pp. 521-522, 1982.

Ridley, Matt, *The Origin of Virtue* (New York: Penguin, 1996). Ridley makes the cultural case for the selfish genes.

Russell, Jeffrey Burton, *A History of Medieval Christianity: Prophecy and Order* (New York: Thomas Y. Crowell, 1968)

Russia.
        The failures of the Soviet system are given a human face by two skilled journalists, David Shipler's *Broken Idols, Solemn Dreams* (New York: Penguin USA, 1987) and Hedrick Smith's *The New Russians* (New York: Avon Books, 1991) which ends with the failed coup in 1991. Billington, referenced above, is an excellent cultural history of Russia. The role of religion is reflected in the works of the philosopher Nicholas Berdyaev.

Sahlins, Marshall, "The Origin of Society," *Scientific American*, August 1960, pp. 2-12.
_____, *Stone Age Economics* (New York: Aldine-Atherton, 1972).

Schor, Juliet B., *The Overspent American: Upscaling, Downshifting, and the New Consumer* (New York: Basic Books, 1998).

Science, "Report Paints Grim Outlook for Young Ph.Ds," 11 September 1998, vol. 281, p. 1584.
_____, 'The Next Oil Crisis Looms Large—and Perhaps Close," 21 August 1998, vol. 281, pp. 1128-1131.

Secoy, Frank, *Changing Military Patterns on the Great Plains*, Monograph of the American Ethnographic Society, Harvard University, vol. 21, 1953.
Smith, Tom, "Happiness: Time Trends, Seasonal Variations, Intersurvey Differences, and Other Mysteries," *Social Psychology Quarterly*, vol. 42, no. 1, 1979, pp. 18-30.

Soros, George, "The Capitalist Threat," *The Atlantic Monthly,* February 1997, pp. 45-58.

Stanford Today, "Cynicism for all," Nov/Dec 1998, p. 41.

Tierney, Patrick, *Darkness in El Dorado: How Scientists and Journalists Devastated the Amazon*. (New York: W. W. Norton, 2000)

Tocqueville, Alexis de, *Democracy in America* (New York: Harper, 1988), pp. 297-297, and Knopf, 1960), pp. 309-10.

Tomasic, Dinko, *The Impact of Russian Culture on Soviet Communism* (Glencoe: The Free Press, 1953).

Toynbee, Arnold, *The Study of History* (New York: Oxford University Press). Most readers use the two volume condensation by D. C. Somervell (New York: Oxford University Press,1947 and 1957).
_____, *Civilization on Trial* (New York: Oxford University Press, 1948).

Tuchman, Barbara, *Distant Mirror: The Calamitous 14th Century* (New York: Ballantine, 1987).

Wallerstein, Judith, *The Unexpected Legacy of Divorce* ((New York: Hyperian, 2000).

White, Linda, *The Case for Marriage: Why Married People Are Happier, Healthier, and Better Off Financially* (New York, Doubleday, 2000)

White, Richard, editor, *The Mendocino Gazetteer*, Issue 74, published by the Mendocino Academy of Sciences. (P.O. Box 165, Mendocino, CA 95460). While such information is widely available, it is periodically summarized in this publication, along with other scientific and environmental issues.

Whitehead, Barbara Dafoe, *The Divorce Culture* (New York: Knopf, 1997), p. 54.

Yankelovich, Daniel, "New Rules," in *Psychology Today*, April 1981, p. 40.

INDEX